Globalisation and the Wealth of Nations

Globalisation and the Wealth of Nations

•

Brian Easton

AUCKLAND UNIVERSITY PRESS

First published 2007

Auckland University Press
University of Auckland
Private Bag 92019
Auckland
New Zealand
www.auckland.ac.nz/aup

© Brian Easton, 2007

ISBN 978 1 86940 377 5

National Library of New Zealand Cataloguing-in-Publication Data
Easton, B. H.
Globalisation and the wealth of nations / by Brian Easton.
Includes bibliographical references and index.
ISBN 978-1-86940-377-5
1. Globalization—Economic aspects. 2. Globalization—Social aspects. 3. Globalization—Political aspects. 4. Economics.
I. Title.
337—dc 22

This book is copyright. Apart from fair dealing for the purpose of private study, research, criticism or review, as permitted under the Copyright Act, no part may be reproduced by any process without prior permission of the publisher.

Cover design: Spencer Levine, Base Two
Printed by Publishing Press Ltd, Auckland

Contents

Dedication	vii
Prologue	ix
Preface: Yet Another Book on Globalisation?	x
A Note on Statistics	xiii
Acknowledgements	xiv

Part One • Diminishing Distance

1. Globalisation: An Introduction	2
2. The Significance of Location: Samoa and Hawaii	10
3. When Distance Changes: New Zealand	18
4. Regions and Economies of Scale: The United States	26
5. The Forces of Agglomeration: New York	33
6. Competitive Advantage: Nokia	38
7. Offshoring: India	44
8. Intra-Industry Trade: Motor Vehicles	50
9. Migration: Mexico	56
10. Locating the World's Population: Aging	62

Part Two • The Nation-State and Diminishing Distance

11. Sovereignty: Time	69
12. The Nation-State: Germany	77
13. Cultural Convergence: Canada	85
14. The Diaspora: Australia	92
15. The Social Market Economy: The European Union	97
16. Policy Convergence: Health Care	104
17. The International Trading System: The World Trade Organization	111
18. The International Financial System: The IMF	120
19. Foreign Direct Investment: McDonald's	129

Part Three • Economic Development

20. How Economies Develop: Smith to Solow and Beyond	137
21. Resources: Oil	143
22. Information: The World Wide Web	151
23. Technology Transfer: Japan	157
24. The Rich Club: Argentina	163
25. Poor Countries: Africa	169
26. The Insignificant Middle Club: The Bifurcation Model	177
27. The Pattern of World Development: China	184

Part Four • The Future

28. Options for Nations	192
29. A Confederation of Nations?	200
30. A Multipolar World	209

Epilogue: Democracy in a Globalised World	217
Notes	219
Bibliography	225
Index	228

Dedication

While on a two-month stint in Boston collecting material for this book, I was faced with the reality of distance. My mother died in Christchurch. I knew when I left New Zealand that she was dying, but we expected her to still be with us when I got back. She went earlier.

My family contacted me when it was clear she was near the end. Should I go home? Despite the diminution of distance that this book describes, it would have taken at least 60 hours, given the flying time and schedules. There was a good chance that she would be gone before I got back. So I stayed put, keeping in touch via telecommunications. Phones had their difficulties, for the common windows between Boston and Christchurch are limited, and anyway I could not see her. The internet proved more effective, if less intimate.

If the situation had occurred twenty years earlier I would have been in a worse position: phones and airfares were more expensive, and there was no significant internet. My real luck, though, was to have those extra twenty years of Mum. Perhaps in twenty years' time some reader will face a similar situation, with lower distance costs: direct New York to Christchurch flights; video streaming. But they may still decide to stay rather than return.

As I tried to lead as normal a life as possible, continuing to work on this project in Boston while pondering what was happening in Christchurch, I realised that there was an aspect of distance which this book hardly touches upon: intimacy – the desire to see, to hear directly, to touch, to smell. Sure, we can move human beings to enable such intimacy, and these movements are much more feasible today than they were in the past. Even so, this book has not much about the need to be near.

It would be sentimental – an emotion for which economics texts are not noted – to dedicate this book to my mother. Instead, I would like to dedicate it to the intimacy which makes us human. I first learned of this from Mum.

On our breakfast table lies each morning the toil of Europe, Asia, and Africa and the isles of the sea; we sow and spin for unseen millions, and countless myriads weave and plant for us; we have made the earth smaller and life broader by annihilating distance, magnifying the human voice and the stars, binding nation to nation, until today, for the first time in history there is one standard of human culture as well in New York as in London, in Cape Town as in Paris, Bombay as in Berlin.

– William Edward Burghardt DuBois, Address to the graduating class at Fisk University, Nashville, 1898

[I]n August 1914 . . . [t]he inhabitant of London could order by telephone, sipping his morning tea in bed, the various products of the whole earth, in such quantity as he might see fit, and reasonably expect their early delivery upon his doorstep; he could at the same moment and by the same means adventure his wealth in the natural resources and new enterprises of any quarter of the world, and share, without exertion or even trouble, in their prospective fruits and advantages; or he could decide to couple the security of his fortunes with the good faith of the townspeople of any substantial municipality in any continent that fancy or information might recommend. He could secure forthwith, if he wished it, cheap and comfortable means of transit to any country or climate without passport or other formality, could despatch his servant to the neighbouring office of a bank for such supply of the precious metals as might seem convenient, and could then proceed abroad to foreign quarters, without knowledge of their religion, language, or customs, bearing coined wealth upon his person, and would consider himself greatly aggrieved and much surprised at the least interference. But, most important of all, he regarded this state of affairs as normal, certain, and permanent, except in the direction of further improvement, and any deviation from it as aberrant, scandalous, and avoidable.

– John Maynard Keynes, *The Economic Consequences of the Peace*, Macmillan, London, 1919

Prologue

In the nineteenth century a vigorous debate took place among those who disliked the trends of the day – trends which they thought of as 'industrialisation', but which we can now see as the early stage of globalisation. The French anarchist, Pierre-Joseph Proudhon, appalled by the human costs of industrialisation, argued for a reversion to an earlier rural way of life – an Arcadia which had never actually existed.

But was there an alternative to retreat? Must the world surrender to the forces of globalisation, with helots toiling in the fields and in dark satanic mills? The best-known rival vision came from Karl Marx, whose thinking is often misrepresented by his twentieth-century followers. Marx argued that industrialisation was an essentially progressive – if unrelenting – force, even though it caused misery to workers caught up in the transformation. Marx argued that the transformation would ultimately benefit workers through the creation of a state in which they would enjoy the fruits of their labour.

With hindsight, we can see that Marx was broadly correct. Sure, no 'communist' state has come into existence; Marx himself was quite vague about what this would look like. But ultimately the workers of the world are better off from industrialisation. Had they retreated to the nostalgia of Proudhon's Arcadia, they would not be, for they would be isolated from the benefits of the technology which drove globalisation and industrialisation. Admittedly, there has not been much equity in the sharing of the fruits of the transformation. Among those who have benefited least are those in Africa, but even here, the material standard of living is about three times higher today than it was two centuries ago.

So the challenge is not how to stop globalisation – as Marx foresaw, that was not a feasible option (and will not be, for as long as the costs of distance continue to fall). Rather it is how to harness it for the common good. That was the challenge our nineteenth-century ancestors took up, despite the awful effects of the industrialisation of the day. Thanks to them, we live in a much more benign society than they did. That is the challenge and the prospect for this bout of globalisation, too: to harness the forces of globalisation, rather than to deny them or pretend we can reverse them.

Marx's last thesis on Feuerbach famously asserts that 'philosophers have only interpreted the world in various ways; the point is, to change it'. The task I have set myself in this book is to provide an interpretation of globalisation for those who wish to understand it.

Preface • Yet Another Book on Globalisation?

Towards the end of the twentieth century, the word 'globalisation' became very fashionable. By 2007 it appeared in one form or another in almost fifteen million websites, while one internet bookshop stocked more than 5000 books with the word in the title. Why add yet another one? For two reasons: time and place.

This book will be read for a long time to come. It is neither coincidental nor a promotional gimmick that the title alludes to Adam Smith's most famous book, one still remembered after more than two centuries. That is because he tackled contemporary issues by providing an analytic framework and insights which are still robust. This is not a book which claims that globalisation has just started. It began shortly after *The Wealth of Nations*, and we can learn from those two hundred years. This book offers not dramatic facts and confident predictions, but an analytical framework – enhanced by Adam Smith's successor economists – enabling the reader to think about current and future issues. So yes, this is a textbook, but one written for informal as well as formal students, with the objective of helping them think about the changing world economy and its political and social implications.

The vast majority of globalisation books are parochial. Most have an American or European perspective, because most are written and read by Americans or Europeans. So often the writer makes unconscious assumptions which the majority of readers unconsciously accept. The outsider finds these assumptions usually interesting, sometimes implausible, and almost always challenging. This book, written from the perspective of another place, offers conventional inside readers the same challenge to think differently about their nation and its future. Readers from great powers – Americans and Europeans – are invited to see the world from the perspective of a small rich economy. That is, after all, the locality most of us live in, even if we think we belong to some greater nation. We need to think outside the comfort of our commitment to our nation's prospects – even if this book concludes that there is still a place for the nation-state.

Even the best books often do not use recent developments in economic theory which throw much light on what is happening; those that do are usually not written for lay readers. This book aims to fill the gap. It is an economics book for a non-economics audience, based on some of the recent developments in economic theory and economic history. It also extends the argument into wider concerns of political economy such as the role of culture and the nation-state.

This goal led to five key decisions. First, the book tries to set out a simple version of current developments in economic theory, specifically those which underpin *The Spatial Economy: Cities, Regions and International Trade*, written by Masahisa Fujita, Paul Krugman and Anthony J. Venables.[1] Such studies, if not always easy to understand (even by good mathematicians), are an exciting development. While there has been some awareness of a spatial dimension in economics since J. H. von Thunen's work in the nineteenth century, its rarity is illustrated by the lack of maps in most economics texts. Typical theories of international economics are not greatly concerned about whether two countries have a common border or are on opposite sides of the world. It is common to ignore transport costs. Much economic theory also treats nations as givens. Such simplifications are no longer tenable.

Once the costs of distance are introduced, location becomes a vital element of economic behaviour, especially where there are economies of scale, with average costs falling as the amount produced increases. In this case interaction with the costs of distance generates outcomes quite different from those thrown up by the standard theory, which ignores the costs of distance and has only diminishing returns (average costs rise as the scale of production increases). This is the frontier of economic theory. When economists have perfected the analysis and found a way to communicate their intuitions in comprehensible language, it will amount to a major advance.

Second, the book is grounded in history and geography, the dimensions in which globalisation actually occurs. Much of the popular debate is about the 'now' of globalisation, with little recognition that the phenomenon has existed for more than two hundred years. Historical and geographical examples help us understand both the theory and the future.

This realisation led to the third consideration. Originally I was going to focus on New Zealand's place in a globalising world. But that would be too narrow, and I have written the book for an international audience. Because I am a New Zealander, my country appears more often than it would had the book been written elsewhere. In doing this I am no different from every other writer who uses their local experience to guide their global thinking and writing. Such an approach is both in the spirit of globalisation and more compelling and informative for the reader.

The fourth factor is the ethical stance of the book. In my view, asking whether globalisation (or just about anything) is a good thing or otherwise is not helpful until it is defined and analysed. Even so, at an early stage my analysis led me toward the view that globalisation – or more precisely, the falling costs of distance (often coupled with economies of scale) – has been one of the great forces of history, largely unstoppable but to some extent governable. The book aims to inform readers and enable them to better make their own decisions about how to harness globalisation. My goal is not to promulgate my own political views, but to help you form yours.

My fifth decision was to not consider the implications of globalisation for military and diplomatic activities. It is written, after all, by an economist. There is, of course, a story to be told about how war, like much of the economy, has been shaped by effective distance. It took the United States 2½ years to get their troops onto the European continent during the Second World War; 60 years later it took them just three months to invade the apparently harder logistical proposition of Iraq.

It will be evident, I hope, that I see myself on the teacher end of the preacher–teacher spectrum, aiming to open up readers to fresh ideas, fresh insights, fresh understandings. Although I do not know what will actually happen to the global economy in the future, I believe that the insights which I share in this book will mean readers experience fewer surprises than had I not ventured on this journey.

Brian Easton
www.eastonbh.ac.nz
April 2007

A Note on Statistics

This study relies heavily on Angus Maddison, *The World Economy: A Millennial Perspective*, published by the Organisation for Economic Co-operation and Development (OECD) in 2001, references to which are given as 'Maddison Data Base'. Details can be found at www.ggdc.net/Maddison/. This is the best comprehensive (in the sense of consistency over long periods and between concepts and countries) data base available.

Some supplementary data has also been used. This has not always been as carefully calculated – even when it is 'official'. I remember looking at the estimates for the German Democratic Republic (East Germany) for 1989, just before its reunification with the Federal Republic of Germany. The GDR's statisticians thought that their per capita gross domestic product (GDP) was about two-thirds that of West Germany – high enough to put East Germany in the Rich Club (see Chapter 24). After the merger, the data was recalculated to nearer one-third of the West German level (see the Maddison Data Base). The East German statisticians had doubled the true figure. How?

Consider the Trabant, the GDR's ubiquitous car. One might value it as equivalent to a Volkswagen, or alternatively as inferior. Once the 'Trabi' could be bought anywhere in Germany, it became clear that the public did not equate it with a Beetle. Before the Berlin Wall fell, such market comparisons were impractical. Value was assigned by the all too human judgements of official statisticians.

Statisticians acknowledge that even the best available data is subject to error, especially in the case of earlier estimates, and may be revised. While I recognise the possibility of errors in data, this book's arguments are robust in relation to likely ones.

Acknowledgements

While one name may appear on the title page of a book, in practice it is the collective work of many people. Many are dead or writers yet to be met. Others are friends and colleagues who patiently read all or part of the text, or answered particular questions: Richard Benton, Rob Bowie, Rolf Brendich, Ken Carlaw, Andrew Coleman, Joan Druett, Peter Elkan, Tilman Enders, Jim Flynn, Paul Gandar, Don Gilling, Bryan Gould, Alan Gray, Malcolm Harbrow, Tony Hooper, Graham Kelly, Peter Lindert, Angus Maddison, Gerald McGhie, John McKinnon, Malcolm McKinnon, Les Oxley, Ian Pool, Michael Powles, John Ralston Saul, Dennis Rose, Bill Rosenberg, Herman Schwartz, Jane Scott, Susan St John, John Tizard, Tony Venables, Robert Wade, Nelson Wattie, Jeffrey Williamson and John Yeabsley.

Funding for such a major task is critical. I am grateful to acknowledge:

The Marsden Fund of the Royal Society of New Zealand, provided by the Government of New Zealand, which made the main grant that enabled me to work on the book over a three-year period;
Fulbright New Zealand, which awarded me a Distinguished Fulbright Fellowship and enabled me to spend time at Georgetown University and Harvard University;
The Federal Government of Germany, which provided me with a travelling fellowship in Germany hosted by the Goethe Institut;
The Claude McCarthy Fellowship, administered by the New Zealand Vice-Chancellors' Committee, whose grant contributed to the completion of the study.

The journey from pen to paper requires specialist skills. I am especially grateful to Spencer Levine, who designed the cover; to Igor Drecki and Tim Nolan, for preparing maps and figures; to Ginny Sullivan, for the index; to David Green, for his sensitive editing of the manuscript; and to Elizabeth Caffin, former director of Auckland University Press, and her staff of Katrina Duncan, Annie Irving, Anna Hodge, Christine O'Brien and Daniel Porter.

If there is one name on the title page, it is because he (in this case) takes responsibility for the errors and omissions, despite the efforts of those named above.

Part One • Diminishing Distance

One | Globalisation • An Introduction

This book is underpinned by five propositions about globalisation:

1. Globalisation is the economic integration of regional and national economies.
2. It is caused by the falling cost of distance.
3. It has exceptionally powerful effects when the reduced costs of distance combine with economies of scale.
4. It first became important in the early nineteenth century.
5. It is not solely an economic phenomenon in a historical and geographical context. It has political and social consequences. In particular, it impacts on, but does not eliminate, cultural differences, and it reduces, but does not eliminate, the policy discretion of nation-states.

I will introduce the book by elaborating on each proposition. (Chapter 20 gives a brief introduction to the standard theory of economic growth.)

1. *Globalisation is the economic integration of regional and national economies.*
It is possible to write an entire book on globalisation without defining the term. Fortunately, in recent years economists have moved towards a common definition, although the one used here is slightly wider because it includes regional as well as national economies. From a historical perspective, the integration of nations was preceded by the integration of regions. The standard economic definition presupposes that regional integration is no longer important. But there are four reasons why regions still matter.

First, we can learn much about national integration by studying regional integration. Second, regional integration and relocation is still going on within nations. And we must also explain the role of cities, intensely local phenomena which are nevertheless integral to globalisation. Additionally, two regional integrations provide possible models for the future world economy. The US economy may be thought of as an early example of a mini-globalised world in which states are not very powerful. The European Union is a more recent mini-globalised world in which states have retained more authority. Each offers a possible system of world economic arrangements, a topic explored towards the end of the book.

2. *Globalisation is caused by the falling cost of distance.*
Comprehending globalisation requires an understanding of the role of space (geography) in economics, for economic space is connected by the costs of distance. These are much more than transport costs. They include the costs of storage, security and insurance, information transfer, timeliness and those arising from lack of intimacy.

A quantitative indication of their significance can be found in a study of paper trade costs by James Anderson and Eric van Wincoop.[1] They calculate that the average American manufacture incurs a mark-up of 55 per cent between the factory door and the domestic consumer. This covers such things as shipping, storage and the retailer's margin. But for exports the total mark-up is 170 per cent. On average a product going out an American factory door worth $100 sells in America for $155 and overseas for $270. One might associate the 55 per cent mark-up with regional trade costs, and the 74 per cent mark-up from $155 to $270 with international trade costs.

Clearly trade costs are a large part of the cost to a purchaser. Actual figures vary greatly on the basis of both destination and product. A Barbie doll manufactured in Asia for $1 sells for $10 in the US, a mark-up of 900 per cent.

Anderson and van Wincoop attribute about a third of the export trade costs (the 74 per cent mark-up) to transport costs – both the costs of direct freight and the time value of goods in transit. The other two-thirds are incurred by border-related barriers – barriers raised by differences of language, currency and information; the costs of contracting and insecurity; and barriers erected by policy (both tariff and non-trade). Policy barriers contribute just a seventh of export trade costs, less than currency barriers, freight costs and the time value of goods in transit, and only slightly greater than information and language costs.

Tariffs are treated here in a similar manner to any other cost of distance. Economists have a substantial theory on tariffs (which largely ignores costs of distance). Converting these other costs into tariff equivalents means that the economic theory applicable to tariffs also applies in most respects to these costs.[2]

Despite this insight, an investigation of the consequences of distance is not high among economists' priorities. An American textbook which I greatly admire, Paul Krugman and Maurice Obstfeld's *International Economics: Theory and Policy*,[3] devotes just two pages of more than 750 to transport costs. In contrast, there are some 40 pages on tariffs, even though these are

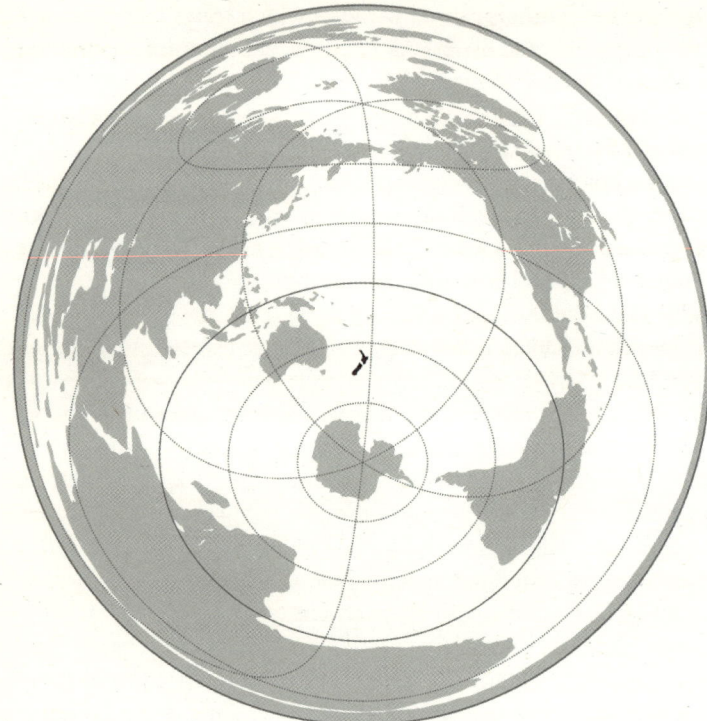

New Zealand's world 150 years ago

such a small proportion of total trade costs. This is all the more surprising, given that Krugman is one of the pioneers of the modern theory of spatial relationships in economics.

Throughout the book we will see examples of the dramatic fall in trade costs over the last two centuries. (There is no comprehensive study of the extent of this decline.)

Geoffrey Blainey entitled a history of Australia, *The Tyranny of Distance* (and New Zealand was even further away from the places that mattered). But effective distance has been changing. In the early nineteenth century it took the Brontë sisters a couple of days to get from their Yorkshire vicarage to London, longer than it takes today's Australasians to fly in from the other side of the globe.

Because the phenomenon has so many dimensions, and because it applies to so many things – different products, people, information – it is difficult to illustrate the falling costs of distance except by giving examples. One study suggests that the cost of ocean shipping relative to general prices fell by more than 86 per cent between 1790 and 1990.[4] Even this figure does not allow for the additional savings from trips becoming shorter and safer (or for declining wharf costs).

Time is money – and easier to measure. The travel time between New Zealand and England has fallen dramatically over the last 150 years. In the mid-nineteenth century it took a boat three to four months to sail from New Zealand to England, then the centre of its economic world. Imagine that effective distance is symbolised by the circle shown on the opposite page with the diameter of the width of this page.

Today a boat – faster (and safer) and using the Panama Canal – can do the trip in three to four weeks. The circle now, shown below, has a diameter of a quarter of the width of the page.

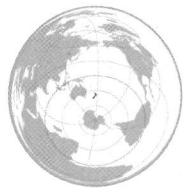

New Zealand's shipping world today

Even this underestimates the reduction. While goods largely go by ship, nearly a fifth of New Zealand's merchandise exports and imports are now airfreighted. Most people fly to and from New Zealand. A direct flight to England takes just over a day. Relative to the time it took 150 years ago, this takes up almost no width on the page.

New Zealand's air travel world today

Information travels even faster. It can be electronically transferred between New Zealand and England (or just about anywhere else) almost instantaneously. Whereas a nineteenth-century letter was carried by ship right across our notional page, today's travel time is smaller than the full stop which ends this sentence.

There are many more instances of this dramatic reduction in effective distance. However, while the tyranny of distance has diminished, reports of its death are exaggerated. The world itself is not a full stop.

Nor has the shrinkage been uniform. Costs have diminished at different rates for different sorts of goods and services, for people, and for information. Tariff theory predicts complex outcomes where tariffs are not reduced to zero and the reductions are not proportional. In fact, a partial reduction in some tariffs can make an economy worse off.[5]

Once the point of the importance of costs of distance is grasped, it is astonishing how often one observes their significance – and how often others do not. Chapters 2 (Samoa and Hawaii) and 3 (refrigeration in New Zealand) illustrate how much the world can change when costs of distance change. Which leads us to the next proposition.

3. Globalisation has exceptionally powerful effects when the reduced costs of distance combine with economies of scale.
Economists often assume that producing more requires an increasingly greater effort, a notion captured in the phrase 'diminishing returns' and signalled by rising unit (or average) costs as output in a fixed time period increases. This is perhaps no more than an example of the laws of thermodynamics. The introduction of a new technology may mean that more can be produced for less (at a lower cost), but for a particular technology it is usual for diminishing returns to apply.

However, over some ranges of production, unit costs may fall. The second item usually costs less to produce than the first. But the unit costs of some processes continue to fall even within the normal range of production. The reasons for economies of scale are numerous. They include indivisible inputs (as when a machine costs the same whether it produces a single item or many); start-up costs; learning effects; specialisation; the economies of increased dimensions (insofar as the thickness of the wall of a tank is fixed, its cost rises with the square of its dimensions, but its capacity with the cube); greater use of flow production rather than batch production; smaller inventories; the division of labour. Any short list is inevitably incomplete.

Economies of scale are important in economic growth (and are frequently realised when the costs of distance fall). But they generate some deep analytic problems for economists. It would take another book to explain them in detail to a lay audience – and the explanation may be so complex that this book cannot be written. A central problem is that once there are economies of scale the standard account of competitive markets does not work properly. While markets will continue to produce and distribute products, they may no longer do so efficiently, using the minimum of resources.

Once there are economies of scale odd things can happen – or do they just seem odd because we are so familiar with the outcomes of the standard model? It may be that we so often use the assumption of diminishing returns that outcomes caused by other factors strike us as unusual. Yet the reality may be the other way around. It was appropriate for economists to focus initially on diminishing returns. Having got that analysis broadly right, in the last quarter-century they have moved on to more analytically complicated cases in which there are increasing returns.

In particular, falling costs of distance enable economies of scale to be reaped. The theory is superbly developed in *The Spatial Economy: Cities, Regions and International Trade*, by Masahisa Fujita, Paul Krugman (again) and Tony Venables ('FKV'). Do read this book if you are able. But be warned: it is based on mathematical models, some of which are quite challenging – even for its authors.

An illustration may be useful at this point. Suppose that steel mills have enormous economies of scale, so that the unit cost for large production is very much lower than when production is small. If costs of distance are high, the mill's market may be local, and so small that no steel is produced and the locality – and all localities – has no access to cheap steel. Now suppose the costs of distance fall. The potential market increases to the point that it is commercially viable to supply it from one large plant. A whole range of uses – many hitherto unknown – appear. As we will see in Chapter 4, the forces unleashed may be powerful, dynamic and transformational.

The results can be unexpected. In Chapter 6 we see that the location of an industrial plant with large economies of scale is determined by luck and history. (The phenomenon could also be illustrated for cities in Chapter 5, but here the principle of agglomeration effects – industry economies of scale – is the focus.) Later in the book there is an account of the world economy. Because of economies of scale, countries go down one of two distinct development paths: one in which the economy benefits from economies of scale (the Rich Club), and one in which it does not (the Poor Club), with hardly any countries in between. The result is both a powerful account of the history of the world economy and an extraordinary – yet plausible – suggestion of how it may develop in the future.

Subsequent chapters in Part I extend the underlying notions to intra-industry trade, services in international trade and migration.

4. Globalisation first became important in the early nineteenth century.
There is much argument as to when the processes of globalisation began. Some scholars make the case for the fifteenth century. The fall of Constantinople in 1453 cut Western Europe off from its land routes to Asia, forcing the exploration of alternative sea routes. Bartolomeu Dias' rounding of the Cape of Good Hope in 1488 opened a sea route from Europe to India. Just four years later, Christopher Columbus crossed from Europe to America, which would be a main driver of subsequent globalisation.

On the other hand, in 1433 the Chinese gave up exploring the rest of the world. A decade earlier a giant flotilla under Zheng He had reached Madagascar. However, following a coup, China turned inward. Whether ocean-capable boats were banned or the Chinese simply lost interest is disputed by scholars. Zheng's exploration seems to have been undertaken to assert Chinese hegemony rather than to stimulate commerce. The subsequent turn inward meant that, unlike Europeans, the Chinese were not to be challenged by new lands, new peoples, new things, new ideas. Insofar as Europe dominated the latter half of the second millennium – China is generally judged to have been more technologically advanced in the fifteenth century – it was because Europeans were engaging with the unfamiliar.

This is a phenomenon we shall observe throughout the book: some economies succeeded only because they were interacting with others. Fifteenth-century China chose an inward-looking strategy analogous to the twentieth century's 'import-substituting industrialisation' (ISI), while the European outward-looking strategy was akin to 'export-oriented industrialisation'. Despite the Chinese domestic market being a quarter of the world market, their 'ISI' strategy proved as limiting as it would for other countries in later epochs.

Another mid-fifteenth-century event was crucial to globalisation (and indicative of a theme in this book). Once Johannes Gutenberg (Gensfleisch) had introduced the printing press with movable type (though the Chinese had a related technology centuries earlier), information could be moved long distances relatively cheaply. We often use the trade of goods as a marker of globalisation, but the information revolution may be more important in the long run.

Access to cheap information generated scholarship, much of which was not always well received. Because Europe was politically fragmented scholars who were out of favour could move to a more tolerant milieu – Erasmus and Martin Luther are well-known examples. Jurisdictional boundaries created an environment for the competition of ideas and innovation.

Attractive though the fifteenth century is as the era when globalisation began, the costs of distance remained high and interactions between regions were small. At the beginning of the nineteenth century, goods exports were still only about 1 per cent of world production (GDP). So while there were globalising forces earlier, it is hard to argue that these were powerful.

By the end of the nineteenth century, more than 7 per cent of global production was exported (and production itself had increased more than sixfold, meaning that exports were almost 50 times as high). Today merchandise exports are nearing 20 per cent of total production – and in addition there are exports of services. It seems clear that globalisation became a powerful force early in the nineteenth century.

It is true that there was stagnation – even some backsliding – between 1914 and 1950, as nations attempted (with only temporary success) to reverse the tide. Some writers argue for a second wave of globalisation starting in 1950, while others support a more recent surge under the impact of information and communications technologies. Because it is hard to identify new historical phases without the benefit of a good deal of hindsight – and since it is not necessary to do so – this book suspends such judgements. Perhaps there were new phases; perhaps the way in which the costs of distance fell changed, but the same drive to globalisation continued.

This study is greatly influenced by *Globalisation in Historical Perspective*, a collection of review essays in economic history edited by Michael Bordo, Alan Taylor and Jeffrey Williamson. Although it does not always agree with the contributors' conclusions, they demonstrate convincingly that focusing on recent decades is to ignore rich and illuminating historical insights.

5. Globalisation is not solely an economic phenomenon in a historical and geographical context. It has political and social consequences. In particular, it impacts on, but does not eliminate, cultural differences, and it reduces, but does not eliminate, the policy discretion of nation-states.

This issue is the subject of the second part of the book. Here I will merely sketch the central questions involved. A common public concern is that globalisation is undermining the sovereignty of the nation-state. (Ironically, as will be shown, the nation-state is itself largely a creation of nineteenth-century globalisation). The course of sovereignty can be explored by considering two 'convergence' theses.

First, the nation-state requires its people to distinguish themselves from those of other nation-states. If globalisation were to result in cultural convergence, a *raison d'être* for the nation-state would be undermined. So the first vital question is, *Does globalisation cause cultural convergence?*

Second, a nation has de jure sovereignty and in principle can do whatever it likes. But in practice its options may be extremely limited in particular policy areas, where it has little de facto sovereignty. So the second vital question is, *Does globalisation cause policy convergence?*

While neither answer is unequivocal, I conclude that the nation-state will continue to play a significant role for the foreseeable future.

Two | The Significance of Location • Samoa and Hawaii

> It is said that the three most important features of any property are 'location, location, location'. Location is one – but only one – of the key elements of economic and social development. This chapter tells the story of two countries whose location changed at the dawn of globalisation. It introduces the further themes of distance, population movements, society, and culture.

Once upon a time, the islands of Samoa were near the centre of the universe. About 5000 years ago some peoples from the shores of China began wandering their way across Melanesia. Their descendants settled in Samoa and nearby Tonga and Fiji some 3000 years ago, evolving into archaic Polynesians. Following improvements in maritime travel around 2300 years ago, they sailed across up to 3000 kilometres of ocean – there were no coasts to hug in the manner of their contemporaries (Vikings excepted) – to Eastern Polynesia.

From the Marquesas and Society Islands (the best known of which is Tahiti), they dispersed into the rest of that Pacific triangle we call Polynesia, with its last-settled vertices of the Easter Islands to the south-east, New Zealand to the south-west, and the Hawaiian Islands to the north. Some Polynesians sailed back west to settle in Melanesia.[1] There was an ongoing interchange in central Polynesia where sailing distances were shorter, but each vertex seems to have had only one major migratory wave, with the possible exception that Hawaii's first settlers (from the Marquesas) 1700 years ago were perhaps followed by another wave (from the Society Islands) 700 years later. The Tahitian chief Tupaia, who accompanied the English navigator James Cook in 1769, knew about the other islands of central Polynesia, but not the vertices.

Whatever the social interaction within Polynesia, the islands retained commonalities in their culture for a thousand years. Tupaia was able to converse with the New Zealand Māori. (Cook's last tragic Hawaiian trip was affected by his not having a Polynesian speaker on board.) 'Hawaii', the name for the largest island in that group, is cognate with 'Savaii', the largest island in Samoa, and 'Hawaiki', the mythical homeland of the Māori, the name New Zealand's indigenous people eventually took to distinguish themselves from later arrivals. It means the 'ordinary people' of the Polynesian universe.

Cook was not the first European to visit Polynesia. Ferdinand Magellan had crossed the Pacific in 1521, and in the next two centuries a scattering of explorers enhanced European knowledge of the central Pacific. But it was Cook who proved that there was no great southern land – the hypothesised Terra Australis – and whose mapping established the world's general understanding of the interior of its greatest ocean.

As much as we may admire Cook's captaincy and his humane views towards both his crew and Polynesians, his task was simplified by the improving technology of sea travel, including his testing of the first reliable chronometer, which fixed longitude and so enabled precision navigation and mapping. After 250 years of only occasional visits, within a couple of decades European and North American ships were swarming over Polynesia. Their purpose was generally no longer discovery, and they rarely respected their fellow humans as Cook had done. They came to exploit natural resources: whales, seals, timber.

Resource exploitation and the accompanying environmental degradation were not new. The idyllic environments that the first Europeans thought they saw were not the original ones. As Polynesians moved to each new island they first over-exploited what was available. By the time of the first European visits the locals had learned to manage the remaining resources in a sustainable manner. Sometimes they learned too late. The destruction of the Easter Island forests – crucial to the erection of the large lonely stone heads – is not just one of the best-understood examples of pre-commercial environmental degradation. It reminds us that the phenomenon is not exclusively a response to market forces. The greater environmental pressures exerted by the Europeans were caused not so much by the number of their sailors, but from the demands of large populations on the other side of the world.

Hawaii

Perhaps the most tumultuous events centred on the Hawaii Islands, a 250-kilometre-long chain of volcanic islands, eight of which were inhabited when Cook first visited them. The islands of the once forgotten northern vertex of the Polynesian triangle are midway between the North American and Asian continents. So they were not only ports for whalers plundering the then bountiful cetaceans, and a source of sandalwood. They became a key staging post in east–west trade in the larger world which Polynesia joined, an effect reinforced by the limited access the Japanese allowed the *gaijin* (foreigners).

The European invasion of guns and germs, religion and commerce changed native politics. The islands had been governed by warring chieftains, whose conflict intensified when guns were introduced. One chief, Kamehameha, who in his youth had met Cook in 1779, obtained cannons which he mounted on outriggers and carts, and by brutal conquest and alliances became king of all the islands in the 1790s. His base was the largest, most eastern, and volcanically still active island of Hawaii, which became the internationally accepted name for the whole group in place of Cook's 'Sandwich Islands'.[2] Today Kamehameha's island has to be called 'The Big Island' to distinguish it from the state of Hawaii.

Kamehameha located his government on the island of Maui, immediately to the west of the Big Island – but not far enough west. The outsiders congregated on Oahu, with its splendid Pearl Harbor and burgeoning town of Honolulu. Initially the settlers were there to provedore the passing boats – with fresh water, sweet potatoes, melons, vegetables, banana, coconuts (and women) – and to export sandalwood to China. Later they farmed sugar and pineapples. With not enough native Hawaiians willing to work the plantations, Filipinos, Chinese, Japanese, and Koreans were imported to make up the numbers.

After the arrival of the first missionaries in the 1820s, the kingship accepted Christianity while, like other Polynesians, maintaining older and sometimes conflicting traditions – and joining in the commercial exploitation. Under pressure from foreigners, from 1844 the system of feudal landholding was converted to private ownership, with most of the land reserved to the monarchy, nobility and government. The fee-simple titles were rapidly sold to the foreigners. By the end of the nineteenth century, 'the great division became the great dispossession'.[3]

By this time, the kingship had also been dispossessed of its political authority, following a coup led by American commercial interests based in Honolulu and supported by United States marines. At the time of the overthrow, only 26 per cent of the population had any Polynesian ancestry. It was indicative of the islands' integration into the world economy that the new capital was on the smaller island of Oahu, which possessed the best harbour and where later the best airport was built. An Hawaiian independence movement still argues that their independence was 'stolen' in 1893.

If so, the United States became a 'receiver of stolen goods' in 1898, when the 'Republic of Hawaii' became a territory of the United States of America (and eventually the fiftieth state in 1959). The commercial interests were concerned that an independent state faced an American tariff when competing against subsidised sugar grown on the mainland. The United

States, at the time embroiled in conflict with Spain over the Philippines, saw the advantage of a forward base en route to Asia. Today the military is one of the largest industries in Hawaii – behind tourism, but now well ahead of agriculture. Hawaii may be America's most militarised state. It ranks fourth highest among states in net federal funding per capita. (Washington DC tops them all, of course.)

How have the Polynesians fared since this turbulence? Today the Maoli – Hawaiians of Polynesian descent (note the cognate with 'Māori') – are about 13 per cent of the state's population. Their poverty rates are higher than average, but their standard of living is also higher than that of most Polynesians. They also have ready access to the United States. As well as the 240,000 in the Hawaiian Islands, there are 160,000 Maoli on the American mainland, 60,000 of them in California.

More problematic is the recognition of Maoli culture in Hawaii. It is presented to tourists as a unique selling proposition – aloha, hula and lei – but this is but a superficial veneer on a society which has largely marginalised its indigenous culture. One reason is that Hawaii is a multicultural society; some of its Asian communities are more numerous than the Maoli. Moreover, the Maoli comprise less than 0.2 per cent of the US population.

Among the Christmas muzak I heard broadcast in Hawaii was 'Walking in a Winter Wonderland', a song which makes as little sense in Hawaii as it would in Jesus's Palestine. It has become redolent of the North American and northern European Christmas. Once played religiously in New Zealand during December, it is scarcely heard here today.

The Māori – about 15 per cent of the New Zealand population are (partially) descended from the first peoples – while anxious about the survival of their culture, are far more despondent about the state of the Maoli's. There does not appear to be the same vigorous attempt in Hawaii as there has been in New Zealand to maintain the native language, and one gets less sense of the dominant culture's willingness to incorporate Polynesian culture into its texture. For while there are complicated tensions, even the Pākehā – New Zealand's non-Māori – have some enthusiasm for integrating the indigenous culture into the national one, contributing to a distinctive nationhood. In contrast, the dominant visual image in the advertising of the Oahu-based Polynesian Cultural Centre is a New Zealand Māori wero – the ceremonial martial challenge to determine whether the visitor is friend or foe.

Samoa

If the islands of Samoa, also of volcanic origin, were once near the centre of the universe – Samoans still make the claim – when Polynesia was the whole world, they are on the margins of the world they joined in the nineteenth century. Dutch admiral Jacob Roggeveen identified the 'Navigation Islands' for Europeans in 1722. But it was not until after Cook – who knew of them via Tupaia, but did not call in – that Europeans began to visit them regularly again for provisions – yams, poultry, pigs, coconuts, tropical fruit, water, firewood – and timber.

Reflecting its inferior location in world terms, the European impact on Samoa came later than in Hawaii, with the first missionaries arriving in the 1830s. As in the case of Hawaii, the political weight shifted from the harbourless biggest island, Savaii, to (the more eastern) Upolu with its Apia. But there was no king, and the villages absorbed Christianity, continued Fa'a Samoa (the Samoan way), and retained ownership of their land. Again it was Europeans who developed plantations, primarily for copra; and again there was insufficient willing local labour, so Melanesians and Chinese were imported.

In 1899 a contest among several great powers was resolved: Britain withdrew in exchange for concessions elsewhere; Germany took over Savaii and Upolu, where its nationals were planters and merchants; and the United States took the smaller Manua islands and Tutuila to the east, thus acquiring Pago Pago, the best harbour in the central Pacific.

In 1914, New Zealand wrested Western Samoa from Germany, ruling it as a trust territory for almost 50 years. At first the administration did not distinguish itself. There were tensions with the Mau, the Samoan independence movement. The nadir occurred on 'Black Saturday', 28 December 1929, when three hundred Samoans were welcoming an exile home. The police killed eleven and wounded more than 30 others. (One European constable also died.) Within a few years, the process commenced which led to the full independence in 1962 of Western Samoa, later renamed 'The Independent State of Samoa'.

American Samoa remains a territory of the United States, one of the few island groups of the Pacific which still lacks self-government. The division between the two parts of Samoa is artificial, but not without its conveniences. The American Samoans have access to the rest of the United States, and there are fewer in American Samoa than there are in America – mainly in Hawaii and California. The migration chain is fed by western Samoans replacing their eastern kinsmen who have gone north.

From the perspective of an isolated state, Samoa has been remarkably successful. The philosophy of 'Samoa mo Samoa' (Samoa for the Samoans) is evident in the ethnic makeup of the independent nation-state, 95 per cent of whose people are Samoans (most of the descendants of the nineteenth-century indentured labourers were sent home). Strictly speaking many are of part-Samoan descent, for it is only the most isolated populations which can be racially pure. Even so, Samoans are less outbred than Hawaiians or New Zealand Māori. Samoan culture and language is dominant, and the somewhat laid-back 'Fa'a Samoa' remains the 'Samoan way'.

The Significance of Social Structure

The story of these two peoples is not solely about location. The different outcomes were influenced by the Polynesian social structures that met the European invaders. Maoli Hawaii, like other Eastern Polynesian societies, was hierarchical. Samoa was typical of Western Polynesia societies in being decentralised, based on villages. The former succumbed more readily to European mores, not only in Hawaii but also in the Cook Islands and the Society Islands. Fiji and Tonga, like Samoa, maintained more of their indigenous social structure. Today Samoan political and social life still resides in villages centred on the local church, having adapted in a manner more consistent with the old ways. If decentralised Samoa had been on an important European route, its culture would have survived less well the extraordinary pressures of colonialism – but still, arguably, better than Hawaiian culture did.

The best clue we have to this comes from the New Zealand Māori, who were less hierarchical than most peoples originating in Eastern Polynesia, probably because of the abundance of land. It was that abundance which attracted the European, and put the Māori under pressure, albeit less pressure than the Maoli. But despite being dominated by the European population by a factor of six (even ignoring the fact that most of today's Māori have European ancestors), they have maintained a vigorous culture, which has incorporated Christianity, European technologies and European ideas while remaining distinctively their own – although not as distinctive as the Samoans'. As Douglas Oliver remarked, Samoans 'remain one of the few examples of a Pacific Island people surviving the strong impact of Westernization without losing their numbers, their dignity, their pride in their own way'.[4]

Yet we must be careful not to idealise the Samoan situation. While there are around 180,000 Samoans in Samoa, there are another 60,000 in American Samoa, 130,000 in the United States and 120,000 in New Zealand (plus a scattering throughout the rest of the world). So Samoa itself houses less than 37 per cent of the total Samoan population. Even were it to incorporate American Samoa, Greater Samoa would still contain less than half of all those who identify themselves one way or another as Samoans. Such are the attractions of affluence and opportunity, it seems likely that were it easier for Samoans to obtain entry to the United States, New Zealand and other richer countries, the home population would be even smaller. New Zealand

Samoans have material incomes twice that of their island compatriots; the ratio in the United States may be even higher.

Fa'a Samoa is more culturally sustainable than its Hawaiian equivalent – tourist-oriented superficialities aside. Even so, it is not obvious that the descendants of Hawaiian Polynesians are worse off than their cousins in Samoa. It is not even clear how to make a rigorous comparison, except on conventional material (GDP per capita-type) measures. One test might be where people choose to live. Even then, the net population flow from Samoa to Hawaii may be accompanied by regrets later in life. This need not mean that Samoa is failing, but rather that its long-term survival cannot be assured simply within the home islands. Economic success is likely to depend upon both remittances from overseas and spending on visits home by migrant kinsfolk.

If so, the cultural sustainability of the Samoan diaspora will be critical. More than half of today's New Zealand Samoans were born in New Zealand. Even the parents of some Samoans of full descent were not born in Samoa. Perhaps the islands of Samoa need to become a Samoan version of Hawaiki – in this case, a reality reinforced by actual pilgrimage.

The development of this broad Samoan culture is likely to involve other Polynesians – Cook Islanders, Marquesans, Nauruans, Niueans, Tahitians, Tokelauans, Tongans. Some islands' populations are so small that they may lose their ancestral culture as it melds into a broader Polynesian one. How will central Polynesia relate to the vertices? Easter Islanders are extinct, and Native Hawaiians – churned up in the United States mixing bowl – may become overwhelmed as a cultural community. (This is a challenge facing indigenous tribes in North America.) More complicated is the fate of the New Zealand Māori, a community as numerous as all central Polynesians and who occupy a political and social environment more benign to their interests than the United States.

Samoa may remain near the centre of Polynesia, but its peoples will be defined less geographically and more culturally – which Polynesians might say has always been true.

Conclusion

The technological improvements in sea travel at the end of the eighteenth century contributed to the globalisation which followed by effectively moving coastal communities closer to one another. Each could tell an analogous story of transformation – typically one in which there were both gains and losses to the community involved. Few have been more vividly affected than Polynesians, isolated from the rest of the world for 3000 years, who moved from the centre of one universe to the margins of a greater, and commercial, one.

Their experience illustrates that falling costs of distance can have pervasive consequences – to the environment, to populations, to the economy, to how people live – ramifications which are at the heart of the book. What may appear to be non-economic issues, such as population movement and sovereignty, are integral to understanding the globalising economy.

As the responses of different societies indicate, location is not everything. Even so, when it interacts with other powerful forces such as diminishing costs of distance and economies of scale, location shapes the way we live, our opportunities, our aspirations.

Three | When Distance Changes • New Zealand

New Zealand may well be the worst-located affluent economy. Like a number of pastoral farms far from Europe, its economy and society was transformed by the introduction of refrigeration. This chapter shows that distance is a complicated notion; for New Zealand it has been both a disadvantage and an advantage. The story is told using a variation of a standard international trade model which underpins much economic thinking.

Rudyard Kipling described New Zealand as 'Last, loneliest, loveliest'; others may dispute the last adjective. Unquestionably it was the last substantial land mass settled by humans. A standard map which places New Zealand in the centre of the world shows it is largely surrounded by ocean, with the nearest significant land mass being Australia, 1200 kilometres to the west. The prevailing winds were favourable for discovery from there, but Australia's first inhabitants – who arrived there 40,000 years ago – did not have the necessary seafaring technology. Instead, voyagers from central Polynesia to the north-east of New Zealand arrived about 800 years ago, their descendants evolving into the New Zealand Māori. Dutchman Abel Tasman arrived at New Zealand's western coast in 1642, but found both the country and the natives too hostile to land. In 1769 Englishman James Cook stepped ashore. His navigation demonstrated that Tasman had found islands of total area a little larger than the two main British Isles, rather than the edge of a large non-existent continent that had tentatively been named Terra Australis.

New Zealand split from the super-continent of Gondwana some 85 million years ago. Its continental shelf is about half the size of Australia, but most is under-sea. The various dunkings as the land rose and fell changed an already evolving ecology. When the first Pacific Islanders arrived there were no land mammals other than two unique species of bats, although there were marine mammals such as seals and whales. The fauna was dominated by birds – the land birds were largely unique, but there were also species that migrated to and from the central Pacific and Siberia, and sea birds common to the Southern Hemisphere, including albatrosses, penguins and seagulls.

The flora, isolated for so long, had evolved independently from the rest of the world. A biologist has described New Zealand as 'another universe'.

The arrival of the first humans, bringing with them cultivable plants – such as kumara and taro – and two other mammals – dogs and rats – ended the isolation. We can only guess how rich the fauna and flora was before their arrival, but we know that shortly after, some of the birds became extinct – notably the large flightless moa. It also seems likely that seal colonies, which had previously ringed the coastline, retreated to less approachable sanctuaries as the more accessible were hunted out.

Devastating as the impact of Pacific Islanders was – the Māori who evolved from them eventually learned to manage, rather than exploit, their environment – the Europeans who arrived in numbers 600 years later, in the nineteenth century, did far more damage. Species were extinguished, ecological systems were destroyed. Two hundred years on, New Zealand still struggles with the notion of sustainability.

The Quarry

Sustainability was not the concern of the transitory visitors who followed the first European explorers. They came to exploit the resources, 'quarrying' the whales, seals, timber, minerals (notably gold) and kauri gum that Europe demanded, and then move on. They were followed by missionaries determined to both save the souls of the Māori and teach them 'civilised' European ways. Later came the settlers who aimed to live in New Zealand, although not a few hoped to retire back 'home' in Europe.

Their settlements faced the problem of how to pay for the goods they imported. In the short term they could be financed by borrowing, but in the longer term the debts would have to be serviced from the proceeds of exports. The quarry was one answer, and many of the settlements were at first based on supplying the resource exploiters. Inevitably the exploited resources ran out. In the mid-nineteenth century the British crown financed the settlers in warfare against the Māori – Auckland was then a military town – but London was unwilling to do this indefinitely. Land speculation – many foreign speculators lost their savings – was another interim strategy to generate a cash inflow to pay for imports. But, ultimately, the settlers had to find a sustainable export base which would support their import requirements.

An early option was wool and tallow, for sheep thrived in the new environment. New Zealand also sent fruit and vegetables to Australia. Grain was not much of an option, because suitable land was limited. In the twentieth century New Zealand was to learn that it was an efficient grower of plantation forests of the Californian radiata pine, which substituted for the depleted native forests as a source of wood. New Zealand could grow meat, but with no way to transport it, sheep carcasses were often left to rot once their wool had been removed.

The tyranny of distance that had isolated New Zealand was overcome for explorers, quarriers and missionaries by the early nineteenth century. But it hung over the settlers, who were not only cut off from the land they thought of as home, but had little to offer it in exchange for the goods they wanted. The most likely future seemed to be as a settlement based on extensive sheep-for-wool farming – the Falklands of the South Pacific.

Refrigeration and After

In 1889, the New Zealand politician Julius Vogel, writing in England, suggested in his futurist novel, *Anno Domini 2000*, that there were prospects for exporting canned fruit and meat. He had missed the boat, which was already increasingly laden with not cans but refrigerated chambers of meat and, later, butter and cheese. Intensive sheep farming for both meat and wool, and dairy farming, began to take over from extensive sheep farming for wool alone.

These pastoral exports were possible because, following the 'Corn Laws' debate about the advantages and disadvantages of free trade, the British government had removed restrictions on imports of food in 1846. Had it protected its farmers, the story of New Zealand would have been very different. So would Britain's. Robert Fogel argues that better nutrition was the key to the economic gains of the late nineteenth century.[1]

The story of how refrigeration created the industries which transformed New Zealand's economy and society is obvious enough, but we set it out here to illustrate one of the standard models of international trade theory – including some features that are not always discussed. Its essence is that refrigeration slashed the cost of transporting meat and dairy products around the world from prohibitive to a small proportion of the selling price. This dramatic change was reinforced by the introduction of faster and safer steamships with iron hulls, the cutting of the Panama Canal, which greatly shortened the distance to market, and the use of the telegraph for virtually instantaneous communication between buyers and sellers.

The Formal Model of Economic Trade

We might think of this as a reduction in a tariff from infinity to (near enough to) zero. The formal economic model predicts that New Zealand and similar countries with a comparative advantage in pastoral production would expand, while British farming would contract, its resources being transferred into making manufactured products which New Zealand and its peers could now afford to purchase.

Deploying more of its resources to pastoral farming gave New Zealand a higher return than alternatives such as manufacturing – the economy became more productive. Similarly, Britain could deploy more resources into manufacturing, where its comparative advantage lay, so that it too had a more productive economy. Both economies were, in principle, better off. The conclusion is so familiar that its astonishing insight is often overlooked. This model assumes that the factors of production – capital, labour, land – are fixed in location and cannot move between economies. Yet the standard economic model (we use this in the next chapter) assumes these factors are mobile and will go to where there is the highest return. But some cannot. British land cannot move to New Zealand, nor New Zealand sun to Britain. And sometimes factor movement is not allowed: there are widespread restrictions on migration, for example.

The model says that some of the gains that would arise from factor mobility can be obtained by trading the goods instead. It is as if some of the immobile factors are embodied in the goods that are exported.

This brief description of the standard international trade model, first articulated by David Ricardo during the Corn Laws debate in the early nineteenth century, has skipped over a number of assumptions which may be important in practice:

- To benefit from the potential gains from trade – in this case from falling costs of distance rather than reduced tariffs – resources must be redeployed so that there is effectively no unemployment of land, labour or capital. This assumption may be true in the long run, but the short-run transition may be difficult for those who move from jobs to unemployment to new jobs in expanding sectors.
- Trading prices are assumed to reflect the actual economic costs of the resources involved. They may not.
- The model assumes no effect on the terms of trade – that export prices will not fall relative to import prices. The importance of this assumption will be explained in Chapter 24 and in Part IV, where we consider the future of the world economy.
- Where economies of scale are involved, the model becomes more complex and conclusions are less certain, We explore this complication in the next few chapters.[2]
- The distribution of the gains and losses is a very important issue.

Distributing the Gains From Trade

Very often the outcome of trade liberalisation is assumed to be that both economies are better off. But economies are inhabited by people. As a Brazilian colonel remarked after a particularly harsh set of measures was taken: 'the economy is doing well, but the people are not'. What the formal models show is that – under certain circumstances – the additional consumption can be distributed so that no one is worse off. In practice, this redistribution rarely happens.

Thus while the flood into the British market at reasonable prices of refrigerated sheep meat from Australasia and the Americas improved the diet of British workers, British sheep farmers found their markets for fresh meat undercut, their incomes diminishing, and the local industry contracting. In principle British workers could have subsidised British farmers and still been better off. But they did not.

Trade liberalisation and falling costs of distance always have a distributional impact. Some people are always potentially worse off. Frequently they are actually worse off. Hence the strong political lobby against 'free trade'. Meanwhile, those who will benefit from free trade glide over the distributional impact, for the gainers prefer not to compensate the losers.

We need to be alert to such distributional quarrels. Economies are inherently unfair, in the sense that some people are better off than others for reasons that can only be explained by the idiosyncratic impact of markets, and not by any theory of justice. The incomes British sheep farmers got before the advent of refrigeration cannot be justified scientifically; neither can the lower incomes they got after refrigeration had undermined their market. One situation is not inherently fairer than the other.

Sometimes the poor are heavily affected by the trade liberalisation. This is not always true – sometimes the workers laid off are among the top wage-earners, and hitherto well-off businesspeople may lose their safe protected markets. Where the poor are affected, measures to ease their losses can be taken. But people well above the poverty line took their chances when choosing their life paths. If these prove to be less prosperous than was hoped, or if an economic change reduces prosperity to more modest circumstances, then so be it.

This discussion of the distributional changes resulting from altered trading patterns is intended to be sensible and dispassionate, an illustration of (Matthew) Rabin's Law that a policy change almost always makes someone worse off. It is difficult, however, to be dispassionate about the sanctimoniousness of those – and their economist acolytes – who advocate trade liberalisation when this is in their own interests, while ignoring the fact that it will make others worse off.

How Big are the Gains from Trade?

While the standard model of international trade predicts gains from trade liberalisation, it does not say how large these will be. Careful measurement often concludes that the increase in output from eliminating tariffs, quotas and subsidies can be very small – typically less than 1 per cent of GDP. While it is possible to include in the model assumptions that will generate fabulous gains, these never actually happen. Retrospective studies following trade liberalisation usually find actual gains even smaller than those promised. Often the winners get far more of their gains from the losers than from increases in productivity.

We should not be surprised. Those who are made worse off are rarely compensated. Were the gains really large, compensation could be provided readily from the resulting boom in tax revenue. If there is not much gain, compensation is much harder to fund.

The studies referred to here are usually of trade liberalisation in the late twentieth century. Possibly earlier trade liberalisation was more beneficial, since protection levels were much higher. However, productivity gains from the falling costs of distance may have been even higher, with lower transport costs releasing resources for other purposes.

The formal model underpinning the last few paragraphs is a static one. The significant gains from trade come from the dynamic processes they trigger. Such gains are both harder to model and harder to measure, but experience shows that they can also be dramatic.

The Dynamic Gains from Trade

The standard model assumes that technologies are unaffected by a change in trading relations. This is not usually true. When the New Zealand pastoral industry supplied meat and dairy products only to the local community it faced no great pressure to innovate. As the industry expanded to supply Britain, the pressures increased. New Zealand became one of the world's major meat and dairy produce exporters because of technological innovations which otherwise may have occurred much more slowly, or not at all. It was not just a matter of growing 'two blades of grass where there had been one', as the grasslands revolution is sometimes summarised. It involved breeding better livestock and husbanding them more efficiently to ensure they ate the grass. (Jonathan Swift's remark in *Gulliver's Travels*, 'that whoever could make . . . two blades of grass to grow upon a spot of ground where only one grew before, would deserve better of mankind, and do more essential service to his country, than the whole race of politicians put together', was nevertheless a shrewd one.)

Beyond the farm gate, there has been a constant search for higher productivity in the collection, processing and distribution processes. New products have been identified and marketed – today pharmaceuticals are derived from the offal of cows and sheep. Related products – electric fences, dairy equipment, farm management software – have become New Zealand exports too. (The dairy factory's need for hygiene resulted in expertise in piping which was applied to wine-making.) These examples involve the 'hard' technologies of the natural sciences. But there was also innovation in 'soft' technologies as the industry created new organisational forms – such as the dairy cooperative – to meet its needs.

The previous paragraph's story of an industry progressing by creating new technologies is familiar in many other instances of increasing trade. These are the real gains from trade: not the static gains detailed painstakingly in the standard economics model, but the dynamic gains from innovation as a result of international competitive pressures. Chapter 6 explains that these gains arise not so much from 'comparative advantage' as from 'competitive advantage'.

In the long run the technological gains do not accrue to the producers. Initially they do benefit from the innovations – otherwise they would not introduce them. But the new methods and products are soon adopted by other producers, and competition between them drives down their prices. The long-run beneficiaries are consumers, most of whom will live overseas in the case of an export industry: third-world children eating milk biscuits, British workers enjoying cheap Sunday roasts.

Yet producers cannot ignore technological innovations, even though these give them only temporary profits. Failure to innovate will see them soon overtaken by other producers. Succeeding in business is a matter of generating temporary profit after temporary profit from innovation after innovation.

Social and Political Consequences
While the story thus far has been an economic one, such transformations have social and political repercussions. The changes in production methods as a result of refrigeration changed social relations, with hierarchical class-bound sheep stations eclipsed by egalitarian family farms serviced by local towns.

New Zealand began to behave as if it were a sustainable economy and society. The first political party – more permanent than the loose and shifting coalitions which governed the quarry – was established in the early 1890s, a decade after the first refrigerated exports. Women, whose motherly qualities are hardly necessary in the transient quarry, became a political force, gaining the national vote in 1893 (the first nation where they did so) and leading the campaign against the 'demon drink', the social lubricant of the quarry. From 1890 New Zealand Prime Ministers chose to retire in New Zealand. It was becoming a green and pleasant land.

The formal models with which economists explore economic relationships largely ignore social and political relationships, assuming the institutions which regulate the economy to be fixed or irrelevant. As we report in Chapter 23, those who study societies and political systems have been unable to develop equally rigorous models. It is harder to track the social and political consequences of the changing costs of distance, yet we must. The New Zealand experience shows that to ignore them is to miss the greatest consequences of all.

Four | **Regions and Economies of Scale • The United States**

Globalisation began with the integration of separate regions into single national economies. An early example was the transport system's creation of the United States economy in the nineteenth century. But success depended upon the way the economy was regulated. The result was the twentieth century's greatest economy, which provides one model for a globalised world.

In 1767, Catherine the Great asserted that Russia covered an area so large that it 'requires absolute power vested in the ruler'. She did not know that on the other side of the world, another country would soon solve a similar problem of territorial extent by taking the opposite approach, the decentralisation of power.

Although it is very difficult to measure such things, in the mid-eighteenth century the per capita production of the British colonies which became the United States of America seems to have been much the same as that of Russia. Today US material output per person is about six times higher than Russia's, and even that magnitude may not capture the difference in quality of life. There are a number of reasons why the performance of the two – each rich in resources – differs. A major one has been the different governance arrangements, a lesson relearned just a decade ago when Russia shed communism. It was hoped that post-communist Russia would flourish. Sadly it has not, in part because it did not have a governance – the 'meta-technologies' which are elaborated in Chapter 23 – providing a basis for economic success.

That the United States discovered such a system more than 200 years earlier is astonishing, all the more so if one recalls how primitive the pre-revolutionary economy was by today's standards. As an American scholar remarked to me, 'they were closer to the medieval economy than the modern one'. The northern states were based upon largely self-sufficient yeomen farmers, who, while not characteristic of the European lands which they had left, were hardly modern. Further south, where more settlers lived, the farms with their indentured labour and slaves were more like the feudal society the settlers had – geographically – left behind, even though some had moved from serf to lord.

Although we think of the United States as 'the New World', the American Revolution occurred some 150 years after the *Mayflower* sailed in 1620. The European settlement of the US is several hundred years older than the settler states of Australasia. Both George Washington and Catherine the Great were contemporaries of James Cook – all three were born around 1730.

The US Constitution

The US constitution originated in a commercial dispute between Maryland and Virginia in 1784 over customs duties on the Potomac River that separated them. James Madison had helped settle the matter, but the possibility of further disputes under the confederation arrangement which followed the American revolution led to a convention in 1787 with the limited task of recommending revisions to the articles of confederation. Presided over by Washington, with Madison attending every session, the convention instead submitted a constitution for a federal United States of America, which was adopted after public assemblies in most states agreed to it. However, they also sought guarantees of individual liberty to complement the proposed constitution, which regulated relations between the states and the federal authority. Their proposals became the first ten amendments (the Bill of Rights), which were immediately adopted.

The key economics player was Alexander Hamilton, the founding father who was the best read in the discipline. Although he was a minor participant in the constitutional convention, as the majority contributor to *The Federalist Papers* and the first Secretary of the US Treasury he had a major role in the constitution's development.

The New York Historical Society exaggerated when they described Hamilton as 'The Maker of Modern America', for his vision was based on the economy of the day, with only the dimmest awareness of how this might evolve. It is true that Hamilton promoted manufacturing, but this was a very different activity from what was to come. It would be foolish to think that he, or anyone in those times, envisaged the organisations such as US Steel, General Motors and Microsoft that would later dominate American commerce.

Even so, two of Hamilton's aims laid the foundations for the future American economy. He wanted to prevent the kind of conflict between the states which the 1784 dispute presaged, and he wanted to have a central government which could effectively fight a foreign power.

The constitution severely limited the commercial powers of the states, reducing both the opportunities for interstate conflicts and the financial wherewithal to settle them by military means. Secretary of the Treasury Hamilton reinforced this by having the federal government assume the debts of the states, reducing their need to raise finance to service such debts – a revenue flow which could potentially be used to finance wars. (To obtain a majority for assumption, Hamilton sacrificed New York's claim as the future capital of the USA.) He also put the federal government's finances on a sound footing, paying off old debt and consolidating revenue. As quartermaster under Washington during the War of Independence, Hamilton was well aware of the difficulties of financing effective warfare.

The resulting federal arrangement is so familiar today that we overlook how revolutionary it was two hundred years ago. Many of the founding fathers wanted to maintain the autonomy of the states in which they lived, in the spirit of the articles of confederation. Perhaps their vision was of continental Europe, with its plethora of independent states, although they wanted rule by the people rather than by petty potentates. Even today, this vision of a confederation in which the individual states maintain considerable powers over the central government is practised on the other side of the Atlantic, insofar as the nation-states of the European Union have more fiscal and other powers than the states of the US.

America's federal arrangements stripped its states of significant fiscal and economic power – from the beginning they had no power to control commerce across their borders. They had another unexpected outcome, the empowerment of the market. Although the ideas behind it were in circulation, Hamilton does not seem to have read Adam Smith's *Wealth of Nations*, published in 1776, until after he ceased to be Secretary of the Treasury in 1795. Nevertheless, in consequence of the constitution and his tenure of office, the market became the primary economic regulator. Power was not simply shifted from the states up to the federation. Much was shifted down to the voluntary transactions of individuals participating in a market.

Not only were there prohibitions on artificial barriers to cross-border movements of goods and services. The constitution also rejected restrictions on capital and labour. It enabled the United States to be a sort of globalised (regionally integrated) economy some two centuries ago, although the natural barriers to trade of distance costs were at first high. In a regulatory sense the US was more globalised then than the world is today, because there were (and are) no restrictions on labour mobility within the US.

Thus if factors of production – labour and capital – were more productive in one part of the US than another, the rewards to them – wages and profits – were higher, and more would be attracted from less productive regions. This is not to assume that factor mobility was easy, or that it did not generate personal suffering. But it allowed the economy to exploit potential productivity gains. Had there been restrictions on mobility, not all the productivity lift from the widening of the American market – promised by Adam Smith's theory of specialisation – could have been achieved. Here was the market functioning at its economic best, albeit with political and social stress.

This internal mobility was reinforced by inflows of migrants and capital. Once in the US, both could move to wherever prospects were most promising.

Diminishing Distance
At the beginning of the nineteenth century the US population was small, just over five million, and scattered in isolated settlements. President Thomas Jefferson took three days to reach Washington from his farm at Monticello, outside Charlottesville, a trip which today takes a couple of hours by road. Whatever its implications for human intercourse – Jefferson stayed overnight with James Madison and James Monroe, two future Presidents – and information flows, isolation limited the possibility of trade, so settlements had to be largely self-sufficient.

Over the next century America was integrated by roads, canals connecting waterways, and later railways. By 1850 almost 6000 kilometres of canal supplemented the natural waterways and seas. The most famous – indeed the only one which proved commercially viable – was the Erie Canal in upstate New York, which linked Lake Erie – and hence the Great Lakes and the landlocked Midwest – to the Hudson River, the Atlantic Ocean and international commerce. We will see in the next chapter how the canal, opened in 1825, was a catalyst for the development of the global city of New York, at the junction of river and ocean. That the other canals were not commercial successes does not mean they were economic failures. In some cases the benefits were captured by people other than those who invested and lost their savings. Railways were begun a little later but by 1860 covered almost 50,000 kilometres across the USA.

The resulting falls in the costs of distance were spectacular. The cost of land transport of bulky products fell by 95 per cent in 40 years. Freight rates on the Mississippi–Ohio river system fell about 75 per cent for travel downstream and 90 per cent upstream. Between Buffalo and New York they fell from $100 a ton to $8. The speed of freightage quintupled, for a freight train travelled at 10 to 12 miles an hour compared to the stately 2 miles per hour of a loaded wagon on a turnpike.[1]

Robert Fogel, who was awarded a Nobel Prize in economics for his contributions to economic history, concluded that the impact of the railroads on American economic growth was small. Whatever the truth of this assessment – caveats about the neglect of economies of scale appear below – it would be idle to ignore the impact of the elaboration of the transport infrastructure – road, canal, rail – as a whole. This evolving transport network unquestionably changed the nature of the US economy.

Gains from Economies of Scale

We saw in the previous chapter how the advent of refrigeration changed New Zealand. The effect of reductions in the cost of distance is much greater where there are economies of scale, as there are in much manufacturing. Here is a simple arithmetical example.

Consider two cities, one twice the size of the other, whose citizens each buy one particular manufactured item each year. Initially there are industrial plants in each city, using identical technology. The plant in Small Town produces the item at a unit (average) cost of $1.20. However the plant in Big Town produces twice as many, and with economies of scale its unit cost is only $1.00.[2]

Suppose the cost of transport is 30 cents an item. The Big Town plant cannot ship to Small Town for less than $1.30 an item, and so the Small Town plant flourishes. But if the unit cost of transport falls to 10 cents, the Big Town plant can undercut the Small Town plant, forcing it to close. The situation is summarised in the table which shows the selling price in the two towns under different transport assumptions, with the preferred source in **bold.**

	HIGH TRANSPORT COSTS		LOW TRANSPORT COSTS	
	Small Town Plant	Big Town Plant	Small Town Plant	Big Town Plant
Small Town Purchaser	**$1.20**	$1.30	$1.20	**$1.10**
Big Town Purchaser	$1.50	**$1.00**	$1.30	**$1.00**

Following the closure of Small Town's plants, its redundant workers may shift to another local job, perhaps accepting lower pay, or they may move to Big Town, a shift facilitated by the lower transport costs. The productivity of the economy as a whole rises with the concentration of production in Big Town's plant. So does production, once the redundant workers have been redeployed.

In principle everyone could be better off (or at least no worse off); in practice, some will suffer. At this point another effect reinforces the kind of static allocative gains described in the previous chapter. Suppose the Big Town plant reaps additional economies of scale from its increase in production, and now produces at a cost of 90 cents an item, selling in Small Town at $1.00

because of the transport cost. This gain is in addition to the static gains from reallocation.

A possible outcome is summarised in the table, which assumes that Big Town purchases 200,000 and Small Town purchases 100,000. When both plants were working the total cost of the items was $320,000. If production costs in the Big Town plant had remained the same after it took over the small city market, the total cost of the items would have been $310,000, a gain of $10,000. However, when there are also plant economies of scale, the single plant can supply the product at a total cost of $280,000, including transport.

	HIGH TRANSPORT COSTS	LOW TRANSPORT COSTS	WITH GAINS FROM ECONOMIES OF SCALE
SMALL TOWN	$120,000	$110,000	$100,000
BIG TOWN	$200,000	$200,000	$180,000
TOTAL	$320,000	$310,000	$280,000

These calculations are notional, but they do illustrate the potential for significant gains from plant economies of scale in addition to the static gains from falling costs of trade.

The previous chapter's story of the stimulus to technological innovation in agriculture arising from the opening up of new markets also applies to manufacturing. Recall that the technologies may already have (almost) existed, but it required the new market circumstances for businesses to implement them. The same applies to manufacturing, where producers can also reap potential economies of scale that were unavailable when markets were smaller.

Thus the productivity gains resulting from a fall in the cost of distance may be enhanced by economies of scale. Fogel's focus on the gains to the agricultural sector resulting from railroads may omit a more important story for manufactures, where economies of scale were being reaped from falls in the costs of distance.[3]

Conclusion

The US constitution created the possibility of a globalised economy within the boundaries of the federation of states, because it allowed goods and services, labour, capital and technology to flow without artificial restriction. As the internal costs of distance fell – in the nineteenth century because of canals and rail, and later telegraph, cars, telephones, planes and the internet – isolated localities were consolidated into regional economies and subsequently into the US economy.

The gains came not simply from being able to exploit the most productive locations for economic activity. There were also gains from economies of scale. This chapter has explained the relevance of plant economies of scale; the next explains the further gains from industry economies of scale.

In 1820, the US population of 10 million people was 1.4 per cent of the world population. By 1913 the proportion had increased to 3.6 per cent (98 million people). Meanwhile, the US share of world GDP (output) had risen from 1.8 per cent to 19.1 per cent. Thus US production per person increased from just above to more than five times the world average as the country reaped the benefits of falling costs of distance and economies of scale that were made possible by a constitution which did not restrict the internal mobility of labour and capital.

The pattern of production changed even more dramatically. Agriculture contributed 70 per cent of US GDP in 1820, but just 38 per cent in 1890. Meanwhile, manufacturing increased from 15 to 24 per cent, and services from 15 to 38 per cent. (Today the shares are 3, 23 and 74 per cent respectively.)

By 1913, North America (including Canada) accounted for 33 per cent of world manufacturing (the US figures alone are not available), compared with about 2 per cent in 1820. Undoubtedly the continent's natural resource base was an enormous advantage, enabling it to absorb millions of immigrants. But its ability to seize the leading edge of manufacturing enabled it to lift its performance further. The United States' constitutional arrangements allowed it to reap the benefits from consolidation and economies of scale to achieve gains in manufacturing productivity that no other country could match.

It would be easy to idealise the achievement of the nineteenth-century US economy. But despite the many individual hardships – even slavery – the US turned itself into the economic powerhouse of the world. This was the power of globalisation in a region, and it indicates the potential for globalisation in the world.

Five | The Forces of Agglomeration • New York

Globalisation unleashes the powerful forces of agglomeration that arise from economies of scale within an industry or cluster of industries. These forces super-multiply the advantages of location into the complex conurbations of many industries and large populations that are exemplified by New York.

In 1674 the Netherlands transferred 'New Netherland' to England in exchange for Surinam (Dutch Guiana). Apparently they valued sugar over the possibilities of the frontier town of New York. Even in 1800 the city, the largest in the fledgling United States of America, contained only around 65,000 souls; London was nearing a million. Had William Wordsworth stood on Brooklyn rather than Westminster Bridge (it was not built until 1883), it is doubtful he would have described 'a sight so touching in its majesty', nor New York as a 'mighty heart'. Yet today one might describe the city – home of the United Nations, Wall Street and so much more, chosen by Al Qaeda as a target for its greatest act of terrorism – as the centre of the modern world.

The story of this transformation began with location, but then powerful industrial economies of scale and externalities – agglomeration – took over, supercharging the growth generated by the falling costs of distance.

Location
The sugar which the Dutch valued more than Manhattan Island began New York's path to prosperity. The shipping path from the West Indies to Europe involved sailing up the eastern coast of America and then striking across the Atlantic to Europe. North America became the source of materials and supplies for the plantations. Europeans did not like living in the Caribbean (although they forced African slaves to), so wherever possible settlements and industry were located on the American continent. There were various potential harbours along this coast, but Philadelphia was too small and Boston too far north, so while there was activity – including sugar refineries

– all along the seaboard, New York became the hub port between Europe and the Caribbean.

Its stronger links south gave New York a greater share of industries such as ship building and repair, and provedoring with locally made supplies. Local producers were well placed to supply the Caribbean too. The city became a financial centre for West Indian investors, linking them to their counterparts in Europe. As the point of first contact for European shipping, it also became the centre for news. And so a group of apparently diverse industries clustered around the port of New York, each the consequence of its location.

New York had another locational advantage. The Hudson River was navigable for 150 miles inland, opening up the interior for resource extraction and farming to an extent no other American Atlantic waterway did. New York's dominance of access to the interior was enhanced by the Erie Canal, opened in 1825 to connect the Hudson to Lake Erie and thence to the vast plains of the American Midwest. Previously it took anything from 15 to 45 days for an eight-horse wagon to travel over dirt roads from Buffalo to Albany – at a cost of $100 a ton. The canal shortened the journey to nine days and reduced the cost to $6 a ton. Other states tried to construct canals through the Appalachian Mountains, which divided the seaboard from the interior, but with much less commercial success. The Erie Canal took $42 million in tolls for a construction cost of $7 million. Even the financing of its building strengthened New York as a financial centre.

New York was located at the seaward end of this canal/river system. Whether it was produce from the Midwest out, or migrants and manufactures in, the harbour prospered, and so did the city. Perhaps the migrants were the greatest import. Many arrived at the dock expecting to move on. Enough stayed to give the city its bustling ethnic mix, with the talents, skills, experiences and entrepreneurship to seize in New York the opportunities offered by the New World. Such was the concentration of services in the city that it also became one of the transhipment centres for cotton. When new forms of transport diminished the significance of water, New York remained a hub for the railroads, highways and airlanes.

New York is not well located for all purposes. Manufactured goods exported from China to the US were unloaded in America's Pacific ports for shipment across the continent by road and rail. Custom was pulled back with the advent of huge container ships around Cape Horn. There are now proposals – not surprisingly emanating from New York shippers – to widen the Panama Canal to take boats bigger than a Panamax (the largest which can go through the Canal). If global warming melts sufficient Arctic ice, the ships from East Asia will travel via the Bering Strait across the seas north of Canada to New York, as well as other Atlantic American and European harbours.

Agglomeration

In the nineteenth century New York's population grew from 65,000 to 3.4 million, doubling about every 15 years.[1] Much of this increase can be explained by the growth of the economic base arising from industries which were sustained by 'exporting' goods and services to other regions. Activity in the base is 'multiplied' by the provision of a second round of suppliers of goods and services to those who work the base, there is a third round of activity supplying the second round, and so on.

The full multiplier – the ratio between total activity and that generated by the export base – varies for each urban centre. But typically, the larger the export base, the larger the multiplier. This is reminiscent of the Parable of the Talents: 'For to everyone who has, more shall be given, and he will have an abundance'. Moreover, the multiplier is dynamic. One New York 'talent' led to another. That the city was already the financial capital of America made the funding of the Erie Canal that much easier. The financiers were further rewarded in abundance when the canal's role as conduit into the interior strengthened New York as a financial centre.

The exact mechanisms by which this multiplier is sensitive to the size of the region and local dynamics are poorly understood. Obviously economies of scale are important, since a larger region can support activities which would be too costly in a smaller region. But while they help explain the overall growth of America (see Chapter 4), they do not explain why economic activity concentrated in nodes like New York.

We have already described economies of scale for a firm. The agglomeration of industry – where many businesses produce similar things – seems to derive from economies of scales of industries rather than firms. As the overall industry gets larger, the costs of individual firms fall. Because they are competing against one another, the benefits of these falling costs do not go to the firm, as they could were it a monopoly, but enable the local industry to undercut businesses elsewhere, thus reinforcing its dominant position. This need not occur in the largest centre. Sometimes, for reasons of history or by accident, an industry will evolve in a smaller centre (see Chapter 6). Nevertheless, larger centres are likely to have clusters of industries supplying the nation.

Exactly why there are industry economies of scale is a puzzle. The English economist Alfred Marshall (1842–1924) suggested they arose in markets rich in specialised skills (and the benefits from such specialisation), from knowledge spillovers (where individual firms cannot prevent other firms learning their technological innovations), and from backward and forward linkages (where other firms benefit from being close to the core business).

More recently, Masahisa Fujita and Jacques-François Thisse identified 'the relevant externalities for the formation of [industrial] clusters':

1. Mass production (the internal economies that are identical to scale economies at the firm's level);
2. Availability of specialised input services;
3. Formation of highly specialised labour force and the production of new ideas, both based on the accumulation of human capital and face-to-face communications;
4. The existence of modern infrastructure.[2]

It is characteristic of economic development that such agglomeration effects are dynamic. They do not all happen instantly, but feed on one another over time.

The industries which benefit are not always obvious. Being a centre of finance increases the likelihood that other businesses will locate their headquarters in the city. They too require lawyers, accountants and other business services. Much of the work of such people involves sophisticated, discretionary decision-making. So while they enjoy a ball game they are also more likely to go to the theatre or purchase a painting – an effect reinforced by the conspicuous consumption of the rich and the need for venues outside business in which to build interpersonal networks. Thus finance and headquarters activities generate a group of sophisticated cultural activities that spill over into creative industries such as art, publishing, fashion, design, writing, and music. And so New York became a major cultural centre. Not surprisingly, it also has a world-class university. (Another 'industry' which generates cultural activity and 'business' servicing is government. New York is not the political capital of the United States, or even of its state. But after 1945 it became the headquarters of the United Nations, which reinforced those activities in the city.)

These agglomerative forces were certainly powerful in the evolution of New York up to the beginning of the First World War, when the city's population neared 5 million. But size brought its own problems.

Congestion and Poor Governance

Throughout its history, New York has experienced tension between positive agglomerative forces for growth and the negative effects of congestion when its infrastructure cannot meet the increased demands placed on it. Water and sewerage are part of the story, but the obvious example is transport.

Population growth increased the need for commuting, and it also increased the volume of goods transported between businesses (including the port). Repeatedly New York introduced new systems which enabled more to be carried further and faster around town – roads, trams, elevated railroad, subways, lifts. (Elevators are currently the fastest way to move people in urban settings – as is nicely illustrated by New York's famous skyscrapers.)

Another inhibitor has been governance. The question of just how badly New York has been governed need not detain us here, nor whether this is inevitable in so decentralised a polity as the US. The fact is that in recent years the municipality has been nearly or actually bankrupt. The quality of municipal services has suffered, and the rich have taken refuge outside the city boundaries where taxes are not so onerous, compounding the city's financial woes.

New York reached 7 million in 1950 and has hovered around that level ever since – still the largest city in the US by a factor of two. Is this stagnation a consequence of the base moving somewhere else, the agglomerative forces weakening, or the congestion and governance costs predominating? It is too soon to tell.

But there is another kind of explanation. What are New York's boundaries? While the Hudson River was certainly a route into the interior, it also stopped the city expanding across it. So its west bank became part of New Jersey rather than the state of New York. Are not the nearly 300,000 people living in Newark really New Yorkers? Indeed, despite the many jurisdictions, is not the 45-million-person conurbation, sometimes called 'BosWash' or 'Bosnywash' or 'Boshington', occupying the corridor between Boston 400 kilometres to the north and Washington 350 kilometres to the south, an economic unity? In which case, Amtrak plus freeways and airways are its commuter services. This question will not be answered here. It is posed simply to point out that with falling costs of distance, the economy and daily life may ignore the jurisdictional and statistical boundaries which frame our thinking. This conclusion will be repeated in later chapters in relation to countries.

From such a perspective, New York did not stagnate so much as grow outside its jurisdictional boundaries. The agglomeration effects remain powerful, while the congestion and governance problems were resolved by this enlargement – for the time being, at least.

Six | Competitive Advantage • Nokia

One consequence of economies of scale is that the location of economic activity no longer depends upon the local particularities which underpinned the comparative advantage that drove the first two centuries of globalisation. Rather, an activity begun for contingent reasons will succeed if it can maintain its 'competitive advantage' through constant innovation that promotes product differentiation and reduces costs.

In folk singer Woody Guthrie's children's song, a tot asks her parents questions such as, 'Why is the sky blue?' The parent gives unsatisfactory responses. The final question, 'Why don't you answer my questions? Why, oh why, oh why?', elicits, 'Because I don't know the answers.' From childhood, we expect answers to questions. As we get older, we expect the answers to be couched in general theories. But sometimes a general answer does not exist, or it lacks the precision to make the kind of prediction we expect.

The Nokia Story
Consider the question, 'Why is the world's biggest mobile phone producer based in Finland?' Journalists often answer with anecdotes – it is cold in winter, so Finns need a means of communication; Finnish boys are so shy that they had to devise texting to contact girls. These are hardly general explanations. Other places just as cold did not develop a mobile phone industry; boys can be shy just about anywhere.

Some accounts are essentially a historical sequence setting out how Nokia, a forestry company, developed the technology, and step by step became the supplier of 40 per cent of the world's mobiles. But how can a company from a country of just 5¼ million people do a deal to provide China with 300 million phones in one year? (Not all are produced in Finland, but the designers and top management are based there.)

A third approach is to say, humbly, that it was an accident that Nokia in Finland rather than business XYZ in country ABC got into the mobile market, and came to dominate the world. The story is all the more curious because Nokia's rivals started producing mobile phones as a result of their involvement in related areas, as you might expect: electricity, radio, telephony, consumer electronics. Nokia does not fit this business model at all.

Nokia began in 1856 as a forestry company with a pulp mill near the river Nokia – the Finnish name for a weasel-like creature, the sable. When in 1903 Nokia built its own power plant, the Finnish Rubber Works built a new factory nearby to share the cheap energy. Rubber Works began to buy Nokia shares, and in 1922 Finnish Cable Works joined them. However, the merger of the three companies was completed only in 1967.

This is still some distance from the consumer electronics for which Nokia is world-famous. Perhaps its origins lie in the expansion of electricity into homes and factories in the early part of the twentieth century, which led to the establishment of Finnish Cable Works and then to the manufacture of cables for the telegraph and telephone industries. In 1960 Cable Works set up an Electronics Department. By 1963 they had built their first radio telephone, followed in 1965 by data modems. In the 1970s the company developed the Nokia DX 200, a digital switch for telephone exchanges.

Nokia tried to develop personal computers, monitors and television sets in the 1980s, but later sold its interests in them. When the world's first international cellular mobile telephone network was introduced in Scandinavia in 1981, Nokia made the first car phones for it. Its 'transportable' mobile phones were huge and heavy. By 1987 Nokia had produced its first 'hand-portable' mobile phones. These have continued to shrink in size while expanding in technological complexity ever since. The 1980s and 1990s saw widespread deregulation of telecommunications and the radio spectrum, which stimulated competition and customer expectations. In 1987 the European Union (as it became) adopted the goal of wire-free telecommunications by 1991. Helping Finland meet this goal launched Nokia on the road to world domination.

Today between 30 and 40 per cent of the world's cellphones are made by Nokia, the market leader in every country except the US (where Motorola leads). Its almost 60,000 employees are scattered across 120 countries and five continents. Each year the company assembles more than 200 million phones (excluding its China sales) from 6 billion components – one for each person on Earth.

How did Nokia do it? Undoubtedly Finnish design and business skills were important, but these exist in other Scandinavian countries. One crucial decision was made in the 1960s, when it was exporting 20 per cent of its output to the Soviet Union: Nokia decided to seek western markets. But so did other companies. In the end, without downplaying the achievement of

Nokia or the talent of those who worked for it, one concludes that it was luck that the world's biggest cellphone producer originated in Finland and remains based there, contributing 3.7 per cent to Finnish material output (GDP) while manufacturing its products throughout the world.

Such an explanation may seem unsatisfactory in its imprecision. But to the extent that it is true, it has the profound implication that in a world with low costs of distance, a firm with a world-dominating technology can pop up in just about any conducive environment. That means that high-technology firms need not cluster in a few central locations, with the rest of the world relegated to resource providers – hewers of wood and drawers of water.

To explain this new phenomenon, sometimes called 'competitive advantage', we need to look first at 'absolute advantage' and 'comparative advantage'.

Absolute Advantage

High costs of distance discourage trade. In 1800 only 1 per cent of the world's GDP was exported (and imported), and even domestic trade over long distances was uncommon. Today internationally traded merchandise amounts to about 20 per cent of GDP, to which can be added services.

Two hundred years ago, a country or region imported products it either could not make itself, or could make only with extreme inefficiency. Thus Europe imported spices from the east and sugar from the west. Typically these were expensive luxuries. The vast majority of products consumed by locals were produced nearby, if not on the farm on which they lived.

A simple, although not quite accurate, term for such trade is 'absolute advantage'. This exists when the resources required for an exporter to make a product are less – considerably less, given the cost of transportation – than the resources the consuming country would need to use to make it. Absolute advantage dominated the pre-globalisation era.

Comparative Advantage

As the costs of distance fell, countries began to import products which they could now make themselves at reasonable cost, but remained cheaper to import. Such trade had a 'comparative advantage'. The theory of comparative advantage – the first deep insights came from David Ricardo in the early nineteenth century – need detain us only briefly. It is sometimes said that the notion is counter-intuitive, but it is no more surprising than the familiar concept of specialisation. Instead of a person specialising, a country does. How much poorer would each of us be if we were only allowed to trade in those (absolute advantage) commodities which we could not make ourselves?

Many of the ideas underpinning comparative advantage which appear complex can be simply explained. For instance, a person or country that is better at a number of activities than another person or country may devolve some of these in order to reap the advantages of specialising in those they are comparatively best at. Or suppose – in contrast to the experience described in Chapter 4 – that labour had not been able to migrate across the Atlantic. America could still to some extent have benefited from that labour by importing the goods it made – importing the embodied labour rather than the labour itself. However, as a general rule, greater economic/material gains arise when labour migrates to the most productive sites. The theory of international trade says that the trade in goods only partially offsets labour mobility.

Comparative advantage occurs where countries differ in their resources (factor endowment), labour, capital and/or technology, and there is some hindrance to the redistribution of the resources to the most profitable uses. Land and related resources cannot be transferred internationally (boundary changes aside), labour and capital movements may be restricted, and two countries may not have equal access to the same technologies (although Chapters 18 and 23 argue that today capital and technology are relatively mobile). Any immobility of factors is offset, in part, by trade under conditions of comparative advantage.

The theory of comparative advantage is sometimes used to justify an uncritical support for free trade. However, the benefits of free trade are sometimes outweighed by the downsides. While some people may be better off, others may suffer (as when the price paid for one's speciality falls). Redeployment from domestic-supply activities closed down by imports to others in the export sector can mean great hardship (and loss of income) for those involved, especially during the period of transition (the length of which is also important). Where there are economies of scale, the economic analysis and the assessment of the benefits of free trade become murkier, as will be shown in Chapter 26.

Absolute advantage trade has become much less important. Until well into the second half of the twentieth century, comparative advantage dominated international trade, with each country exploiting its relative advantages in resources or technology. While this did not necessarily make everyone better off, it usually represented a kind of progress. (In a famous parody on the injustice of trade, candlestick-makers present a petition complaining of the unfair advantage possessed by the sun.)

The next stage was competitive advantage, where factor endowment (along with consumer demand) ceased to be the most important determinant of what was traded.

Competitive Advantage

Finland has no obvious advantage in natural resources which would give it a superiority in producing mobile phones, so we cannot explain Nokia's success by the factors which make up comparative advantage. It succeeded by becoming superior in technology, design, marketing and business practice, and developing a reputation for being the best. At an early stage in the evolution of the market for mobile phones, Nokia happened upon a combination that was favoured by the market. It was one of the first companies to recognise that mobile phones were partly fashion accessories – hence its introduction of changeable coloured covers.

Competitive advantage is usually said to be won by either reducing costs or differentiating products. While this may be true at any given point in time, it can be maintained only by continuing both to lower costs and introduce new products.

Getting the combination right once does not guarantee permanent success. While it is possible to prevent (or restrict) direct competition through secrecy and by taking out copyrights and patents on key technologies, this only reduces the competitive pressure. In any case, the telecommunications sector has been experiencing such rapid technological change – in a system which requires interfaces between equipment supplied by different producers – that restrictive mechanisms have had little effect. A firm which wants to continue dominating an industry must keep innovating. Nokia found this to its cost when it did not recognise quickly enough the demand for 'clamshell' phones (with folding covers) and lost market share temporarily.

But was this solely a matter of innovation? Markets mature. Sometimes product differentiation becomes less important and costs become key. Nokia has responded not only with new designs but by cutting its profit margin. Especially important may be the introduction of mobile phones into poor countries lacking comprehensive systems of traditional telecommunications, bypassing fixed-line technology. Their phones will need to be much cheaper than the fashion accessories of the rich. The medium-term implications for the industry are unclear. Perhaps it will be split between a cheap end with simple functions and an expensive end with complex functions and fashionable design. What about the middle?

At the cheap end, where product differentiation and innovation are less important, a product becomes a 'commodity' sold primarily on the basis of its price, the main arena of competition between products produced on the basis of comparative advantage. We will meet such commodities in later chapters, especially Chapter 24. Another curiosity of competitive advantage, intra-industry trade, is described in Chapter 8.

Coda: Technological Change

In the early 1990s, this writer scorned the suggestion that the monopoly embodied in the telephone line to each house in the developed world was under threat from mobile phones. The judgement remains broadly true a decade and more later, even though the cost of using mobile phones has fallen considerably. In the rich world, Bell wired houses but Nokia (Motorola in America) is wiring persons. As a twenty-something said to me, referring to his relationship with a girlfriend, 'I can't imagine how you lived before cellphones.'

This is not a story about the courting habits of the young, nor even modern telecommunications. The mea culpa is that at the time this writer had no sense of the revolution that mobile phones would create: the personal phone, the text messager, the emailer, the BlackBerry, the . . . .

This example illustrates a crucial feature of new technology. At the beginning we think of it as replacing old technologies. Often, however, a new technology creates new uses which have extraordinary and unexpected impacts on how we produce, consume and live. That is why the shape of a future in which the costs of distance change is so hard to predict.

Seven | **Offshoring • India**

The telecommunications revolution enabled some service activities to be located far from their customers, similar to manufacturing. India is a beneficiary of this offshoring, but because it differs in some ways from the offshoring of manufacturing, the social implications are different.

Economies are usually portrayed as consisting of three (mega-)sectors: a primary sector based on natural resources, a secondary sector based on manufacturing, and a tertiary sector based on the provision of services. Why are they grouped this way, especially as the distinction involves ambiguities? (Is repairing motor vehicles manufacturing or servicing?) While any justification for these divisions is lost in the history of economic ideas, one important aspect is where the economic activity can be located.

The primary or natural resource sector – farming, fishing, forestry and mining – is characterised by businesses which must be located near their most important inputs. Their product is transported to their customers. At the other end of the spectrum, businesses in the tertiary (service) sector – including communications, education, government, health, restaurants, and retailing – are located near their customers. In the middle are activities whose location is not simply determined by the location of inputs or customers. The key factor is the minimisation of costs, including those of transporting inputs and getting products to customers. Such activities are usually placed in the secondary or manufacturing sector.

This explains why fast food is classified as a service, even though it has elements of manufacturing. It also explains why manufacturing has been so central to policies for economic development. Policy-makers cannot do much to affect the location of either primary-sector businesses – which must be near their natural resources – or tertiary-sector activities – unless people are to be moved. But the location of secondary-sector activities can be influenced through policy instruments such as tariffs and subsidies.

The classification is not without its problems. What about industries which shift the customer to the site of production? Tourism is the most prominent example in a category that includes students travelling for education and the sick travelling for medical treatment. While it is usual to call such industries 'services' – since the transaction occurs close to the customer – perhaps they should be put into a separate (fourth) division.

A further anomaly arises when activities which have traditionally been treated as 'services' take on the locational characteristics of manufacturing. Cheaper telecommunications enable some services – call services, some business services, online consumer and business purchasing, information services, software development (although perhaps this should always have been classified as 'manufacturing') – to be located at the end of a line far from the customer.

Not surprisingly, some of the traditional policy battles over promoting manufacturing in particular countries, as an alternative to going 'offshore', are being repeated with respect to these services. But first we need to consider the origins of offshoring in outsourcing.

Outsourcing

Like many neologisms, 'outsourcing' has various meanings. Perhaps the most common definition among those writing systematically is that it occurs where services or components are provided by an outside supplier. (Another term associated with this phenomenon is 'contracting out'.) Sometimes the definition is narrower. Our broader one covers a motor-vehicle assembler sourcing a component from a factory across the road.[1]

On this definition, outsourcing is a common phenomenon. Are publishers outsourcing when they go to a printer for their book? In Gutenberg's day, publishers and printers were the same business. Subsequently they became separated at which point one could say that the outsourcing began. Today this separation is so familiar that few pay much attention to it. Thus the term tends to be applied around the time that an activity which has traditionally been within the firm is outsourced. This typically involves some disruption, with workers laid off (they may or may not be re-employed as subcontractors).[2]

Outsourcing involves the boundary between the firm and the market, an issue raised in a classic paper in 1937 by the economist Ronald Coase, who asked why some economic activities occur within the firm regulated by administrative practices, whereas others occur between firms and are regulated by market practices.[3] Do they 'make' it or 'buy' it?

Most firms use a mixture of the two arrangements. At one end of the spectrum, a subsistence farm may produce the entire product, take it to the local market and sell it. At the other end is a firm which designs computers but outsources their marketing, production, selling and distribution. This business never actually touches the product it supplies.

The prime factor determining what is made in the firm and what is bought from outside is, of course, cost-minimisation. Coase focused on the different costs of monitoring the two sorts of transactions, but outsourcing may also provide advantages in terms of specialisation and economies of scale (where the outside firm has more than one customer for a product), risk-taking (sub-contractors may be more exposed to market volatility) and business culture (if the outsourcing firm wishes to focus on its core competencies).

Concern about outsourcing increased late in the twentieth century as businesses found it cheaper to outsource a range of activities which had traditionally been conducted inside their firm or which were new – frequently with a different business culture, such as information technology. The exact reasons for this shift need not detain us. What we observe here is that in principle outsourcing had little to do with globalisation, insofar as – initially – the beneficiary was a local business. However, it led to 'offshoring'.

Offshoring and the Protection Debate

Offshoring is outsourcing to a business in another country.[4] It is made possible by falling costs of distance. The phenomenon has been around for a long time, insofar as components have long been made in one country and assembled in another, as we will see with respect to the motor-assembly industry in Chapter 8. Today's debate centres on the dispersal of services which cheap international communications make possible. But it is really a replay of the earlier debate about manufacturing moving offshore, facilitated by lowering costs of transport, as occurred when American and European steelworkers protested that they were losing jobs to plants with lower input costs in Asia and South America.

This time it is white-collar rather than blue-collar workers who are suffering, while the traditional remedy of tariff protection is difficult to apply to services. Nevertheless, the service workers in rich countries demanding protection from low-wage workers in poor countries are using broadly the same rhetoric as their manufacturing compatriots. And those who oppose such protection also use parallel arguments.

The rigour and subtlety of the debate against or for protection – be it of manufacturing or services – is far greater than the rhetoric suggests. The narrow argument against is that protection reduces overall national welfare even though it may improve the lot of the workers whose jobs are saved. The other side argues that while abolishing protection may (or may not) increase overall national welfare, it unquestionably reduces the welfare of those who lose their jobs. Each side tends to emphasise the portion of the argument that favours them and ignores the rest.

Despite the rhetoric, there is probably no valid single short generalisation about the effect of protection or its removal (with the possible exception of this one). The nearest to it may be that as a general rule the aggregate gains from ending protection are small in the short run, but some groups will benefit enormously while others will suffer grievously. In the long run, it seems, nearly everyone will be better off, although those who initially suffered but survived may have gone through considerable hardship (and some will not have survived). There are numerous caveats, including, as we shall see in Chapter 26, that economies of scale seriously complicate the argument.

Insofar as the generalisations of the previous paragraph are true, they explain why the protection debate is so heated. If there are no significant (measurable) aggregate gains from the abolition of protection, those who are worse off cannot be easily compensated. Were the gains big, they could be. Meanwhile those who will benefit from the ending of protection, partly at the cost of those worse off, are likely to be very keen advocates of free trade.

As was observed in Chapter 1, protection is but a small part of the total costs of distance. Its levels have been reducing – for manufacturing, if not so much for agriculture. Even so, the debate remains heated and has been re-energised with the advent of offshoring.

Offshoring in India

The most prominent location for offshoring services has been Bangalore (now Bengaluru) in southern India. It is by no means unique. For example, Europeans offshore translation services to Australasia, where it is day during the European night and the work can be finished in time for the next business day in Europe.

India dominates offshoring not just because it is large, nor because it is located on North America's anti-meridian. A key factor is the quality of its workforce. One heritage of the Raj (the British occupation) is a large population which is both well-educated and fluent in English. (It is said that Indian-English – Inglish? – is the largest dialect in the English-speaking world.) Thus offshoring services which depend upon the ability to speak English (call centres) or where this is an advantage (software development) are likely to be located in India. In effect, India has a comparative advantage in 'offshorable' English-speaking processes which it can reap thanks to the low cost of transporting information. In that sense it is doing for these services what China is doing for manufacturing. But there is a difference.

China, with its population of 1.3 billion, has for all practical purposes an unlimited supply of suitable factory workers, although recruitment from the interior of the country will take time. (Eventually some factories on the coast may move inland as internal transport costs decline.) The workers recruited from manufacturing come from the agricultural sector. They are cheap.[5] Since there is a labour surplus on the land, a reduction in the agricultural labour force will not lead to a proportional fall in food supplies. Moreover, the additional manufacturing productivity can finance the purchase of food imports.

India, with a population of 1.1 billion, is only a little smaller than China, and it dwarfs any rich country. (The US population is just over 300 million, the EU's just over 450 million.) But while just about any Chinese (or Indian) peasant can transfer to a production line, even the simplest offshoring activities require less readily available skills. Only about a third of Indians (say 350 million) are able to converse in English, and not all of these can do so well enough to provide offshore services.

How many can? We don't know. But there are already shortages of suitable workers for Indian firms providing offshore services – wages are rising as firms compete for scarce skilled labour. At some point they will rise to a level which will make the sector just competitive with the same services in the rich countries. (Because of distance costs, Indian wages will still be below the counterpart American and European rates.)

This does not mean that the Indian offshore industry will decline. Rather it will cease to expand rapidly, growing more slowly through productivity improvements, as long as the comparatively high wages and good working conditions continue to provide an incentive for young Indians to master Inglish. There are other low-income countries with sub-populations fluent in English. As India reaches its limit, the offshoring of services will expand elsewhere in a process that will continue until all the poor world's possibilities have been exhausted.

Other offshoring services, such as computing, depend upon advanced vocational skills generated by the educational system. (But speaking English still helps.) The supply of such skills is also limited, and other countries are in a position to compete with India. Technical education was strong in the Soviet empire, and some software development is moving there.

There may not be a lot of 'trickle down' from these new industries in the poor countries. Peasants cannot move into the high-paid jobs without mastering advanced skills. Those who are well paid will – directly or indirectly – employ the less-skilled workers in local service industries. Inequality within these countries is likely to increase. In 2004 the government of 'Shining India' was ousted by peasants disgruntled that the sun had not smiled on them. The long-run prospects of Shining India may depend on the ability of the children of the peasantry to take full advantage of the education system.

Are There Limits to Offshoring?

As a general rule, services which interface directly with the consumer cannot be offshored. Offshoring typically arises from outsourcing, where the provider relocates part of the production process in another business. The consumer may still interact directly with the offshore centre: the air tickets are bought from the outcall centre, but they must be used in a plane on which the purchasers embark.[6]

Even so, the possibilities for outsourcing and offshoring are far from exhausted, especially as experience with existing activities continues to throw up improved methods. With the rise of cheap telecommunications, an extraordinary range of service activities which once had to be located near customers need no longer be. While manufacturing may be a decreasing proportion of the world's economic activity, footloose industries may grow as parts of the service sector join the shift to low-cost locations.

Eight | Intra-Industry Trade • Motor Vehicles

Intra-industry trade, in which two countries exchange very similar products, now amounts to perhaps a quarter of the world's trade. It involves different principles from the traditional comparative advantage. Competitive advantage is characterised by low costs of distance, product differentiation, economies of scale, the outsourcing of components and service inputs, ongoing innovation and monopolistic competition. The principles are illustrated here by the motor vehicle industry, the world's largest manufacturing industry, which exemplifies also the increasing ambiguity of the nationality of firms and products.

David Ricardo's seminal exposition of comparative advantage in the early nineteenth century was based on inter-industry trade – England trading its cloth for Portugal's wine. It did not envision intra-industry trade, in which two countries trade the same product. ('Inter' here means between countries, 'intra' within a group of products.)

Some intra-industry trade is obvious. Northern Hemisphere apple producers send apples south in their peak-season, and import Southern Hemisphere apples in their off-season. Tourists also flow both ways, and not only seasonally. But how are we to explain the fact that two countries may both import and export cars of similar size and design? One may argue that a Toyota sedan is different from a Ford sedan – marketers will insist on it. But if all Toyotas disappeared from this earth, one could switch to a Ford without great loss. There is not nearly so much substitution between cloth and wine, although there is intra-industry trade in both products, for there are countries today which import and export each.

It is difficult to measure the size of intra-industry trade, since this depends upon defining how similar or different two products are.[1] But roughly a quarter of the world's goods trade by value involves intra-industry exchange, with the remaining three-quarters divided about equally between oil, other primary commodities, and manufactures which are traded between industries. (Including services changes the proportions.)

Fifty years ago, all trade was inter-industry. Even today, many countries have little intra-industry trade, which typically occurs between rich nations. In 1996, 57 per cent of US international trade took place within rather than between broad industry product groups.[2] Intra-industry trade constitutes more than 60 per cent of trade between European states and about 20 per cent of Japanese trade, with its huge demand for imported resources. The proportion is lower for primary product exporters such as Argentina, Australia, New Zealand and oil suppliers.

What drives intra-industry trade? Not low costs of distance alone, although these are necessary. Indeed it seems that intra-industry trade may be more sensitive to distance effects than inter-industry trade. Economies of scale are not critical. There is intra-industry trade in wine, for instance, even where producers are quite small. What is critical is product differentiation, with broadly similar products distinguished by style, shape, size, colour, texture, quality, location, packaging, advertising, level of service, and so on. It is common to argue that sellers create differentiated products through marketing, advertising, packaging, or physical differences. This cannot be done with all products. Many are sufficiently homogeneous for buyers to consider them identical and seek the cheapest and most conveniently available (despite the best attempts of sellers to get consumers to perceive differences).

The seller of a 'differentiated' product enjoys a favoured position over its rivals, in that some buyers consider it a superior product and are willing to pay a premium price rather than accept the substitutes offered. (Hence sellers often go to considerable trouble to differentiate their product.) The resulting market structure, sometimes called monopolistic competition, consists of a limited number of sellers each producing substitutable, but slightly differentiated, products.[3] Each producer has some flexibility in setting its price and sales volume. In contrast, in a purely competitive market, where each of many sellers is producing what is seen by buyers to be the same product, the seller is a price-taker.

Monopolistic competition may involve many or few firms selling closely related products, and it may have low or high barriers to entry and exit to and from the industry. In practice, whatever the situation in the short run – and the industry can be very profitable in that short run – in the long run the firms compete vigorously with one another. The industry may mature into one where the product is no longer differentiated, or it may remain dominated by innovation and product differentiation. Its location may also change over time as consumer markets flourish and mature, and the costs of distance diminish.

The Motor-Vehicle Industry

The motor-vehicle industry is commonly thought of as the largest manufacturing industry in the world. It accounts for more than 5 per cent of US GDP. It encompasses much more than vehicle assembly, although the producers of the final product are the most prominent. Today's car is typically assembled from many components produced by firms which may or may not be independent of the assembler and may or may not be produced in the same location, or even the same country. Other similarly situated firms supply the raw materials which go into the components. Entire industries exist as a consequence of the motor-vehicle industry – dealers, fuel suppliers, road builders. Some 14 per cent of all jobs in the US are generated by motor vehicles (including trucks) when the upstream and downstream activities are included.

Walt Rostow went so far in his *The Stages of Economic Growth* as to put the industry at the centre of the growth of the twentieth-century US economy, despite giving little prominence to its impact on reducing the costs of distance, which would have reinforced his conclusion.

Motor-vehicle production has probably been equally important in some other rich economies, and the downstream activities – even if the vehicles are imported – have influenced them all. In many rich countries, the penetration of motor vehicles seems near saturation, yet replacement purchases still represent a major proportion of total expenditure. In the developing world, motor-vehicle consumption – and probably production – is likely to rise in the twenty-first century as penetration rises, so sales will be proportionally greater. (Everywhere the industry is challenged as the price of oil – historically the main source of energy for internal combustion engines – rises. Chapter 21 will argue that while the practicality of using alternative fuels will cap how far the oil price can rise, it will still be much higher than it was when the car became king.)

At the beginning of the twentieth century, motor-vehicle production was domestic, scattered in numerous small firms (some of which had been blacksmith shops), using mainly locally sourced materials and largely self-sufficient in the construction process. But demand was so strong – there were fifteen personal automobiles in the US for every 100 people by 1920 – that production methods improved and costs fell. Henry Ford's first Model T assembly line, applying the principle of mass production, is a famous example. The industry in each country consolidated into a few producers (although many retained the names of original producers as marques – brands). Economies of scale were important not only in production but because of the expense of model development and the accompanying production re-equipment.

Product differentiation between manufacturers was enhanced by internal differentiation. Not only might there be different versions of a vehicle – sedan, station wagon, hatchback – but manufacturers differentiated their products with marques to appeal to different market segments. At one stage General Motors had twelve different brands. Mazda once experimented with giving the same basic vehicle five or more model and marque combinations, although the strategy was abandoned when consumer confusion hurt sales. On the other hand, Toyota has successfully developed the Lexus as a luxury car, distinguishing it from the company's traditional mid- and lower-market products.

Initially, transport costs reinforced reasons such as prestige and military security to ensure that many countries set up their own assembly lines, usually sheltered behind protective barriers, although in some cases many components were imported. As the costs of distance fell and economies of scale in assembly increased, protection became increasingly expensive, and some countries consolidated or even closed down their assembly lines.[4] Today it is large economies which assemble cars (although there are still countries where the industry hides behind high levels of protection).

The interaction between protection, economies of scale and falling costs of distance could be powerful. Many assemblers formed alliances or even merged with assemblers in other countries, exchanging the marques made by subsidiaries. One of the strangest developments came when the US, fearing greater penetration by Japanese imports, imposed 'voluntary' quotas. The Japanese avoided these by establishing their own assembly lines in the US, usually on greenfield sites, without some of the costs incurred by traditional US plants in relation to labour unions and pension funds.[5] Toyota production surpassed General Motors in the first quarter of 2007.

A focus on assemblers fails to capture the complex nature of component suppliers. While some have to be close to the assembly plant, others can ship their products long distances, including across borders. This was inevitable when the labour-intensive assembly process was protected and final costs were kept down by using cheap imported components. Today it occurs even where there is no protection.

The Nationality of Production

Robert Reich observed in *The Work of Nations* that in the early 1990s a 'Japanese' car sold in the US had more local content than its 'American' equivalent.[6] This phenomenon arises from what is sometimes called the 'value chain', in which the product goes through a series of transformations (including distribution) while moving from firm to firm. Today the firms need not be in the same countries, and the 'nationality' of the producer changes as the product moves along the chain. The linear quality evoked by 'chain' may be misleading. The process is more like a river system, in which many streams combine to form a river, just as components come from numerous sources to contribute to the final assembly. Even that may be misleading in cases where a producer sends a partly made product out temporarily to undergo a specialist process, then gets it back. Just as the components may be made in different countries, the process of manufacturing the final product may involve two or more countries.

Is a car's nationality determined by where it was designed? where it is assembled? where the assembler's headquarters is based? where the assembler is traditionally domiciled? where the majority owners of the assembler's equity live? where the greatest value has been added (including raw materials)? In fact, what is the meaning of being a motor-vehicle firm? Is it not almost all component production now, with a handful of firms designing the final product and sourcing (or sometimes manufacturing) the engine, transmission system, body panels and other components?

The issue is not peculiar to cars. As simple a product as a jacket made in East Asia may contain components from six countries and be assembled in a seventh. Thomas Friedman asked Dell to identify the countries in which they had produced parts for or assembled his laptop computer.[7] There were seventeen, which I estimate contribute more than 60 per cent of the world's GDP. (Treating the European Union as a single economy, rather than just allowing for the Republic of Ireland and Germany, would push the figure above 80 per cent). So, even though they are assembled in only five countries, where are Dell computers 'made'?

The nationality of a product is becoming less clear. We can resolve the paradox by observing, as Michael E. Porter – famous for *The Competitive Advantage of Nations* – points out, that it is not nations which export, but firms. Yet firms come and go, while the industry remains. Who is, or was, the biggest (or the second-biggest, or whatever) car producer in the world matters very much to the firms themselves and, in the short run, to consumers. But whatever the rankings, they will change. Toyota's rise occurred in part because the Japanese firm invaded the US heartland and became a significant American producer. Thus the industry seems to be more stable than the firms within it, and national markets continue to play an important role.

So what is the significance of intra-industry trade? A German-assembled Ford Taurus sold in France may contain components from France and many other countries. We know this because they are recorded when they cross national borders. Is intra-industry trade no more than a statistical artefact?

In one sense the answer has to be yes. But assent obscures the lesson which intra-industry trade teaches. Today international trade – especially among the rich – is increasingly unlike the comparative advantage which began with globalisation. International trade is no longer just in finished products and raw materials, on the basis of a comparative advantage between countries liberated by the falling cost of distance. Increasingly it involves a world with low costs of distance, product differentiation, economies of scale, and outsourcing of components and service inputs. It is a world of constant innovation and competitive advantage, one that may seem paradoxical in the way we officially think about it, but is familiar in our practical experience of production and consumption.

There is one further heartening thought from this. The 1951 Treaty of Paris established the European Coal and Steel Community, in which six countries – Belgium, France, Italy, Luxembourg, the Netherlands and West Germany – pooled their steel and coal resources. This was the precursor of the European Union (which originated in the Treaty of Rome of 1957). A free trade area in coal and steel made economic sense, but that was not the main idea behind it. Rather, the aim was to so tangle up the production of coal and steel – then the sinews of war – that the six countries could not fight among themselves again as they had done twice in the last half-century. Consider the Dell production chain, which cuts across 80 per cent of the world economy, and repeat that for all the other company supply chains. It is going to be very hard to have another world war.

Nine | **Migration • Mexico**

Nineteenth-century migration flows were large and faced few restrictions for cultural or economic reasons. Today there are restrictions for such reasons. But because of high wage differentials there is still a persistent flow of illegal migrants across the Mexico–US border. The North American Free Trade Agreement was meant to reduce this pressure by substituting the flow of goods (embodied labour) for migration. But because not everything can be traded, there are still economic opportunities for Latinos to their north, and illegal migration persists.

A world in which labour cannot migrate between countries is well explored in international trade theory. It finds that instead of importing the labour directly via migration, this (and other resources) could be embedded in produced goods and imported indirectly without as many cultural hassles. However, labour is more mobile than the models assume. As long as there are significant geographic differences in payments for the same labour, there will be pressures to migrate from low-paid places to high-paid ones.

Mexico and the United States have one of the largest cross-border income differentials between any two countries. US output (GDP) per person is about four times that of Mexico.[1] For many Mexicans the lure of higher incomes is irresistible. Just over half of the 12 per cent of US residents born outside the country are Mexicans and other Latinos. It is thought that between 3 and 4 per cent of all US residents are 'undocumented' (illegal) residents.

In contrast to its nineteenth-century practice, the US rigorously protects its borders to prevent the infiltration of the illegals. In some places nature makes a contribution. Having sneaked past border control, many 'wetbacks' – a reference to having swum the Rio Grande – must walk across the desert with insufficient water to survive the journey. (US charitable groups put up water depots, but Mexicans still die of thirst.)

While there are concerns about health and, increasingly, security (against terrorism), the main reasons for this American policy are economic and social. Yet had the US maintained a similar migration regime for the previous two hundred years (assuming it to have been practical), it would today be an economically and socially poorer nation and a less powerful player on the international stage.

Nineteenth-Century European Migration
Some 60 million people left Europe for the New World in the century after 1820, 36 million of them going to the United States. In 1820 the population of Europe was about 220 million. It was 320 million in 1913, so around one in five people had migrated. Over the same period, the population of the countries most went to – the United States, Canada, Australasia, South Africa, and the South American cone – soared from about 14 million to 134 million. The migrants, their children and grandchildren were the main source of this spectacular growth.

Migration has occurred since the beginning of human history. But these migrants were neither coerced – slaves or convicts – nor indentured (contracted) labour. Nor were they primarily refugees from war or terror (although religious persecution of Jews and others, and the Irish famine, played their part). They were 'free' labour. Nineteenth-century European migration was driven by economic factors such as the greater opportunities offered by destination countries and the falling cost of distance which made the passage affordable (more distant destinations offered subsidised passages to offset America's competitive advantage). Because of the cost of migration, the earliest migrants came from richer Western Europe.

Although many migrants faced hardship and even death, those who survived (and their descendants) generally became better off than they would have been had they stayed at home. Those left behind also benefited. Had there been no migration from Europe, the continent might have had an extra 100 million souls by 1913 – though perhaps less, because of higher mortality from greater disease and poorer nutrition. This would have been a more turbulent society (which would have added to the mortality), and possibly the continental wars would have come earlier and had even more horrendous outcomes.

Thus the growth of the New World contributed to the development of the Old World, both by taking surplus population and by supplying food and other resources. It was rich in land and other resources, but lacked the labour to work them. The (relatively) free flow of labour enabled the land to meet the rising demand for food in Old World countries.

We saw in Chapter 4 that the nineteenth-century United States, with its abundant resources and the size of the market – by 1870 its population was greater than that of any European country except Russia – was able to industrialise more successfully than any other New or Old World country.

What can be added is the effect of migration on wages (more precisely, the remuneration of workers and peasants). The reduction of the labour force in (especially rural) Europe increased the wages of those who remained. Meanwhile, the additional labour in the US depressed wages, although these remained higher there than in the origin countries. As the wage differential narrowed, migration fell.[2] But as the costs of distance fell, new streams of migrants from poorer Northern, Southern and Eastern Europe crossed the Atlantic. In the mid-nineteenth century about 300,000 migrants left Europe each year. By the century's end the numbers had doubled, and early in the twentieth century, before the Great War, the annual figure doubled again to well over a million.

However, the convergence of wages meant that migration eventually became less attractive. Today Europe is a minor source of America's immigrants. The official data suggests that Americans still have higher incomes than Europeans, but when lifestyle (including leisure time) is taken into consideration, most western and northern Europeans are happy where they are (and those unhappy in other parts of Europe need only migrate to their nearby north-west).

Restricting Migrants

Today the migrant pressure on America comes from poorer continents – especially Latin America, but also Asia and to a lesser extent Africa. Some Asians – especially Chinese and Indians – migrated in the nineteenth century (sometimes as indentured labour), although like the Latinos (and, initially, many Europeans) many were too poor to contemplate moving. From an early stage, there were restrictions on non-European migration to the New World. These restrictions became increasingly comprehensive, and by the middle of the twentieth century they were all-encompassing. All the New World countries introduced restrictions, but it makes sense to tell the story from a US perspective because this dominated the other destinations. Indeed, had the others not imposed restrictions, they would have been overwhelmed by migrants barred by America.

America's resource base was huge and growing as it expanded to the west, and the economy was also reaping the benefits of economies of scale. Chapter 4 described how the surplus of land and other natural resources, coupled with these economies of scale, enabled the incoming migrants to be paid well in comparison to wages in their homelands.

Rising incomes from economic growth meant that, despite their impact on relative wages, the new migrants were at first not generally seen to be depressing the incomes of the existing labour force. But this rapid rise would not go on for ever. For while voluntary migration is in general good for both the migrants themselves and those they leave behind, the impact on those they join is more complicated (which is why migration policy is so bitterly disputed). The owners of resources and capital will be better off by having more workers to choose from. Workers whose jobs are not threatened by the immigrants will also generally be better off. But those who are in direct competition with the migrants for jobs – historically the unskilled and semi-skilled – will have their work and conditions undermined by the new arrivals.[3]

So as the numbers of new migrants increased and the growth in wages slowed, the rhetoric became 'the migrants are taking our jobs' or 'they are under-cutting our pay'. The irony that the complainants were migrants or the descendants of migrants was obscured by the fact that the later migrants were coming from other parts of Europe. (A further irony was that the expanding industrial centres needed labour, so when external sources of new labour became unavailable they turned to African-Americans from the South. This internal migration, with all its ramifications for race relations and the US nation as a whole, was almost certainly not intended by those who opposed immigration.)

This resistance was associated with the rise of organised labour among those who were directly affected, and the identification of an ethnic nationalism which evolved into political lobbying for restrictions on migration. The rumblings reached the United States Congress in the 1890s, and over the following decades there was a steady tightening of access for migrants to the US (and elsewhere). At first this was imposed most on Asians, then on those from Europe. Latin America was initially ignored because it was then too poor to constitute a major source of migrants.

Today the US (and European) restrictions on skilled labour are far less onerous than those on the unskilled, for it is cheaper to obtain workers who have been trained at another country's expense. (Even so, there has been no great pressure to universalise professional qualifications, perhaps because the professions are well aware of the way it would put downward pressure on their incomes.) The world is now much less hospitable to migration than it was in the nineteenth century. Does trade liberalisation offer a means of reducing pressures for migration?

International Trade as an Alternative to Migration: Mexico

There were many justifications for the North American Free Trade Agreement (NAFTA) of 1994. One argument was that making it easier to import goods from Mexico would create more jobs there, and therefore reduce the incentive to migrate to the US. It was illustrated by the possibly apocryphal story of the Mexican who sneaked across the border, lived illegally on the margins of California society for many years, and eventually got documentation as the result of an amnesty, only to find that the factory where she worked was moved south because labour was cheaper in Mexico. Yet, unsurprisingly given the wage differentials, NAFTA did not do much to abate the pressure for Mexicans to migrate.

The wage differentials must be for comparable skills. In the United States, there are still job opportunities for the unskilled for which US citizens tend to be reluctant to accept the going wages. These jobs are typically in industries that cannot move south. Land cannot move, and farms are worked by low-paid unskilled (often seasonal) workers. Neither can personal services (although some Americans do move south to live in retirement villages). Were there no migrants willing to accept such low-paid jobs, employers would be forced to pay much higher wages and pass the costs on to consumers. So not only are employers beneficiaries of the (often illegal) migration, but so are consumers – providing they have not lost their jobs.

Because consumers make only modest gains, they rarely lobby for policies which benefit them. And there are not a huge number of employers (although their influence is greater than their numbers). When in 2006 a Republican Congress tried to clamp down on the undocumented, it raised the wrath of the documented Latino community, which saw the measures as a direct attack on their kith and kin, and an indirect attack on themselves. It may be that, unintentionally, this action has revived the political involvement of recent migrants that was so central to the Democrats' political hegemony in the mid-twentieth century.

If migration – legal and illegal – is once more changing the face of America, it has probably done less for Mexico than was hoped. Jobs to supply the US have not been created to the extent expected. Instead they have moved to even cheaper East Asia (an area to which few Mexicans wish to migrate).

The Future of Migration
As long as there are significant wage differentials and the costs of distance are not too high, there will be pressure to produce traded goods in low-wage economies, and for poor workers to migrate to higher-wage economies to find jobs in the service and land-based industries. Both pressures generate some wage convergence – well-paid workers' fear of imports is parallelled by their fear of migrants. Yet today the rich economies' barriers against imports are low and getting even lower (agriculture products possibly excepted). Meanwhile, they defend their borders ever more vigorously against migrants – particularly low-skilled ones – in a reversal of the nineteenth-century pattern.

Most likely the barriers will slow migration of the unskilled down, rather than prevent it altogether. As we shall see in Chapter 10, the aging population of the rich countries will need more personal services. The good fortune of the European peoples who populated North America and Australasia is likely to spread to those outside Europe. In contrast to the nineteenth century, Europe will also become a net recipient of migrants.

Ten | Locating the World's Population • Aging

The character of international migration changed between the nineteenth and twentieth century, from almost unlimited opportunities for unskilled Europeans to much greater restrictions, with skilled workers privileged. The aging of the populations of the rich countries is likely to result in twenty-first century migration consisting of both of these modes. The cultural mix of the new migrants will differ, providing a dynamic for both cultural convergence and cultural uniqueness.

United Nations population projections – the best we have, but almost certainly wrong – expect the world's population to increase by about half, from 6.1 billion to 9.3 billion, between 2000 and 2050.[1] Different regions will have quite different rates of growth. At the extremes, Africa's population is expected to rise by more than 1½ times from 780 million to 2.0 billion, and Europe's to fall by 18 per cent from 730 million to 600 million. India is forecast to have a larger population in 2050 (1.5 billion) than China (1.4 billion). A host of assumptions underpins these projections. Those relating to migration are explored shortly. The crucial factors with respect to the world as a whole are increasing longevity and the fertility transition.

Over the last century, the average number of daughters born to females in Europe, North America, Japan and China has fallen to or below the replacement level of just over one (given that some females do not reach maturity). In other parts of the world the fertility rate is still above replacement level: in Africa it is 2.5 daughters per woman. Economists explain the fall as a consequence of affluence.[2] While more affluent families want to have more children, the cost of raising them (including keeping mothers out of paid employment) rises even faster, so they tend to have fewer. With the notable exception of China (and its state-enforced one-child policy) these effects have not yet had much impact on the poor world. However, the UN population experts expect most regions to be down to or below replacement fertility levels by 2050.

As well as slowing down population growth (eventually), this fertility transition will age the population structure. The worldwide median age (the age of the middle person when the population is ranked by age) is expected to rise from 26.5 years in 2000 to 36.2 in 2050. In the 'more developed world' it is already 37.4 years and expected to rise to 46.4 in 2050; in Africa it was 18.4 years in 2000 and may rise to 27.4 in 2050.[3]

The effect of declining fertility on the age structure will be reinforced by increasing longevity. In the more developed world, life expectancy at birth is forecast to increase by about five years to near 85 in 2050. Countries with the lowest life expectancy can anticipate an increase of about ten years, although this will leave the ten lowest (all in Africa) under 50.

The Aging Rich

The aging of the wealthy countries will be quite spectacular. It is projected that there will be almost the same proportion of over-80s in more developed countries in 2050 (9.6 per cent) as there are over-65s today (9.9 per cent in 2000). More than a fifth of the population will be over 65, roughly the proportion that is over 55 today. The change in the world as a whole will be less dramatic, with the proportion of over-65s rising from 6.9 to 11.0 per cent, and over-80s from 1.1 to 4.1 per cent. The aging problem in the next 50 years will occur mainly in the more developed world.

In another book, one could explore the implications for each country. In principle the proportion of those in working age groups to the total population falls, and so per capita output falls relative to worker productivity (even though the proportion of children in the population also falls). That assumes that the conventional upper working age (the age of retirement) remains constant. Today, older people are healthier. It seems unlikely that their extra years of life will bring as many additional years of leisurely retirement. Instead, they may have to work longer. The changing age structure resulting from falling fertility means that there may not be enough people in the traditional working age groups to provide for all the needs of the elderly (including sustenance and health and care services).

For most of human history, provision for elderly people who are no longer able to produce has come from their family (especially children and grandchildren) and the local community. With the uprootings from industrialisation and migration this support became less practicable and provision was made increasingly by internal transfers (the welfare state is the best-known example) and from private savings. However, it is rare for the average individual to save enough. An individual living for 70 years from the age of 15 and working for 50 of them must save approximately 30 per cent of their annual income if they want to maintain their position in relation to the average standard of living after retiring.[4]

But even if they manage to save enough, will retirees be able to obtain the services they require? If they have invested wisely – including offshore – they will be able to purchase goods even if there is insufficient local labour. However, some of their requirements – notably health and care services – must be sourced locally. It is possible that equipment such as robots will eventually substitute for some labour, but it is hard to envisage that this will be sufficiently sophisticated to provide the intimate personal care inhabitants of rest homes require, or visiting (domiciliary) services for those living at home.

Will there will be sufficient workers to carry out these tasks? The forecast of relatively smaller workforces with upgraded skills suggests that the answer may be 'no'. How then to meet these needs of the elderly?

The UN Assumptions

The assumptions about international migration in the UN projections may be misleading. In contrast to the assumptions in the forecasts, there will be pressures for increased international migration. In contrast to the implicit assumption of increasingly skilled migrants, this additional labour force may be less skilled, its purpose being to provide services for the growing elderly. Thus population aging is not just a global phenomenon (pervasive throughout the globe), but a globalisation one (involving interactions between economies).

Net international migration to the more developed regions rose from almost nothing in 1950 to around 2.5 million a year in 2000. The UN's projected rate for the next 50 years is just under 2 million a year.[5] If the trend of the last 50 years continues, there will be close to 5 million migrants in 2050. The underlying assumptions reflect those of individual countries, which are often wary of migration for cultural and political reasons. But is the projection realistic?

Suppose that international migration was greater. What would be the effect on the distribution of world population? Unless the net migration rates are very high, they will not solve all the age-balance problems of the more developed regions. However, they are likely to alleviate them. Some projection variations involving later retirement from work and higher migration rates suggest that many countries may be able to manage the aging transition.[6]

Because key services needed by the elderly cannot be imported, there will be considerable pressures in the more developed world for more liberal migration regimes than are currently being contemplated. History enables us to explore the implications.

Two Kinds of International Migration[7]

As the experience of Polynesia indicates, migration is as old as humankind. Typically it occurred between adjacent regions. However, in the last two centuries migration has involved much longer distances because of the falling cost of distance. But migration was different in the twentieth century from in the nineteenth.

Aside from slavery and indentured labour, most nineteenth-century international migration was from Europe. As a rule there were few restrictions, and migrants were typically reasonably well-educated but not especially skilled, many coming directly or indirectly off the land. In the first half of the century the dominant source of migrants was Britain. Germans became important from the 1840s, followed by others from North-west Europe, especially Scandinavia. Emigration from Southern and Eastern Europe surged after 1880. (The Irish deserve separate mention. Following the famine of the late 1840s, Irish emigration averaged more than 1 per cent of the population annually until the end of the nineteenth century.)[8]

The emigrants settled mainly in Australasia, North America, Southern Africa, and the Southern Cone of South America. Sixty per cent went to the United States of America, by far the largest single destination. Except in Southern Africa, the new settlers numerically overwhelmed the First (indigenous) Peoples.

In a typical year, 300,000 people left Europe for the frontier societies between 1850 and 1880; 600,000 in the remainder of the century; 1,300,000 early in the twentieth century. The tide turned with the First World War, and numbers fell to below 200,000 in the 1930s. After the Second World War migration built up again, but in comparison to the more than 700 per million people who were migrating each year at the beginning of the twentieth century, only 300 per million were doing so at its end.[9]

This fall-off is the result of restrictions imposed by the destination countries, where the descendants of the earlier migrants had settled in and felt themselves culturally and economically threatened by new arrivals. Moreover, the pattern of migration changed. Initially it continued to be from Europe. But these days more than 100,000 people migrate annually from each of China, India, Indonesia, Iran, Iraq, Kazakhstan, Mexico, Pakistan, and the Philippines. Europe is now a destination for migrants rather than a source of them, although the United States remains the largest single destination.[10]

Moreover, especially for Rich Club destinations, a higher proportion of migrants are skilled and fill gaps in the labour force. Nation-states control the entry of the unskilled and refugees in their own economic and cultural interests.

The Implications of Increased Migration

Nation-states are not going to readily give up their power to control who become their residents. However, as the age-structure transition works its way through the Rich Club, we are likely to see a demand for migrants to provide services for the elderly that the local workforce cannot. This new migration stream will be less skilled than is implied in the UN projections. It will also be ethnically different. In the nineteenth-century Western offshoots, descendants of migrants now dominate those of the First Peoples. But with the exception of Latinos in the US, the new migrants are unlikely to constitute a major population sub-group in Rich Club countries – not by 2050, anyway – although they will be changing their ethnic composition.

The ethnic composition of international migration will itself change. The UN projections may overestimate migration from China, since the Chinese population will also be aging, and underestimate Africa as a potential source of migrants, given its burgeoning population growth. Ethnicity will vary by destination. Latinos will generally go to the US; Africans and West Asians to Europe; East and South Asians to most parts of the world.

How countries deal with their economic and ethnic problems will vary. Canada will no doubt celebrate the challenge. At the other end of the spectrum, Japan is much more closed to *gaijin* (foreigners). There are various ways to reduce the ethnic impact of migration, including issuing temporary work permits (creating a diaspora for the poor countries, whose emigrants' remittances will bolster living standards) and pepper-potting (not allowing migrants to cluster together). But these are likely to delay rather than prevent cultural impacts.

The need for immigrants in societies with aging populations will be reinforced by the failure of individuals to save enough while they were working. In practice all the Rich Club countries transfer substantial resources to the elderly through their tax and public spending systems. Even where, in principle, the elderly are expected to look after themselves – as in the United States – the state is likely to increasingly find itself propping up failed private pension schemes as well as funding health and care services and assisting those for whom private provision has failed.

While we know that these inter-generational transfers from the working-age population to the elderly are substantial, there is little internationally comparable data. So we cannot yet undertake order-of-magnitude estimates of the sort that were used earlier to explore the looming shortage of the unskilled. What we may be sure of is that these transfers will increase as populations age. That means that, one way or another, the working-age population is going to have to share more of its market income with the elderly. In effect it is going to have to pay more tax.[11]

Increases in the size of the working-age population will reduce that burden. Migration can make a contribution, and not all of this need be of the unskilled. There will be migration between Rich Club members. More significant will be the raiding of skilled workers from poor countries. The new arrivals will presumably improve their material standard of living, and may enjoy an enhanced physical and (possibly) social environment and greater opportunities for their children. Part of the increase in their market return will have to be transferred to the elderly – a fee for the migrants being let in.

Thus the scale of international migration in the twenty-first century may be even greater than we have thus far foreshadowed. What we may be sure of is that the ethnic composition of each member of the Rich Club will be very different in a century from what it is today. That does not mean that cultures will necessarily converge, but there will certainly be considerable cultural change.

Part Two • The Nation-State and Diminishing Distance

Eleven | **Sovereignty • Time**

Over the ages calendar and clock time was globalised to a common basis. This now seems so 'natural' that it is frequently overlooked that individual countries have largely abandoned their de facto power to determine their time system, even though they retain the de jure power. This is an example of how globalisation challenges the traditional notion of sovereignty.

Local Time and the Common Calendar

Five minutes after nine o'clock, Big Tom, the clock above the quad of the Oxford college of Christ Church, strikes 101 times, a signal to the 101 men of the original foundation that curfew is beginning. The striking time is set by the sun, rather than British Standard Time (also known as 'railway time'), which arrives five minutes later at Oxford than at Greenwich, 100 kilometres to the east. Two hundred years ago every locality had its own time, and such aberrations – if that is the right way to describe them – went unnoticed. The traveller arriving in a new town simply adjusted his watch to the time showing on the town clock, just as we do today when we cross between time zones. Accuracy was both impractical and unnecessary. Did it really matter if a London visitor arrived five minutes early for a meeting in Oxford?

Because it *would* matter if the traveller arrived on the wrong day, calendars had been developed thousands of years earlier. Ours began in Roman times – July and August are named after a couple of Caesars. It was taken over by the Roman Catholic Church, with its present form settled by Pope Gregory in 1582. The Gregorian calendar was immediately adopted by Catholic countries, but others were tardier. Britain, afraid of a papist heresy, adopted it in 1752, Russia in 1918 after the 'October' Revolution. A nice example of the confusion is that Shakespeare died on St George's Day, 23 April 1616 – on the Julian calendar. The equivalent Gregorian date was 3 May. Not that it matters – the day is a convenient one to celebrate the man. (And who knows on what day St George died, assuming he ever lived?)

While God may be a mathematician, he or she was not particularly interested in integers – not to mention ones with many useful factors – when the orbit of the Earth was determined. Its 365-and-a-bit-day annual cycle requires some tinkering with any calendar – leap year is the best known – to synchronise with the movements of the sun and seasons. The moon's non-integer cycle is recorded, but ignored. With divisors of only 73 and 5, the calendar divisions are complicated too. Computers use a daily measure which they convert into the Gregorian calendar for mere mortals.

In 1792, in the heady days of the French Revolution, the Republicans replaced the Gregorian calendar with one of twelve equal 30-day months, plus five or six extra days a year. Weeks were of ten days, which meant that rest days were less common. (Apparently increasing work intensity after the people's revolution was not confined to the Soviets.) Days were divided into ten hours, each of 100 minutes and 10,000 seconds. Napoleon returned France to the Gregorian calendar in 1806. He was not risking troops turning up for battle on the wrong day.

Clock Time

Napoleon and other commanders using clocks to coordinate troop movements did not need an international standard, but navigation did. By one of those curious twists of science – preceding Einstein's notion of space-time by centuries – time became location, and accurate location required accurate time. Any point on a globe requires two coordinates to uniquely identify it. The distance in degrees from the equator – the latitude – is relatively easily measured by using the height of the sun and a sextant. The second coordinate proved much harder to measure.

The natural candidate is the longitude, the great circle from pole to pole which sets the axis around which the earth spins. Various methods were used to determine the longitude a ship was on. Dead reckoning does not work, because speed cannot be measured accurately and there is drag from both current and wind. Astronomical sightings were not accurate enough either. One can but marvel at the navigational achievements of the Polynesian and Viking seafarers.

Accuracy was important (as it was also increasingly becoming for industrial processes). It was not just a matter of avoiding calling into the wrong harbour on a coast, dangerous though that could be. The location of the Auckland Islands, 460 kilometres south of New Zealand, was at first plotted 56 kilometres out of position on maritime maps. Many ships sailing through the 'furious fifties' (latitudes 50 to 59 degrees south), confident of their navigational skills but hindered by poor visibility and bad weather, smashed against the sheer basaltic cliffs on the western coastline.

The eventual solution to longitude measurement was an accurate clock, set on a particular longitude and transportable without error through heaving seas (or on a mule's rolling back). Local longitude could be calculated from the time it showed at the local noon. In Oxford a clock calibrated to Greenwich shows 12.05 at noon. Since the earth spins 360 degrees in 24 hours, or a quarter of a degree a minute, Oxford is 1.25 degrees (1' 15') west of Greenwich. The big challenge was making an accurate enough clock. Eventually the Englishman John Harrison constructed a sufficiently precise chronometer – a large pocket watch which used a fast-beating balance wheel controlled by a temperature-compensated spiral spring. James Cook's expeditions confirmed its accuracy. Chronometers became standard on all ocean-going shipping, reducing the costs of distance by providing more secure navigation and, usually, accurate maps. Telegraph, radio and satellites were to increase accuracy even further.

Location was now settled, but every town still had its own time. A few minutes matter a lot to the running of a railroad. In 1853 fourteen people died when two trains on America's Providence and Worcester Line slammed into each other on a blind curve because, it was said, one conductor's watch was slow. Railways required a consistent standard time, yet late-nineteenth-century French travellers were faced with three: station courtyard and departure lounges set at Paris time, platform clocks set to give the traveller a margin of error, and the local time in the town outside. It was almost the end of the nineteenth century before many countries achieved a nationwide time system.

Even then, countries insisted on their own standard times and there was no international coordination. In 1897 France was 9 minutes 21 seconds ahead of Germany, despite being to its west. As telegraph cables ringed the earth, the chaos could only increase. But since they transmit information almost instantaneously, once the convention which settled time in locations had been agreed, they made its implementation simple. International conventions setting scientific standards began in the mid-nineteenth century. The Convention for the Metre of 1875 was the first major one; the international standard was housed in France. The World Time Conference held in Washington in 1884 set the prime meridian, from which longitude would be measured, at the Greenwich Observatory in England. Its 'sun time' became world time, with each country able to set a local time (or times, for those wide from east to west: Australia, Canada, Russia and the United States).

While Greenwich time may seem natural today, the location of the prime meridian was bitterly contested. Some of the proposals were nutty or nostalgic; scientific requirements narrowed the choice to Berlin, London (Greenwich), Paris or Washington, where the necessary skills and institutions were available. The Germans, preoccupied with unifying their domestic time, dropped out, and the Americans sided with London, thereby releasing Observatory Circle in Washington for their Vice-President's dwelling.

The French argued vigorously and ingeniously for Paris (and also for the adoption of decimal time). But eventually 21 of the 24 countries at the convention favoured Greenwich, with San Domingo (today's Dominican Republic) dissenting and Brazil and France abstaining. The arguments that 70 per cent of world shipping already used Greenwich time and that its antimeridian passed near Bering Strait may have been persuasive (although it cleft the group of Pacific islands which later became the state of Kiribati).

Today, time and date are such routine matters, with international commerce, communications, science, and travel depending upon them, that we rarely give a thought to an earlier world in which there was little coherence of time and date. The same is true for standards of weights and measures. But by accepting these regimes, nation-states seem to have given up some of their sovereignty.

International Time and National Sovereignty
The international establishment of the notion of sovereignty is usually attributed to the 1648 Treaty of Westphalia, with its principles of the state and sovereignty. The world was divided into territorial parcels, each to be ruled by a separate government. The state was 'sovereign', exercising comprehensive, supreme, unqualified, and exclusive control over its territory. 'Comprehensive' meant that the state had jurisdiction over all the affairs in the country; 'supreme' meant that it recognised no superior authority; 'unqualified' meant that its right to total authority over its territory was treated as sacrosanct by other states; 'exclusive' ruled out joint sovereignty.

The Westphalian order is a historical phenomenon, and its principles, including the implicit notion that the territories are eternal, have often been breached. Moreover, in a globalising world it may not be practical to exercise sovereignty in the way that was envisaged 350 years ago, when there was little international economic intercourse between sovereign states. We can get a sense of the difficulty by considering the amount of freedom a country has to choose its standards of time, weights and measures.

Typically countries determine their standards and have the de jure (legal) power to change them. A sovereign country could pass legislation enacting a different calendar. Some do have their own calendars, although usually only for ceremonial purposes. For practical purposes the Gregorian calendar is used globally. Two of the major exceptions – the Jewish and Moslem calendars – also have a seven-day week cycle, so in practice translation is not difficult. The Chinese calendar, *yin-yang li*, continues to have ceremonial significance – Chinese New Year is the day for the Chinese in Western countries to celebrate their identity. (China itself adopted the Gregorian calendar in 1912.)

In principle, any sovereign country could divide its day any way it wishes, but even the French have not adopted decimal time, perhaps because its conversion to international time would be too complicated for the human mind. The international convention allows for local time different from Greenwich time, but calibrated to it. In practice the difference is a matter of exact hours (or, sometimes, half hours), thus creating a set of time zones. Every country has the de jure power to establish a different time standard from Greenwich Mean Time, just as Oxford did with its sun time. In practice they do not. They may change the time within the time zone – as when the British switch to summer time – but the new time is always anchored to GMT.

In 1995, the Pacific republic of Kiribati, fed up that its scattered islands were divided between two days, decreed that the International Date Line would henceforth run along its many-cornered eastern boundary, giving the Date Line a very noticeable eastward protrusion from the 180 degree meridian, the antimeridian to Greenwich. There is no international convention for the Date Line. The de facto (practical) line is determined by the unilateral choices of time zone by those countries next to it, although even today many maps ignore Kiribati's decision.

So whatever de jure powers a country may have, its de facto ability to set time, and weights and measures, is circumscribed by international practice. San Domingo may have voted against Greenwich Mean Time, but you may be sure that its time practices conform to it. Only a country completely isolated from the rest of the world could do otherwise.

Some countries waited until the twentieth century before adopting the International System of Units based on metre, kilogram, second, ampere, kelvin, mole, and candela. New Zealand did so in stages between 1970 and 1976, the staggered timetable aiming to reduce the cost of the transformation. The change, which caused considerable hardship to older people and expense to business, might have been justified by arguing that the metric system is intrinsically simpler than the imperial system. But, instructively, the rationale was almost entirely the necessity to keep in step with overseas trading partners. While New Zealand has the de jure power to return to the imperial system or to adopt any other, its de facto power over weights and measures is limited as long as it wishes to engage with the wider world.

The US economy, which generates a fifth of the world's total production but exports only a tenth of the world's total exports, is a much more self-sufficient economy, and so has more de facto economic sovereignty. It signed the Convention of the Metre. But while acknowledging the Paris-based system, domestically America uses its own distinctive measures of distance, volume and weight. As one American industrialist put it, 'I export in metric: I import in American'.

Running two separate systems of measurement can have its problems. The Mars Climate Orbiter spacecraft burnt up in the Martian atmosphere in October 1999 because the acceleration data for controlling its thrusters had been provided in pounds of force (the US standard unit) but entered into the spacecraft's computer in newtons (the metric unit). With little information obtained from the trip, most of its US$240 million cost was wasted.

Some might argue that, unlike most conventions, time, weights and measures have a scientific underpinning. This is a matter of degree. The Gregorian calendar is overlain by a host of cultural assumptions – that is why the French revolutionaries wanted to abandon it.

Sovereignty in Theory and Practice

'Non-scientific' conventions are also necessary. Consider the aborted Multi-lateral Agreement on Investment (MAI). Any country which is accepting foreign investment, even reluctantly, needs a framework so that foreign investors know exactly what is expected of them. Currently this is largely administered on a country-by-country basis. Why not have a common set of rules? In 1995, the Organization for Economic Cooperation and Development (OECD) tried to reach an agreement which would provide a broad multi-lateral framework for international investment, with 'high standards for the liberalization of investment regimes and investment protection and with effective dispute settlement procedures'.[1] This was to be a free-standing international treaty open to both OECD members, some of the main net investors, and non-OECD members, who are often net debtors.

Of course any country has the de jure power not to agree to such an investment convention. But had the MAI been adopted, those wishing to attract foreign investment would have been unwise to opt out, since potential investors would be deterred by the uncertainty that a different institutional arrangement generates. In practice a country might have acceded to the convention with specific reservations, or offered a more generous deal to investors. But once it was adopted by sufficient countries, the MAI would have been the framework for all, even implicitly for those which stayed outside.

As it happens, the MAI was not adopted. The debtor countries dissented, and the OECD found that there was not quite the internal consensus it had assumed. The claim that citizen protest killed the treaty is probably an exaggeration. A proposal for a broad multilateral framework for international investment is likely to arise again, and if it is managed more sensitively than on the last occasion, it will probably be adopted by sufficient countries to force most of the remainder to accept the inevitable and accede to it.

That some big economies – characterised by being both large and having high incomes – may have more de facto sovereignty than small economies should come as no surprise. But even they do not have full de jure autonomy.

The arrangements may be unfair to small countries even where there is one country/one vote (as in the World Time Conference), or where every country has a unilateral veto (as applies in most multilateral trade negotiation rounds), because the big countries determine the agenda. Typically, the smaller economies find that an international convention does not meet all their needs. Individually and collectively, they can work to make it a better – a less lopsided – arrangement. But in the end each has to judge whether the benefits of being in a bad agreement outweigh the costs of not being in it. While each has the theoretical freedom to make this choice, in practice there may be only one option.

The globalisation of time shows that there can be practical reasons for a country adopting an international convention. Those reasons can be so strong that while there is a theoretical figleaf of de jure sovereignty, the de facto reality is that the country has no practical option but to follow an international convention over which it has marginal influence.

So what is the future of the sovereignty of the nation-state? The answer can be explored by considering two 'convergence' theses:

- does globalisation cause cultural convergence?
- does globalisation cause policy convergence?

The first question arises because the nation-state requires its people to distinguish themselves from those of other nation-states. The second arises because to continue to be relevant, the nation-state must be able to meet some of the needs of its people.

Chapter 13 uses the example of Canadian–American interaction to conclude that any cultural convergence occurs slowly, and can be upset by particularities of experience, although the nature of the membership of the nation-state is changing because of the increasing significance of diasporas (Chapter 14).

A response to the second question requires some preliminary clarification. First, a country may adopt a policy because it is the best available. Thus some policy convergences may not reflect the forces of globalisation, but rather the application of common sense to the implementation of best practice. Policy convergence is explored in regard to the social market economy (Chapter 15), health (Chapter 16), world trading arrangements (Chapter 17), and the world monetary system (Chapter 18). The latter two chapters focus on international institutions which are seen as a threat to sovereignty; so does Chapter 19, on multinationals. The conclusion is mixed. It is clear that in some policy areas discretion is increasingly limited as a consequence of global economic engagement. But there remain policy areas within which nation-states still seem to have considerable autonomy to pursue their national aspirations and make their own judgements about best practice.

Before taking up this discussion, it is necessary to recognise that, even though most countries claim much older national roots, the nation-state is largely a creation of nineteenth-century globalisation. Chapter 12 illustrates this through the example of Germany.

Twelve | **The Nation-State • Germany**

The history of Germany illustrates that notions of nationalism and the nation-state mainly arose after, and partly in response to, globalisation.

The nation-state lies at the heart of much of the contemporary discussion about globalisation. It is characterised by two key features. First, it governs a region – that is, it is sovereign within defined borders. Second, it tries to reflect the aspirations of the people who belong to it – that is, it has some kind of national identity. As a result, to a lesser or greater extent, it pursues policies that differ from those of other states.

Today's anxieties about the future of the nation-state in a globalising world may be summarised in two hypotheses, both of which – if true – imply that the nation-state will become increasingly irrelevant. The first is that there is pressure for 'policy convergence', with each state increasingly forced to adopt the same polices as every other. The second is that there is pressure for 'cultural convergence' – the distinctive features which characterise different nations of people will eventually disappear, to be replaced by a common world culture. The two processes are not entirely independent, insofar as one of the functions of the sovereign nation-state is seen to be the expression and preservation of the distinctive national culture. This part of the book explores these issues.

I will argue that while these pressures for convergence exist, they are not necessarily overwhelming. Indeed, what the anxious do not notice is that the nation-state was itself a consequence of globalisation. While in the rhetoric of many of its defenders its roots are found in the distant past, most nation-states – and nationalism itself – are no more than a couple of hundred years old. The great- (or great-great-) grandparents of most of the world's peoples did not live in nation-states as their descendants know them today.

Only a score of today's nation-states existed in broadly their present form 150 years ago. Oddly, they include New Zealand, which considers itself a young nation. By 1856 it was a largely self-governing polity which has continuously evolved into today's sovereign New Zealand. Its boundaries have also remained largely unchanged.

Using these not very demanding criteria, today's nation-states in Europe which were there 150 years ago (ignoring their colonies) are Belgium, France (ignoring the chequered history of Alsace-Lorraine), Luxembourg, the Netherlands, Norway, Portugal, Spain, and Switzerland. The United Kingdom is excluded because it lost Eire in 1921. On the American continent there is possibly the United States, although it was still expanding westwards in the mid-nineteenth century, six central American republics (Costa Rica, El Salvador, Guatemala, Honduras, Mexico and Nicaragua) but no Caribbean ones, Argentina and Uruguay; all the other South American states have had significant boundary changes in the last 150 years. The only Asian states to meet the criteria may be Afghanistan, Iran and Japan (ignoring Sakhalin). No African states qualify, and Australia did not federate until 1901. These twenty or so countries are only a tenth of today's nation-states. Only about ten of them existed at the beginning of the nineteenth century.

Many of the more recent nation-states claim an ancient but broken lineage from nations of peoples without states, or from older nations that were temporarily conquered or have changed their boundaries. Often their history recalls wars of national liberation or some other such defining events. As real as such traditions are to those who tell them, the nation-state is largely a nineteenth-century construct which, outside Europe and America, was not implemented until the twentieth century.

Of course there were sovereign states before the nineteenth century. Europe had many. (Their status on other continents was more ambiguous.) Their evolution may be traced by considering the history of Germany, today one of the largest and economically most powerful nation-states.

A Short History of the German State
Germany as a recognisable nation-state emerged in 1871, albeit with different boundaries from today. Until then Central Europe was a mélange of overlapping and changing jurisdictions, including petty princedoms and ecclesiastical estates. (The situation was so complicated that there appears to be no authoritative list.) These entities were loosely organised under the Holy Roman Empire, founded in 800 CE (the common era – previously AD) when Charlemagne was crowned emperor by the Pope. Its boundaries varied, including at various times all or part of today's Austria, Belgium, Czech Republic, Denmark, France, Hungary, Italy, Luxembourg, the Netherlands, and Poland. But Germany was always near its centre.

The empire was justified by the argument that just as the Pope was the vicar of God on earth in spiritual matters, the Emperor was God's temporal vicar. But while the Emperor claimed to be the supreme temporal ruler of Christendom, in actuality his power never equalled his pretensions. Sometimes it amounted only to diplomatic precedence. As Voltaire famously remarked, what he ruled over was 'neither Holy, nor Roman, nor an Empire'. The seventeenth-century political philosopher Samuel Pufendorf described Germany as 'a body that conforms to no rule and resembles a monster'.

The Holy Roman Empire was dissolved in 1806, as Napoleon swept over Europe. Its replacement was first the Confederation of the Rhine and then, from 1815, a German Confederation of 35 monarchies and 4 free cities which lasted (with some mergers) until 1866. Covering a smaller area than modern Germany, this was little more than a loose mutual defence union. There was a similar merging on the economic front. In 1818 Prussia created a customs union in northern Germany. Later more were created elsewhere, and they were all unified as the 'Deutscher Zollverein' (German Customs Union) in 1834. In 1871, following the defeat of France in the Franco-Prussian war, the confederations were subsumed in a unified Germany. Its monarch, the Kaiser (emperor), was the Prussian king and it described itself as the Second Reich (empire), Pufendorf's ruleless monster having been the first.

Germany's defeat in the First World War led to a reduction of territory and then the rise of Hitler's 'Third Reich', its promise of 1000 years echoing the 1006 years of the first one. Germany acquired territory under Hitler, but lost even more – especially to the East – after defeat in the Second World War. Many of the German-speaking peoples in the lost territories were repatriated to the Germany which was left. Occupation by the victors led to two separate sovereign Germanies, which reunified in 1990 following the collapse of the Iron Curtain between them. The western Federal Republic of Germany was the dominant partner, although the capital shifted back east to the Prussian (and the Kaiser's) capital, Berlin.

This brief sketch is enough to indicate that the nature and permanence of the nation-state is somewhat problematic in the case of Germany. The same conclusion could be equally well demonstrated for more than 100 other nation-states. Why then should we expect a nation-state to be there in another 100 years, or even in another 20? Indeed Germany was a founding member of the European Union, so its sovereignty is already compromised. (Germans like to joke that the EU is the Second Holy Roman Empire.)

There are two continuities. The first is the need for territorial governance, including governance of the economy. The second is nationalism. Both became important in the nineteenth century.

German Nationalism
Almost all nation-states trace their origins to episodes which occurred before

they existed. Germans might cite the defeat of the Romans by the Germanic tribes at the Battle of the Teutoburg Forest in 9 CE (Clades Variani – the Varian Disaster), which meant that Germany east of the Rhine was never integrated into the Roman Empire. Or perhaps 800 CE, when Charlemagne was crowned emperor, or 962 CE, when his empire was split in two, the west becoming France and the east the Holy Roman Empire. The list of key events would have to include Luther's translation of the Bible into German in the early sixteenth century (the whole text was published in 1534), thus formalising a written German language. Every nation has a host of such occasions to incorporate into the story of its historical beginnings.

Such historical events need to be distilled into a kind of myth, a narrative with explanatory power and emotional significance. How does such a need arise? German nationalism can be identified in writings from as early as the sixteenth century. But the modern story begins in the second part of the eighteenth century. It has been argued that German nationalism did not exist even in 1806, when Napoleon abolished the Holy Roman Empire. However, the vigour of the nationalism that appeared just nine years later at the Congress of Vienna with the founding of the German Confederation suggests that it was latent a decade earlier.

The nineteenth-century German-speaking elite were children of the Enlightenment, which destroyed faith in the traditional verities of religion, status, tribe and loyalty to a lord. French thinkers dominated the Enlightenment, arguing that there were universal timeless unquestionable truths which applied to everyone, everywhere. German intellectuals were among those who reacted against this ideological dominance. Not having a single country of their own, they defined their nationalism in terms of their common language. This was a written language, that of the Lutheran Bible. Even today Germans living on the western border may better understand a Dutch speaker than they do Germans on the eastern border, and Bavarian television productions may require sub-titles when broadcast in northern Germany.

Johann Herder (1744–1803) was critical in the broadening of the notion of nationalism to include the ordinary people's culture, believing that a sense of belonging to a culture – something that united a group or region or nation – was a basic human need. Herder argued that mature human life required membership in a community where one could comprehend what others said, shared their understandings, symbols and myths, could move freely, and had emotional as well as economic and social bonds. The twentieth-century psychologist Abraham Maslow placed belongingness above the basic physiological needs and safety in his hierarchy of human needs.

Herder was concerned with folkways, not high culture. Moreover, crucially – and ironically, given a later version of German nationalism – he was a cultural pluralist. After all, he was challenging the supremacy of French culture. Different peoples would have different cultures, none of them superior or inferior. They just dealt with the issues of human existence in different ways.

Why was such a nationalistic theorisation broadly successful? Why did the seeds of German nationalism (and many others) planted at the beginning of the nineteenth century flourish, when earlier seeding had been less successful? Why are nation-states a post-eighteenth-century phenomenon?

The micro-state was becoming largely obsolete as the costs of distance fell and regional trade became important. Helmuth von Moltke famously said that the railways made Germany. The field-marshal was referring to his rapid mobilisation of the Prussian Army which crushed France in 1870. But he could have been describing the impact of railways in widening village communities into regional and national ones. By 1850 Germany had almost 6000 kilometres of railways; by 1880 it had more than 34,000 kilometres.

We saw how the transport and communications network – of which railways were a major part – integrated the United States economy, enabling the efficient location of business and facilitating the reaping of economies of scale. The same process occurred in Europe. Parallel to the integration of economies was the integration of communities.

But state sovereignty required the division of Europe into separate nations. Bilingual communities found themselves torn between different nation-states. Alsace-Lorraine, for instance, moved back and forward between France and Germany after each war. While the region is nominally today a part of France, an ethnic (that is, local) restaurant in Strasbourg will offer a German entree followed by a French main. National boundaries influence, but do not make, communities.

This is why states sometimes emphasise a particular version of their underpinnings in order to bind disparate communities together. Thus did a newly unified Germany wage its *Kulturkampf* ('struggle for control of the minds of Germans', or, more loosely, 'the battle of civilizations'), which was an attack on German Catholics as well as on ethnic minorities such as Danes and Poles.

Such ethnic nationalism is based on exclusivity and antagonism towards others. It may be culturally, racially or religiously based, and can lead to territorial expansion and ethnic cleansing. Although of course it has not been confined to Germany, it was this kind of nationalism which nineteenth-century and early twentieth-century German leaders used to suppress diversity within their boundaries and separate themselves from those outside. Perhaps it was inevitable, given that there was no tradition of a civic Germany (see below), although Britain, which has such a tradition, could be just as chauvinistic.

Ethnic nationalism was one of the factors which involved Germany in two world wars and generated the 'cleansing' of Slavs, homosexuals, the intellectually handicapped and gypsies, as well as Jews. Since then Germans have been nervous about all nationalism. In conversation they tend to play it down, perhaps identifying themselves by their region – Länder – and being scathing about Germans from other regions. Inter-regional rivalry is not a peculiarity of Germany, and often exists within tolerant societies. Yet we may be sure that when watching an international football match, Germans do not care which Land the scorer of the winning goal comes from, providing he is a German.

Nationalism in the European Union

Shortly after the Second World War some visionaries resolved to prevent another great European war by integrating the French and German coal and steel industries, the basis of their armaments production. Thus was born the European Coal and Steel Community, which also included Belgium, Luxembourg and the Netherlands. In 1957 Italy joined them in signing the Treaty of Rome, which established the European Economic Community, essentially a customs union. This arrangement has expanded in number and scope into today's European Union. What has happened to nation-states such as Germany?

The states that merged into the United States of America were hardly nation-states. It would be anachronistic to think they could have been. They were originally in a confederation following the end of the American Revolution. The federation of the United States arose out of conflict between states – the particular incident involving a quarrel between Maryland and Virginia over the allocation of customs duty. The resulting constitution, together with the policies of the first Secretary of the US Treasury, Alexander Hamilton, had the effect of weakening the states both fiscally and militarily. The purpose was to prevent them fighting among themselves – the American Civil War has been the only failure – and to create a strong federal government capable of staving off foreign threats.

Two hundred years later the nation-states of Europe were well-established, and they have been reluctant to surrender their powers to a 'United States of Europe'. The member states are prominent in the daily deliberations of the European Union, whereas in the US government is by the representatives of the people, albeit selected on a state basis.

Who knows what the EU will look like in 200 years? Some visionaries hope that it will become a US-style federal democracy. The fact is, however, that in its first 50 years the member states have been unwilling to abandon the sovereignty which the American states did not know they had. The nation-state will make only a reluctant exit from the world scene.

On the other hand, while each European nation-state remains more powerful than any American state ever was, they are arguably less powerful than they were 50 years ago, with less control over their economy and laws, and less ability to act unilaterally in the military area (although in 2003 Britain went to war in Iraq without the blessing of most of the rest of the EU). The role of the nation-state is changing.

Whatever the reasons for the explicit French and Dutch rejection by referendum in 2005 of the proposed new EU constitution, and the likelihood that other countries would also have rejected it had they had the opportunity (see Chapter 15), there appears to be no great popular appetite for reducing the role of the nation-state.

Conclusion

Throughout Germany today, three flags fly beside one another: those of the European Union, Germany, and the local Land. The German flag flies in the middle. Despite perhaps being the people least comfortable with nationalism, Germans value their membership of the German nation-state and expect it to act in their interests. In contrast to the ethnic nationalism which betrayed them, Germans exhibit a civic nationalism, a nationalism which emphasises citizenship and political and social participation.

Aristotle tells us that society is not a market, because one can do business with foreigners; it is not a mutual security pact, because one can have military alliances with foreigners; it is not intermarriage, because one can marry a foreigner; it is not occupying the same territory, because the occupants of the same city can treat one another as if they were enemies; it is not doing no harm to one another, because one can be kind to foreigners. There must be a cherished way of life woven out of friendships, civic cooperation, and social pursuits; but even this is not enough, unless it is crowned by mutual moral concern among fellow citizens. All must count as worthy of justice; none must be denied full participation.[1]

In such a society there is a sharing of common values, a sense of belonging to a community, and an allegiance to a nation which is typically, but not always, the nation-state of residence. A key common value for a civic nationalism is tolerance of diversity, a tolerance which perhaps makes possible the hierarchy of allegiances symbolised in the three flags: proud to be European citizens, proud of their local community, and proud they are Germans.

Even so, civic nationalism (or 'positive nationalism', as John Ralston Saul calls it) has a tension that cannot be easily resolved. Ethnic and civic nationalism might be thought of as analogous to Karl Popper's closed and open societies. Ethnic (or 'negative') nationalism limits the possibilities for change in a manner similar to what occurs in closed societies. At its worst, the leader is an ideologue who claims to know absolute truth; and its crowds can be just as intolerant of difference. In an open society, nobody has a monopoly on the truth, different people have different views and different interests, and there are institutions that allow them to live together in peace.

Peter Munz cautions that open societies can be too open. Living together also involves common rules and understandings about how the members are to function.[2] Such institutions are integral to culture, yet their very existence limits the openness of society. (Consider the example of legislation against hate speech – an intolerance of intolerance.)

Often the rules and understandings entailed in civic nationalism are informal. They are never entirely rational; there is an emotional as well as a rational commitment to civic nationalism. As Herder understood, civic nationalism needs a mythic narrative to explain its heritage and future. For Germans, that involves navigating past the chaos of the Holy Roman Empire and through the unhappy waters of ethnic nationalism. Their Enlightenment forebears may have been correct: nationalism may be better based on language, culture and history than on state boundaries. Without such myths, a German may face a cultural convergence into an ersatz European. It is more likely that as recent history fades, a new mythology will evolve.

It seems likely that the 300-odd million Europeans will have a variety of myths. Yet they will not have a common culture in the foreseeable future. We can see this from the experience of Canada that is described in the next chapter.

Thirteen | Cultural Convergence • Canada

One test of the cultural convergence thesis is the degree to which Canada's culture is converging towards that of the United States. The two nations remain culturally distinctive despite 150 years of friendship and economic intercourse, suggesting that globalisation's pressures for cultural convergence are not sufficiently strong to outweigh the distinctive experiences of communities.

From the point of view of someone living in rural Africa, the peoples of any two rich countries will have a lot in common. But cultural convergence means more than all rich countries looking much the same to someone from a poor country. The thesis is that the processes of globalisation mean that even an observer from a rich country will be increasingly unable to tell the difference between the inhabitants and the communities of other rich countries (having made due allowance for any effects of topography and climate, and ignoring looks). The thesis postulates a *tendency* to converge, a process which may take generations. While one can recognise differences today, they are smaller, it is argued, than they were a generation ago, and will be still smaller in a generation's time.

If any such tendency exists, it ought to be evident in a comparison between Canada and the United States which, having had friendly relations for over 150 years, meet at the world's longest undefended border, across which flows the world's greatest international trade in goods and services. If globalisation's pressures for cultural convergence are strong, there should already be considerable cultural convergence between the two countries, beyond what can be explained by affluence and technology.

Because Canada has about one-ninth of the population of the US (33 million versus 300 million) any cultural convergence is more likely to involve Canadian culture shifting towards US culture. So the focus here is on Canada.

Canada is the second largest country by area in the world, a federation of ten provinces and two territories spanning six time zones. It can also be divided into Francophone Québec and the Anglophone rest, although as many as 1.5 million Canadians outside Québec are Francophones and most Canadians are bilingual. Roughly 31 per cent of Canadian citizens are first French-speaking and 25 per cent are of French-Canadian descent. Not all French speakers are of French descent, and not all people of French-Canadian heritage are exclusively or primarily French-speaking. The sentence remains true if 'French' is replaced by 'English'. (More than 50 other languages are also recognised in Canada.)

Another source of divergence is ancestry. These are predominantly the First Peoples (Indians and Inuit), the British and the French, with some other Europeans. (Those of mixed First Peoples–European ancestry are called 'Métis'). Chinese are another prominent but small minority.

Culture is about symbols. A couple of key events may help explain Canadian culture.[1] There were armed uprisings in 1837 in response to frustration at the lack of responsible government. The Lower Canada (Québec) Rebellion against the British colonial government was the larger and more sustained of the two. (Lower Canada is the region that is 'lower' on the St Lawrence River.) It inspired a much shorter rebellion in Upper Canada. Although both uprisings were crushed, more moderate reformers proved to be influential with Lord Durham, who was charged with investigating the cause of the troubles. Among his recommendations was the establishment of responsible government in Canada, which came about with the British North America Act of 1867.

The moderates were led by Robert Baldwin of Upper Canada and Louis-Hippolyte Lafontaine of Lower Canada, whose 'binding' (or 'golden') handshake in 1839 represented a commitment for their two regions to work together in the partnership that founded the bilingual Canadian nation. (In a nice touch, Baldwin then had his children educated in Québec.) Perhaps the deal was not always fully applied in the past, and more recently the Québécois separatist movement has challenged it. That story comes later in this chapter.

This commitment to cultural diversity was reinforced by Wilfrid Laurier, Prime Minister in 1905, when the recently settled regions of Alberta and Saskatchewan were made provinces. 'We do not anticipate, and we do not want, that any individual should forget the land of their origin or their ancestors. Let them look to the past; let them also look to the future; let them look to the land of their ancestors, but let them look to the land of their children.'

A Celebration of Migrants

Today, 18.2 per cent of Canadians were born overseas. Despite the US's reputation as a country of immigrants, only 11.1 per cent of its current population were born outside its borders.[2] The population of Toronto is almost half foreign-born. Currently about a tenth of each year's immigrants are explicitly refugees: two recent heads of state (Governors-General) have refugee origins. Canadians give the impression that they are more hospitable to immigrants than other nations. Many communities actively welcome new immigrants and go out of their way to help them adjust.

Yet immigrants inevitably challenge the rules and understandings which underpin the community's culture. In the closed society of ethnic nationalism, the challenges are dismissed by the requirement that immigrants assimilate themselves to the mores of the majority. The open society of civic nationalism welcomes the contribution of immigrants to cultural diversity.

But an open society cannot be *too* open to immigrants. Most Canadian immigrants are chosen on the basis that they will fit into Canadian society relatively readily. (The ability to obtain employment is a criterion.) Refugees are more likely to be accepted if they speak English or French (although the parents, spouses and children who subsequently join them may not). In welcoming immigrants, communities enhance their mastery of the conventions and laws of their new society. Even so, the ability to absorb migrants – culturally as well as economically – sets a cap on the rate of immigration. A society based on civic nationalism cannot be a totally open society.

What is a Canadian?

Given this heterogeneity, we have to ask what is a typical Canadian – or, to avoid the choice of gender – a typical pair of Canadians? Their key characteristic is that in appropriate situations, most commonly when overseas, they would describe themselves as 'Canadian'. This is in one sense a trivial definition, but there is little other unanimity in response. The anecdotal accounts which abound provide insights.

For example, according to Stan Persky, an immigrant from the US:

> The striking thing I've noticed about Canada is its fundamentally social democratic character. That is, most of the country's political parties, and the majority of its polled population, accepts capitalism, however grudgingly, but favours some regulation of the marketplace. The country also thinks some goods ought to be in the public domain, including a segment of the media. And it believes there ought to be a collectivization of some of the risks of living, in the form of public health care, welfare, and education. Unlike European social democratic nations, however, its population is not ethnically homogenous and yet, as a multicultural assemblage it has managed to avoid ethnic riots and large-scale slaughter....
>
> [T]o be a Canadian means to speak one of the two national languages, and to formally adhere to the Canadian Constitution and its values. But there is no official Canadian national identity.... National identity in Canada is consciously weak,

especially compared to countries like Germany, France and the US, where there is a strong sense of being French, German or American, even if more in myth these days than in reality.

Once, I was on a literary panel that was prattling on about 'the writer and the state in Canada.' An elderly woman in the audience couldn't stand it any longer, and got to her feet to ask, while literally pointing a finger at us, 'What makes you proudest of being a Canadian?' My fellow panelist, Brian Fawcett, a Prince George, B.C.-born, dyed-in-the-wool, authentic Canadian (if there is such a thing), didn't pause as long as the blink of an eye to reply, 'What makes me proudest about being a Canadian is that I don't have to be proud of being a Canadian.' The audience, which burst into the laughter of self-recognition, thought that was a good thing, too.[3]

As enlightening as this account is, a commentator from a different background – Australia, or France – would highlight other characteristics, emphasising different differences between their culture and Canada's.

The definition of 'Canadian' cannot be resolved by a questionnaire about beliefs, because it would suffer from a sort of 'Heisenberg effect', with the questions chosen influencing the outcome. Another systematic approach would be to contrast, say, Americans, with Canadians. While not resolving the absolute meaning of Canadianism, that might take us a little closer to the issue of cultural convergence.

As we observed in the previous chapter, ethnic nationalists often define themselves by drawing boundaries to exclude others. Undoubtedly there are ethnic nationalists in Canada, but many are civic nationalists, or what John Ralston Saul calls 'positive nationalists', accepting Canada is the right place for them without necessarily arguing that Canada is the right place for everyone.

They may still say, of course, that some features of Canada are superior to those elsewhere. Canadians take great pride in their public health system, contrasting it to the US one. That the two are so different suggests that there is no inevitability about policy convergence. They are so different partly because there is no broadly agreed best practice for health systems – which are sufficiently independent of cross-national boundary transactions to resist the market pressure from a globalised world.

Also importantly, the US and Canadian health systems differ because of their different systems of government. Even were Americans to agree that the Canadian system was a better one, the US would find it very difficult to restructure in the Canadian direction (or, indeed, in any direction) because of the resistance that would spring up from domestic pressure groups. Of course there are some pressures on the Canadian health system to move in a more market direction. The expectation is, though, that while some will advocate chauvinist resistance and others will advocate colonial submission, the resolution will be – with hindsight – based on the principle of making the proper Canadian response.

In 2005 Canada adopted a statute enabling gay marriage. One view was that this was intended to contrast with the US, which was generally opposed to gay unions, with only one state allowing same-sex marriages and a few others permitting civil unions. This was, I was told, an example of Canadians demonstrating their difference from their neighbours. But that is misleading, since gay marriage is not the only alternative to the US confusion. (For instance, homosexual acts could be made illegal.) Instead, aware of the debate to the south, Canada decided after reflection that, given its commitment to tolerance, statutory gay marriage was the appropriate response. (I conjecture here, for national cultural decisions are rarely so conscious or clear-cut.) Thus the decision was not the result of opposition to the US, but an indigenous response to a problem posed by the US experience.

So while the civic or positive nationalist looks over her or his shoulder to other countries, it is for ideas rather than competitively. But of course Canadians do take pleasure at Canadian international cultural or sporting or whatever success, just like other civic nationalists.

The question of the integrity of Canada remains a vital political issue, with a vigorous separatist movement in Québec. Migrants from Brittany and Normandy were the first European settlers in Canada (or as they called it, 'New France' – today many call themselves 'Canadiens'). Britain acquired Canada by the 1763 Treaty of Paris, when France chose to keep the territory of Guadeloupe for its valuable sugar crops rather than New France (renamed the Province of Québec), thereby echoing the 1674 exchange between the Dutch and the British for the island of Manhattan. By the 1850s, after many decades of British immigration, the Canadiens had become a minority of Canadians.

The separatist pressures are complicated – too complex to relate here. They are by no means unique in the rich world. Although in one sense they are a continuation of the demands for independence by colonialised people in the mid-twentieth century, those usually involved peoples much poorer than the imperial power. More recently there have been pressures within rich powers for an independence based on cultural identity: from Basques and Catalans in Spain, and Scots and Welsh in Britain, for greater self-government; in Yugoslavia (the separation of which into half a dozen countries may not yet be completed); and the break-up of Czechoslovakia.

In part, this illustrates a point to be made later: small populations can be governed more efficiently in a globalised world, provided they are willing to trade internationally to obtain the benefits of economies of scale. It also reflects a cultural independence, which can be best promoted – the separatists believe – by the greater autonomy embodied in the nation-state. Moreover, they value this culture to such an extent that they may be willing to trade off material gains for cultural independence – as the Slovaks did, and the Québécois may yet do.

International Pressures and Cultural Convergence

Not so long ago, it seemed that nation-states might lose the power to promote their own culture(s). Various commercial treaties, agreed under the umbrella of the World Trade Organization, had the effect of preventing states from intervening for cultural ends where there were (kind of) international substitutes. (For instance, subsidies to local cultural artefacts such as magazines and films were successfully challenged by potential foreign suppliers.) The proposed Multilateral Agreement on Investment (MAI) would have required, among other things, the opening up of the creators and transmitters of culture (such as television stations) to those who were unsympathetic to the culture. Rejection of such an approach was one of the reasons the MAI did not proceed.

By 2001 UNESCO had adopted a Universal Declaration on Cultural Diversity, which was followed in 2005 by a Convention on the Protection and Promotion of the Diversity of Cultural Expressions (also known as the 'Convention on Cultural Diversity'). Having affirmed both that culture is 'a defining characteristic of humanity' and the importance of cultural diversity (by implication, both between and within nations) the convention states that a country may adopt measures to protect and promote the diversity of cultural expression within its territory. The measures listed include 'public financial assistance' (such as subsidies) and 'public institutions' (such as public ownership).

The World Trade Organization, with its greater commitment to the private market, is likely to have difficulties with the measures supported in the Convention. The reconciliation of the two approaches is a matter for the future. However, it is clear that the Convention both flags the conflict and offers a justification for rejecting solely private market solutions. Underpinning it, albeit without an explicit statement, is the notion that market relations may be destructive to the protection and promotion of existing culture.

The nation-state is charged with this task. This is in part because it is the institution with which UNESCO deals. But it is also because the nation-state has the power to create institutions and policies to regulate the local market. But note that in its celebration of intra-state cultural diversity, the convention envisions nation-states based on civic rather than ethnic nationalism.

Though Canada was the main promoter of the Convention, this may seem some distance away from this chapter's apparent purpose of evaluating the extent to which Canadian culture is converging with that of its US neighbour. But there is a sense that once this possibility is hypothesised, the thesis can be promptly rejected. Of course there are cultural similarities between the US and Canada, but the differences are great too, and there is little evidence they are diminishing.

Rather, this chapter has underlined the central role of the nation-state in preventing cultural convergence. A further illustration of the failure of globalisation to cause cultural convergence is the US itself, a 200-year paradigm of one sort of globalised world, in which there are no nation-states. And yet there is considerable regional heterogeneity within the US, illustrated by its political bifurcation in the 2004 presidential elections into red Republican states in the south and interior and blue Democrat states on the coasts and around the Great Lakes. Once more we see the integral role of the nation-state in the preservation of culture, a role which also gives it a valued *raison d'être* for its existence.

The effect of globalisation processes which cause cultural convergence is slowed down by the interventions of nation-states, and their long-term effect is thwarted when shocks cause cultures to follow their own trajectories. Differing responses to '9/11' have led Canada and the US to take different paths, even while both are concerned about terrorism.

Certainly globalisation causes some cultural convergence. Most obviously, it will not be long before the entirety of the world's elite has some dialect of English as its first or second language, a consequence of the need for a lingua franca for international communication (not least on the World Wide Web). The accident of current circumstance means it will be English: half a millennium ago it might have been Latin or Chinese. But many countries, fortified by the Convention on Cultural Diversity, will ensure that in the foreseeable future their local languages are preserved and continue to dominate local intercourse.

So this chapter is more optimistic about the unlikelihood of cultural convergence than my tentative position when I first began defining the problem. It is also more optimistic than many commentators, who have a tendency to attribute all cultural change to globalisation.

Culture has always been changing. Inherent in that change is a nostalgia for the culture of the recent past, usually without noticing that this is also different from the earlier culture from which it arose. While the continuities and changes of this process are outside this study, there is much wisdom in the theme of Giuseppe Tomasi di Lampedusa's novel, *The Leopard*: 'If we want things to stay as they are, things have to change'.

Fourteen | The Diaspora • Australia

While we think of a nation-state as encompassing a specific region, its diaspora effectively extends it beyond its sovereign boundaries. There are several kinds of diaspora.

'Diaspora', cognate with 'disperse', is a Greek word meaning 'to colonise' that may have appeared first in Deuteronomy 28:25. Indeed the Jews are the classic diaspora, a people who left their homeland, usually under traumatic circumstances, yet maintained a culture linked to their origins. More recently, with increasing international mobility, the term has been used to encompass expatriate populations who live outside their home countries. Their leaving may not have involved trauma, and their exile may be voluntary. Indeed, the emigrant would often be welcomed home. This modern form of diaspora reflects the falling costs of distance. Telecommunications are cheap: migrants may maintain regular contact with those they have left behind. Travel is cheap: they may return frequently. Some even retain property in their 'homeland', perhaps using this during holidays or planning to do so in retirement.

Australia

There is an irony in considering the Australian diaspora, as that country is usually thought of as a nation of immigrants, with one of the highest proportions of foreign-born at 23.1 per cent, higher than Canada and more than double the US rate.[1] And yet the Australian diaspora was estimated to be 4.3 per cent of the resident national population of 20 million in 2001. Most of these 850,000-odd people were located in Europe (450,000), North America (140,000), New Zealand (70,000) and China (55,0000).[2]

Each location illustrates a characteristic reason for being away from 'home'. Many of those in Europe have returned to the land of their ancestors, while retaining their commitment to Australia. (Some 200,000 are in Britain, 135,000 in Greece.) Others use their above-average skills and talents to earn greater remuneration in North America. Those living in New Zealand – probably more average in terms of skills and talents – are there because of the significant degree of integration between the two labour markets. In China and other developing countries, Australians often work for foreign firms. There is considerable overlap of reasons: health, lifestyle, and marriage can also be relevant factors.[3] Two other (overlapping) groups are those overseas for educational and training purposes, and those on their 'OE', Australasian shorthand for the 'overseas experience' gained by the young for whom travel is a rite of passage.

In a 2002 survey of a (very select) sample of Australian travellers, 43 per cent said they went overseas in search of better employment opportunities, 36 per cent for professional development, 32 per cent to obtain a higher income, and 24 per cent to achieve promotion or career advancement (multiple responses were permitted). Lifestyle reasons came only fifth on the list (23 per cent), followed by marriage or life partnership (22 per cent). Other factors cited by more than 10 per cent of respondents were a job transfer, study, and a partner's employment prospects. So the predominant reasons for migration were 'economic'.[4] (Oddly, none seem to have mentioned 'the burden of taxation'. A vociferous domestic lobby claims that Australians are overtaxed, and driven overseas as a consequence.)

Asked if they still called Australia 'home', 79 per cent said yes and 17 per cent no. Just over half expected to return to Australia to live, although almost two-thirds of this group were going to stay away for at least two more years. A further third of respondents were undecided on this question, often for economic reasons such as employment, professional and career opportunities, and scope for higher incomes. Being established in one's current location, being in a partnership, a partner's employment circumstances, and the presence of local family members and friends also loomed large.

Those surveyed maintained contacts with Australia. More than two-fifths of those over the age of 50 had made at least ten trips back to Australia. Not surprisingly, the better off and those living closer (in Asia) were more likely to have made frequent visits. Some 90 per cent of the trips were to visit family, although 58 per cent also involved holidays. There are other ways of staying in contact. Australian football is an almost exclusively Australian game (its closest relation is Gaelic football) which gets little overseas media coverage. A quarter of all hits on the Australian Football League website come from foreign terminals – around 2.5 million each week in season.

While the falling costs of distance have made it easier to stay in touch, and so to remain an Australian, there is one major difference from the classic diaspora. It is unlikely that the children of Australians settled overseas will think of themselves as Australian. They are more likely to describe themselves as, say, 'Californians with Australian ancestors' than – like their parents – as 'Australians living in California'. It may be a little different for those who grow up in non-English-speaking countries, unless they marry locally. The children of an Australian couple living in Guangzhou are unlikely to call themselves 'Chinese'. Some may return to Australia; others may drift around the world in expatriate communities unsure of their nationality or culture.

This trend echoes some Australians' own experiences. Their nineteenth-century ancestors came for many reasons: some were convicts, others refugees. (Of course, the First Peoples came tens of thousands of years before them.) Some came to build a 'Better Britain'. As they experienced migration from a 'homeland', they might be thought of as a diaspora. But their descendants discarded the notion of Britain as 'home'.

Today Australia describes itself as a 'multicultural society' and many of its new migrants come from outside Europe (especially from Asia). They often live in ethnic communities that are a part of a wider Australian one. While some are recent, there are Australians who celebrate Irish or Italian origins going back generations. (In both cases religion may contribute to this cohesiveness.) Thus there is not only an Australian diaspora, but within Australia there are diasporas from elsewhere.

Samoans Outside Samoa

The economic role of the diaspora of Samoans, who were mentioned in Chapter 2, differs from that of the Australian diaspora. More than half of all Samoans live outside Samoa (treating both territories as a single unit). Those who live in New Zealand, say, are likely to call themselves 'Samoan New Zealanders'. (They make up around 3 per cent of the New Zealand population.) Over half of them were born in New Zealand, but most maintain a distinctive lifestyle. Some 92 per cent of the overseas-born can hold a conversation in Samoan, but so can 48 per cent of New Zealand-born Samoans. The younger generations are more fluent in the Samoan language than elders born in New Zealand.

Many New Zealand-born Samoans maintain their links with relatives and family-owned land, including by visiting and even working back in Samoa. The New Zealand community in which they live may be Samoan, including a Samoan Christian church, and they are likely to marry another Samoan. Those who do not often draw their 'palagi' spouse into their community. As in the classic Jewish diaspora, a land in which they were neither born nor grew up is their 'homeland', and yet like the members of many other diaspora communities they are citizens committed to contributing to the nation-state and culture in which they live. In the case of young New Zealand Samoans this is most notable in art, theatre and especially Polynesian hiphop, which draws on a Samoan musical tradition as well as international trends.

Such an integration, which accepts ethnic distinctiveness, reflects the culture within which it resides. Hindu-Punjabi anthropologist Dhooleka Raj, who grew up in Canada, describes walking through London with Manoj, born and bred in England and a British citizen. 'I was excited and surprised to see all the Canadian flags near Trafalgar Square. My friend said, "You really are a Canadian. You see, I am not British, but you really are a Canadian".'[5] Apparently the British – indeed most European nations – are less welcoming than Canada of the diversity that ethnic migrants bring.

Samoa is not strong in material wealth. It is very dependent on imports, only 60 per cent of which are funded by exports. The gap is mainly covered by remittances from overseas Samoans to their families or for churches and schools – these amount to almost three times what the country receives in foreign aid.

The interactions between economic and demographic factors are complicated. In Samoa, families are large – the typical woman has four children, more than twice the rich-country average. The limited economic prospects on the islands mean there is a steady migration of Samoans overseas that reduces population pressures. Their interaction with Samoans born offshore reinforces the diaspora through generations. Because it remains committed to Samoa, its remittances and visits sustain the homeland economy and society. Although the typically fertile Samoan mother gets little financial reward, her production is central to the economic viability of her nation-state. She is supplying a product – people – which nation-states with lower fertility need. Her overseas children support Samoa through their remittances and visits.

The Significance of Modern Diasporas

What are we to make of these diasporas, whether they transmit a 'homeland' to their children or not? Different countries apply differing criteria to their citizens living abroad. Most will offer consular services if requested. Some restrict dual nationality or the right to vote. Some still require their overseas young to undertake domestic military service (although this can be hard to enforce). The media is quick to seize upon someone with a local connection, however tenuous, to colour an overseas story. By doing so they enable the reader to make a personal connection, in triumph or tragedy.

Sometimes the diaspora is seen as a part of national economic development. For poorer countries – as for Samoa – migrants' remittances and what they spend visiting the homeland are a major source of foreign exchange. The diaspora of richer countries – such as Australia – may not remit such funds, but they can be an important bridge to the rest of the world and speed up the importation of capital, technology and specialised labour.

To reduce diasporas to merely economic terms is perhaps to miss the point. They are a crucial part of the global connectedness of nations, yet another example of its intensification as the costs of distance fall. For our purposes they illustrate that membership in the nation-state remains fluid.

Modern diasporas challenge the notion of the nation-state as a specific region, since they live outside its geographical boundaries while remaining its members, and have no desire to bring the lands on which they live within them. Across the geographical and jurisdictional borders are the invisible links between the community of the diaspora and its homeland families and friends.

Because its children do not connect readily to their parents' homeland, an Australian-type diaspora is probably no threat to the nation-states in which it lives. Nations have long lived with diasporas like that of Samoans in New Zealand, whose children and grandchildren remain connected to a 'homeland' in which they were not born. While on occasions they are seen as threats to a host nation – the most dreadful case being that of European Jews in the first half of the twentieth century – the civic nation open to celebrating diversity as Canada does is likely to benefit from their presence.

This increase in diaspora – in the numbers of those living away from their homeland and yet keeping in touch with it – is a vivid illustration that in different parts of a globalising world, distance and location may have quite different significances.

Fifteen | The Social Market Economy • The European Union

To what extent does globalisation place the social market economy (welfare state) under threat? While there are other pressures, it would appear that increased labour mobility, in particular, is increasing inequalities in wages and reducing the ability to redistribute income for social purposes.

In May 2005, both French and Dutch voters rejected the proposed European Union constitution.[1] It was easy to dismiss the 'non' as a protest against President Jacques Chirac and the state of the French economy, but how are we to interpret the Dutch 'nee'? Few are more European-minded than the Dutch: their small country suffered collateral invasion in 1940 when the great European powers were in conflict, and its location makes it a transport hub. Were the EU's economy to collapse, the Dutch would be among those to suffer most.

In any event, other EU members abandoned plans to hold their own referenda. Had there been referenda, rather than parliamentary votes, in other countries such as Germany, it seems likely that here too the populace would have thrown out the proposed constitution. Such has been the Europe-wide backlash against it that the new constitution has been deferred and further enlargement of the EU has been slowed.

People, especially in the West, often vote on quite different matters from the precise question asked in a referendum. Undoubtedly there was a mix of reasons for rejecting the proposed constitution, including the fact that it was an exceptionally clumsy document (in contrast to the US constitution).[2] But a key motive seems to have been the threat voters saw to the social market economy. (This is the continental term for what English-speakers call the 'mixed-market economy' or 'welfare state'.)

In most of the rich European economies (and Australasia), there was – following the Second World War and in response to the devastation of the interwar Depression – an 'historic compromise' between business, government and unions in which businesses were given considerable market freedom in exchange for social protection of the workers and the population as a whole.³ These welfare states were delivered largely through the market, most importantly through 'full employment', since other protective elements – including health and retirement rights – were mediated through occupational-based schemes. Many voters in the constitutional referenda seemed to think that the social market economy was under pressure because of the enlargement of the EU.

I am not sure this is correct, as while the EU may have exacerbated the threat (see below), economies outside the EU – notably those in Australasia – were experiencing similar pressures. The welfare state faces fundamental problems in a globalising world.

The 'Hollowing Out' of Manufacturing and Tradeable Services

Throughout the rich world in recent decades there has been a steady 'hollowing out' of those manufacturing and service activities whose products are traded relatively easily. Despite the costs of distance, lower-paid offshore workers have become increasingly successful at supplying many products.

The following schematic figure sets out the problem. It divides the economy into quadrants, separating the tradeable sector (the sector exposed to foreign competition) from the non-tradeable sector (which is not exposed directly to foreign competition), and subdividing both sectors according to whether they are dominated by skilled or unskilled labour.

		ECONOMY	
		TRADEABLE SECTOR	NON-TRADEABLE SECTOR
LABOUR FORCE	SKILLED		
	UNSKILLED	hollowed-out sector	

It is the tradeable/unskilled labour force quadrant which appears to be hollowed out by the relocation of manufacturing offshore. There will still be some unskilled jobs in the tradeable sector (such as janitors for high-tech manufacturers), and there will also be unskilled jobs in the non-tradeable sector. But a substantial number of low-skilled jobs will be lost. In this context, 'skill' is not some absolute notion. The issue is whether the particular labour skills are available offshore at wage rates low enough to offset the distance costs. If they are, the product will be sourced offshore and local employment will diminish.

Thus the consequence of such a hollowing out is a fall in demand for 'unskilled' workers from the sector. Their personal options are to move to other sectors, to upskill themselves to levels which the offshore worker cannot meet (at least, not immediately), to become unemployed, or to take wage cuts sufficient to make them competitive with the low-paid offshore workers. Other than upskilling – which is unrealistic for some workers, even if the facilities exist – none of these options is particularly attractive to those involved.

The public policy option might be to protect the industries from the offshore competition by measures such as tariffs and import controls, so that local consumers are forced to purchase the product from the more expensive local producers. However, the historic tendency has been for public protection to fall, while natural protection from the costs of distance have been also falling.

The bitterly fought case for and against protection is discussed elsewhere in this study. Here we observe that if the rest of the economy purchases high-cost products from a protected sector it is, in effect, transferring income from the general populace to those in the protected sector. Thus hollowing out generates pressures which compromise the social market economy, because it removes from some workers the protection that was part of the historic compromise.

Moreover, in the EU, and to a lesser extent in Australasia, there was a second pressure on the social market economy.

The Invasion of Non-Tradeable Services

Although the mountain will not come to Mahomet, Mahomet can go to the mountain: if cheap labour cannot be embedded in exports of goods and tradeable services, the labour may be able to export itself to provide services in the non-tradeable sector. This possibility became a serious one following the enlargement of the EU by the addition of countries from the poorer east and south, where wages are lower.

Using the previous diagram, we focus now on the quadrant in which low-skilled workers undertake non-tradeable activities.

		ECONOMY	
		TRADEABLE SECTOR	NON-TRADEABLE SECTOR
LABOUR FORCE	SKILLED		
	UNSKILLED		invaded sector

The workers in such industries seem protected from imports, because the products have to be produced locally. But they come under threat from low-wage workers migrating to the locality and taking their jobs. The migrant workers may or may not have exactly the same skills as the locals. But they are willing to accept wages and working conditions that are inferior to those enjoyed by the locals after allowance is made for differences in skills and productivity.

The new workers may be employees, in which case the employer has to make a judgement about productivity relative to wages, or they may be self-employed, in which case the purchaser must make this judgement. Either way, there is downward pressure on the locals' wages, who face the same options as workers in the hollowed-out sector – upskilling, unemployment or wage cuts.

In this instance, protection involves restricting migrants rather than products. Australasia does this via immigration controls which are biased against unskilled immigrants. The EU also restricts the entry of workers from outside. And while in principle it requires freedom of movement within its boundaries (as the US does in practice), at the time of its enlargement in 2004 twelve of the fifteen existing EU members imposed 'transitional arrangements' – Brussels-speak for restrictions on labour from the new members – which were still in place some years later.[4]

Thus the jobs of many workers in the affluent parts of the EU are at risk of either being offshored (including to countries which have recently joined the EU) or lost to migrants from the new EU members who are willing to take a lower wage. The promises of the social market economy seem to be under threat.

The Pressure Towards Increasing Inequality

Workers forced to compete – whether indirectly with the cheaper labour embedded in imports or directly with cheaper migrants – will experience a cut in their market incomes through lower wages (and reduced working conditions) and/or unemployment. Such pressures increase the likelihood of greater inequality of market incomes within each country, not only for the population as a whole but also for the pre-migrant population.[5]

The increase in inequality can be moderated by upskilling workers, and more directly by adjusting the tax and benefit system in favour of those on lower incomes. The latter change is not always appreciated by those on whom the tax burden increases. An example will illustrate this.

Suppose jobs are lost locally as a result of a consumer product (say clothing) being produced offshore. The unskilled workers shift to lower-paid employment elsewhere in the economy. (Ignore the transitional unemployment, which may be traumatic.) Meanwhile the skilled workers obtain clothing at a lower price, and so are better off than had the offshoring and redeployment not happened. However, they take the price reduction as a given, whereas any change used to offset the loss of market income by unskilled workers is seen as an imposition rather than a compensation.

Thus one of the key assumptions of the short-term benefits of reducing protection does not apply in practice. Those made better off can compensate those made worse off; in practice the compensation rarely happens. Instead there is growing inequality in both market incomes (wages) and disposable incomes, unless the central government raises taxes on the better-off and lowers them on the worse-off.[6] The story is broadly the same when immigrant workers are willing to accept lower wages, and so press down on the wage rates of the locals.

There is a view that the main cause of the observed increase in inequality is that technical change has recently been biased against the unskilled (and has favoured the employment of more skilled workers). This may be so – but it is not how many of those involved see it. It seems unlikely that globalisation has no role in the downward pressure on workers whose jobs are moving offshore or being taken over by migrants.

Is the Social Market Economy Under Threat?
The numbers rejecting the proposed EU constitution and further enlargement of the union suggest that it is not only those directly affected by offshoring and the migrant invasion who are concerned. There seems to be a fear that the social market economy itself is under threat. Not all the threats are related to globalisation. The increasing importance of women in the employed workforce and the aging of the population are global phenomena, yet not outcomes of globalisation. Likewise, the way in which technological change is increasing job insecurity and eliminating jobs-for-life could have occurred, in principle, without globalisation.

The delivery mechanisms of many welfare states have also contained some fundamental flaws. Insufficient current contributions mean that many funds in areas such as health care are now unable to make 'guaranteed' payouts. This has nothing to do with globalisation. Capitalism (like every other known economic system) just cannot offer guaranteed returns on funds, although the long-run logic can be obscured by optimistic projections. Thus a switch from 'benefit-determined' schemes (where the contributor is guaranteed a pension based on end-of-lifetime income) to 'contribution-determined' schemes (where the pension is based on the amount contributed in the fund plus investment returns) is inevitable. Such pressures, which have little to do with globalisation, can only compound those arising from the increased mobility of labour and capital.

There will be considerable political pressure in America and Europe for governments to bail out faltering private pension funds. That will mean increased taxation. As Jean-Baptiste Colbert, the French minister of finance under King Louis XIV, is famously translated, 'the art of taxation consists in so plucking the goose as to obtain the largest possible amount of feathers with the smallest amount of hissing'. But what if the geese can fly? Globalisation limits the ability to impose taxes. It is not just a matter of the very rich fleeing to tax havens. High-income workers may also move, and international investors treat taxation as a cost when choosing the location of their investment.

The Future of the Social Market Economy

Does this mean that countries are losing their capacity to tax: that there will be a race to the bottom as they compete against one another to offer the most favourable (low) tax regimes? The evidence is equivocal. It is easy to identify instances where a tax change in one jurisdiction led to competing changes in all others.[7] Tax rates on top incomes have been coming down, in part because they caused avoidance within countries, but also because they led to shifting of residence and capital between countries.

On the other hand, the fact that there are substantial and persistent differences in tax regimes between countries (even within the European Union) suggests that any competitive mechanism to lower taxes – any race to the bottom – moves at glacial speed. In part this is because taxation is used to provide public services. Sometimes the taxed may appreciate sufficient of this spending to remain in the jurisdiction while grumbling about the taxes they pay – for good education for their children, quality public health, solid public law enforcement, a favourable environment, the arts and recreation, or whatever. If a lower-taxed jurisdiction cannot provide such valued outcomes, a high-tax regime has advantages.

Cultural considerations are important here. Scandinavians tolerate higher tax and spending regimes than those elsewhere in part because they think of themselves as 'Scandinavian'. Canadians tolerate a higher tax regime than their American neighbours because more generous public spending is yet another way they distinguish themselves from those to the south. Nonetheless there are Scandinavians and Canadians who leave their homelands partly in response to the differences in tax regimes. Are they sufficiently offset by Americans, say, heading the other way? There is only anecdote and prejudice to answer such questions.

Given the mobility of capital, it seems likely that tax rates on capital will increasingly fall to the level necessary for a government to fund the activities which business requires: infrastructure, trade promotion, support for research and development, and suchlike. Those with superior meta-technologies (members of the Rich Club) may be able to charge for them by way of taxation, since they add to business profits. Even so, the traditional left's dream of plundering corporations to fund the welfare state is fading.

In any case, the traditional response of business to such plunder was to add the cost to the price paid by purchasers of their products, for ultimately it is consumers who pay business taxation. Recently there has been a tendency to do this directly by the use of value-added (goods and services) tax. Since this is paid in proportion to local consumption, income tax avoiders who officially reside elsewhere but spend time in a country pay in proportion to the resources which they use (as do tourists and other visitors).

Such expenditure taxes have two major limitations. First, there is a limit to the rates that can be set, for high rates encourage avoidance. Second, thus far it has not been possible to identify an effective means of imposing these taxes on direct imports by consumers (as when products are purchased offshore, say online) or on their overseas travel, both of which seem likely to grow as a share of consumer expenditure. It is little comfort to one jurisdiction that another may be benefiting fiscally from its residents' offshore expenditure.

What about taxation levied on income? Most Rich Club members have been flattening their tax scales – reducing the difference between the top and bottom rates – in part as a response to the labour and capital movements that are possible in a globalised world. Thus the income tax system becomes less progressive, imposing relatively less on those with higher incomes.

So in a globalising world it will be increasingly difficult for individual countries to raise additional revenue to meet the increasing demands for government spending resulting from the aging of the population and rising pressures on health-care systems. Any such taxation is going to be less progressive. The scope for vertical redistribution of income (between people on different income levels) is going to become more limited, so that income inequality after allowance is made for taxes (and benefits) is going to increase, even in the unlikely event that inequality of before-tax (or market) income does not.

There are counter-pressures. Some countries – including their high-income earners – will remain committed to reducing economic inequality for reasons of political philosophy. Others may fear that high inequality will lead to social disharmony. Or they may see that investing in children improves a country's long-term prospects. The demise of redistributive policies is not inevitable. But in a globalising world they become more costly.

Thus there would seem to be some policy convergence between countries in the area of taxation and public spending. But the convergence is partial, not absolute. The social market economy is likely to continue to exist in some form for some time to come. Some of the new members of the Rich Club may have to adopt aspects of it. The social market economy was created in response to the breakdown of traditional forms of social protection which were undermined by increased labour mobility. The Asian economies are likely to go through a similar trauma as they develop.

But the social market economy will have to adapt. It may look rather different in the future, and it is unlikely to be as strongly redistributive as it was in the last decades of the twentieth century.

Sixteen | Policy Convergence • Health Care

While there is much policy convergence, both to best practice and where international trade is involved, this chapter argues that it is not necessary in many areas, such as health care. But even here, cross-boundary movements of goods and people compromise a country's freedom to choose its own system.

We saw in the previous chapter that while globalisation is putting pressure on the organisation of social market economies, the likelihood is that they will adapt rather than end. So globalisation is driving some policy convergence (as policy-makers in different jurisdictions are forced to adopt similar practices). If this convergence became widespread across too many policy areas, little would remain for the nation-state to do (except perhaps – perish the thought – participate in external aggression). In which case, despite representing a cultural entity, the nation-state might fade in significance.

But does globalisation necessarily cause policy convergence? While in relation to business policy it may, in other areas convergence seems less inevitable.

The Canadian and United States Health Systems

Canada and the United States have very different health-care systems, even though more goods and services cross the US–Canada border than any other. Of course the two systems influence one another, but their organisation remains very different. They are likely to remain so, despite some Americans thinking that Canadians have the better system (and some Canadians using the US system when theirs denies them immediate treatment). If there is policy convergence here, it is very slow.

Often policy convergence stems from a drive towards best practice. We expect the treatment of most medical conditions to be much the same throughout the world, subject to the availability of resources. That has little to do with globalisation.

But often there is not only currently no agreed best practice, there is no likelihood of this developing soon. While sometimes such divergence reflects cultural and other specific factors, often we just do not know what is best. For example, we do not know how best to organise a health-care system. Pragmatists discuss policies for improving the current situation, and they look elsewhere to learn from the experiences of others. But there is no agreement as to the optimal system, nor is there likely to be in the near future.

Without an internationally agreed best practice, a country can develop its health system to meet its own cultural and philosophical needs. It is limited by its ability to attract medical personnel (so salaries must usually be internationally competitive), and medicines and equipment must often be imported. But inside the country there can be considerable room for choice. Where health issues cross borders, choice is much more limited. The obvious example is control of worldwide epidemics, but a more instructive illustration is provided by control of the misuse of alcohol – a product (rather than a person) that may be shipped across a border.

Alcohol Control in the European Union

Controlling alcohol misuse (and tobacco use) is one of the most effective contributions that can be made to a nation's health, for the economic and social costs of alcohol abuse are large.[1] In principle, alcohol control policies are the responsibility of individual EU countries, which is understandable given that drinking is partly culturally determined. Moreover, the EU principle of 'subsidiarity' holds that governance should occur at the lowest possible level consistent with efficiency.

COUNTRY	Preferred Drink	Consumption	Liver Disease	Control Index 1950	Control Index 2000	Excise Duties
Austria	Beer	12.6	18.3	4.0	7.0	4.0
Belgium	Beer	10.1	11.8	6.0	11.5	5.9
Denmark	Beer	11.9	21.8	4.0	8.5	12.1
Finland	Beer+	10.4	12.4	17.0	14.5	33.3
France	Wine+	13.5	13.4	1.0	12.5	3.6
Germany	Beer+	12.5	17.0	4.0	8.0	4.3
Greece	Wine*+	9.3	5.0	2.0	7.0	3.7
Ireland	Beer+	14.5	5.8	8.0	12.0	22.8
Italy	Beer+	9.1	13.6	7.0	13.0	3.6
Luxembourg	Wine	17.5	12.8	n.a.	n.a.	1.0
Netherlands	Beer+	9.7	4.5	6.0	13.0	6.6
Portugal	Wine	12.5	14.1	1.0	8.0	1.4
Spain	Wine*+	12.3	10.5	0.0	10.0	2.2
Sweden	Beer*+	6.9	5.4	17.5	16.5	30.9
United Kingdom	Beer	10.4	10.4	8.0	13.0	21.4
EU	Beer*+	10.8	12.7	4.7	11.0	7.8

* Preferred drink accounts for more than 50 per cent of absolute alcohol consumption.
+ More than 20 per cent of absolute alcohol consumption comes from spirits.
Source: E. Österberg & T. Karlsson, *Alcohol Policies in EU Member States and Norway: A Collection of Country Reports*, 2002.

The table tells the broad story of alcohol consumption and control in the European Union (before its recent extension).[2]

- Preferred Drink: Drinkers in most European countries prefer beer. In a handful of 'Mediterranean' countries – mostly with low excise duties – they prefer wine. In many countries more than 20 per cent of the absolute alcohol consumed comes from spirits.
- Consumption (in litres of absolute alcohol per adult – over fifteen – in 2001): Consumption ranges from 6.9 litres per adult per year in Sweden to 14.5 litres in Ireland, averaging 10.8 litres across the EU. A male drinking three standard drinks a day – the level sometimes recommended as the prudent maximum, although some dry days are also advised – would consume 10.6 litres of absolute alcohol in a year; the recommended female level of two drinks a day amounts to 7.1 litres per year.
- Chronic Liver Diseases and Cirrhosis (all ages, per 100,000 people): Alcohol causes harm. The rate of chronic liver disease and cirrhosis is but one indicator, for this does not capture harm from drunk driving, alcoholism or alcohol-induced violence. This measure ranges from 4.5 people per 100,000 for the Netherlands to 21.8 for Denmark, around an EU average of 12.7.
- Control Intensity (out of 20): Control intensity is a summary indicator of the effects of all alcohol control policies constructed by Esa Österberg and Thomas Karlsson. Its six sub-components cover control of production and wholesaling, control of distribution, personal control, control of marketing, social and environmental control, and public policy – taxation is treated separately. The control index is an attempt to capture the intensity of public policy measures to limit alcohol consumption or the resulting harm. In 2000 values ranged from a relaxed 7 for Austria and Greece to an intense 16.5 for Sweden, averaging 11.0 for the EU.

    Levels of the control index in 1950 were much lower, averaging just 4.7, which presumably reflects less willingness to tackle alcohol-induced harm half a century ago. The spread was also greater, with Sweden and Finland having even more controlling policies than they did in 2000. Thus there has been a policy convergence, although this is probably better explained by changing attitudes and shifts towards best practice than by globalisation, except in relation to the spreading of information and attitudes.
- Taxation of Alcohol (Euros(€) per litre of absolute alcohol): Taxation, which raises the price of alcohol, is often seen as the most

effective way to reduce consumption, and thereby harm. It does so clumsily, because it also reduces drinking that is not harmful and may even be benign. However, the majority of health professionals support high excise duties on alcohol.

Yet that may not be the view in all European countries, for there are wide variations in excise duties and other taxes, which range from close to zero in (typically) wine-drinking countries to a punitive €33.3 per litre in Finland. (Northern European countries tend to levy the highest taxation rates.)

Any correlations in the table are crude, and hardly worth pursuing given the limited number of observations. But there is a larger message. The individual countries have very different drinking practices, and their alcohol control policies differ too.

There is a tension between the principle of alcohol control and the principle of freedom of movement of goods and services within an economic union. What is to be done about travellers who cross national borders with goods taxed under the departing jurisdiction at a lower rate than they are at their destination?

The EU has abolished duty-free allowances for travellers between its member countries, while allowing them to carry sufficient purchases for 'personal use'. In the case of alcohol the effective personal allowance is 110 litres of beer, *plus* 10 litres of spirits, *plus* 90 litres of wine, *plus* 20 litres of fortified wine. That amounts to almost 23 litres of absolute alcohol, or more than two years' average consumption for a European Union citizen (and more than two years' consumption at the maximum recommended male rate).

So under the EU rules, travellers can purchase large quantities of alcohol in a low-tax country, and consume it in a high-tax country. The greatest benefit would be gained by a person travelling from Spain or Italy, where the allowance would carry a tax burden of €46 and €53 respectively, to Sweden or Finland, where the tax would be €703 and €688 respectively. The differentials are smaller for countries that border one another, but four Swedes returning from Germany in a light van laden with their 'personal' allowances would save more than €2400 in taxes compared with buying at home. (Finnish alcohol control policy is having a similar problem with its neighbouring new EU member, Estonia. Alcohol is so cheap there that even Britons fly to Tallinn for the weekend to get wasted.)

Thus the opportunities offered by travel to avoid excise duties on alcohol are considerable – enough, it would seem to pay for some trips. The alcohol must be used for personal consumption and not on-sold or exchanged. For public health purposes it might be better if this rule was ignored.

Individual jurisdictions may continue to pursue independent policies in respect of most of the elements covered by the control index. While varying minimum drinking ages may affect the drinking opportunities of young travellers, that will not markedly undermine the alcohol control policies of the home country. However, advertising limitations are being undermined by media which cross international boundaries – television, radio and print media. It may also be difficult to sustain public monopoly provision of alcoholic drinks because of World Trade Organization and European Union rules.

There may well be a convergence of these controls over time, as best practice becomes clearer, but that will be the voluntary decision of the countries involved, and hardly attributable to globalisation, other than in the sense of the sharing of information. Even so, the pressures from the personal shipment of alcohol within the EU may force some convergence of alcohol tax regimes. It would seem, then, that the globalisation inherent in the European Union provides a pressure on high excise duty countries to scale down their tax rates. If these duties existed just to generate revenue, that would be a matter of only fiscal concern. But insofar as they exist to reduce harmful drinking, some European countries may be losing one of their most effective public health policy instruments in relation to alcohol.

The WHO Framework Convention on Tobacco Control
The approach to tobacco control might suggest how such differences can be handled. In many rich countries the consumption of tobacco is falling, partly because smoking is going out of fashion, but partly because of vigorous control measures introduced after its consumption was recognised as a major public health problem. However, tobacco consumption is rising in poorer countries and consequently in the world as a whole.

In order to reduce the long-term effects on public health the World Health Organization negotiated a *Framework Convention on Tobacco Control* which came into force in February 2005, when sufficient countries acceded to it.[3] Its objective is 'to protect present and future generations from the devastating health, social, environmental and economic consequences of tobacco consumption and exposure to tobacco smoke by providing a framework for tobacco control measures to be implemented by the Parties at the national, regional and international levels in order to reduce continually and substantially the prevalence of tobacco use and exposure to tobacco smoke.'

The convention covers the following areas:

- Measures relating to the reduction of demand for tobacco, including price and tax measures; protection from exposure to tobacco

smoke; regulation of the contents of tobacco products; regulation of tobacco product disclosures; packaging and labelling of tobacco products; education, communication, training and public awareness; tobacco advertising, promotion and sponsorship; and measures to reduce dependence on tobacco.
- Measures relating to the reduction of the supply of tobacco, including provisions to prohibit sales to and by minors; support economically viable alternative activities; and deal with illicit trade in tobacco products.

The WHO solution leaves considerable freedom to individual countries; there are no sanctions for non-compliance. Membership is voluntary, and at the time of writing in 2006 many countries – most notably the United States and fourteen members of the European Union – had not acceded to it. Moreover, except for references to smuggling and a commitment to a comprehensive ban on cross-border advertising, promotion and sponsorship (which is likely to be ineffective as long as major media-owning countries have not acceded to the convention), there is little on international trade. Travellers may continue to carry duty-free cigarettes across borders. This is a global convention setting out best practice, but ignoring the implications of globalisation.

Controlling Borders

The European Union has a protocol on alcohol control, but this is honoured more in the breach, since it involves low-duty countries raising their rates.

Given that the European Union is a sort of mini-globalised world, the case study illustrates the possibilities for tension between the principle of free trade in goods and services on the one hand, and public health on the other. This tension does not just apply to alcohol (and tobacco), including their advertising. Other examples include genetically modified foods, unapproved pharmaceuticals and, of course, (illicit) psychotropic drugs. What is to happen if one country requires an additive such as iodine in salt, but others do not?

Nevertheless, the prospect of more international conventions to regulate public health issues across borders is a counterweight to the drive to zero tax levels, despite public health justifications for maintaining higher prices. This involves challenging uncompromisingly free trade in goods and services: restrictions for biosecurity reasons are a precedent.

But even if people cross borders without (licit or illicit) drugs (and without epidemic-generating diseases), there remains a pressure for policy convergence. Who is entitled to treatment? No rich country has an entirely patient-pays system, even where a large proportion of the population have private health insurance. Who is entitled to publicly funded health care?

This is a particularly difficult question for countries where entitlement has been a matter of citizenship, so that practically everyone (or at least every resident) got 'free' care. (Britain and New Zealand have been examples.) Did that mean that tourists and other visitors were not charged either? What about guest workers and their families? In particular, what was to prevent an outsider with a medical condition travelling to a country and using its publicly provided care without payment? It is impractical to give everyone who crosses a border a full medical examination. Completely free-to-(all)-residents schemes may have to become more selective or markedly change their funding principles.

Insofar as insurance schemes, whether public or private, do not cover everyone, the same challenge applies when the 'non-citizen' is not covered. Once more the mobility of people threatens to undermine traditional assumptions of who is entitled to 'free health care', whatever the reluctance to switch to a full private user-pays regime.

Because international boundaries are increasingly porous, policy areas such as public health face new challenges which at first seem to have little to do with jurisdictional boundaries. John Donne famously said that 'no man is an Island, entire of itself'; nor, increasingly, is any public policy.

Seventeen | The International Trading System • The World Trade Organization

This chapter explains some features of the world trading system, especially in the context of the World Trade Organization framework, within which multilateralism and the rule of law are crucial, especially for small countries.

Every couple of years there is a meeting of the trade ministers of the member countries of the World Trade Organization (WTO), accompanied by myriads of officials, to discuss progress in the reform of world trading arrangements. Outside the heavily guarded compound a mass of protesters gather to demand the abandonment of the negotiations and a return to a less-globalised world in which jobs have more protection. Meanwhile, despite the demands from the streets below, yet another economy is applying to join the WTO. If the protesters are right and the world trading system is hostile to the interests of ordinary people, why do so many countries – some of them democracies – bother to join or remain in it?

We might dismiss the arguments of those among the protesters – certainly not all of them – who, despite their public-interest rhetoric, are primarily concerned with saving their own jobs, which they see the removal of protection threatening further: steel workers from the American rust belt protesting in Seattle, farmers from South Korea protesting in Hong Kong. By the same token, we should discount the equally self-interested public-good arguments of the smooth-suited private lobbyists from businesses and trade associations inside the barriers.

Yet the self-interested do represent a truth which is often ignored in the free-trade rhetoric, with its stress on the benefits of lower protection. There is no trade deal from which everybody will benefit. Some people are going to be made worse off by a cut in protection.

I coined 'Rabin's Law' to characterise this cruel fact after hearing the economist Matthew Rabin argue that 'existing policy is always Pareto optimal'. My translation of this is that 'a policy change *usually* makes someone worse off'. Rabin would no doubt have added the 'usually' had his formulation been less spontaneous. On very rare occasions, there is a free lunch for all. Rabin's Law says that all opportunities for everybody getting better off will be seized quickly. Further policy changes – the ones that are not immediately implemented – will improve the situation of some people and worsen that of others.

Rabin's Law is one of the most fundamental ideas in public policy. It does not say that a new policy should never be introduced. Rather, it directs us to ask who will suffer from its introduction and how they should be treated. Reducing protection and subsidies will usually make some people worse off in the short, medium and sometimes long run. Regrettably, the free-trade rhetoric often ignores this truism. No wonder free traders become the target of protestors who angrily engage with arguments that oversimplify reality.

An aside on terminology may be helpful at this point. There is no such thing as 'free trade', because whatever is traded is paid for. Moreover, even those who pursue 'free trade' insist on some government interventions, such as a legal framework to protect property rights. In practice, 'free trade' refers to the removal of tariffs, quota restrictions, subsidies and the like on international commerce. The WTO does not talk about 'free trade' but, more accurately, 'freer trade'.

CER Between Australia and New Zealand

To avoid the narrowness of the free trade rhetoric and counter-rhetoric, consider the 1983 trade deal between Australia and New Zealand – the Australian and New Zealand Closer Economic Relations and Trade Agreement (ANZCERTA, usually shortened to CER). This was wider than a traditional free-trade arrangement since it covered all goods, services and occupations, with almost no exceptions, as well as total mobility of labour between the two countries, and a willingness to, where practical, align commercial laws and practices.

At the time a few vociferous free-trade ideologues argued that the agreement did not go far enough. However, the vast majority of politicians and their advisers were more pragmatic. They considered that the Import Substituting Industrialisation (ISI) phase of economic development had come to an end (and perhaps had never been much of a success anyway) in Australasia, and that the two countries – especially their manufacturing sectors – should switch towards a strategy of Export Oriented Industrialisation (EOI).

But how to do this? Fifty years of ISI had generated both a public mind-set in favour of the strategy and significant lobby producer groups – business and unions – whose immediate interests would be served by maintaining protection against foreign imports and ignoring opportunities to sell offshore.

Under an earlier free-trade arrangement (the New Zealand Australian Free Trade Agreement – NAFTA) tariffs had from 1966 been timidly reduced on a select set of products. It was hard work extending the list. (One negotiation added 'seawater' as something which could now be traded without restriction across the Tasman Sea.) But as a result of the deal a small, but growing, group of manufacturers – the main sector to be affected by the proposals – got into exporting. They gained prestige through their success, and had greater weight in public discussions than those hiding behind protected barriers. That was one small lobby for a CER.

An even greater key to the success of the negotiations was acceptance of the principle that protection between the two countries was to be phased out, with only a handful of exceptions. This left each industry in a dilemma. It could either make a case to be one of the exceptions, thus implicitly conceding the general principle, or it could argue against the whole policy. There was no significant coalition in opposition to the policy. Those who were already exporters favoured further opening up; others saw export opportunities; many realised they would not be much affected anyway. Those firms that expected to suffer had little political pull individually, and many were given some assistance during the transition.[1]

Admittedly, the deal was limited to two economies, each of which – it was sometimes said – was opening access to the highest-cost economy in the world. The perhaps pardonable exaggeration was to suggest that neither was under threat from 'cheap wages'. In addition, protection was phased out over a decade, giving businesses a chance to adjust rather than close down.

Two conclusions can be drawn. First, most of the trade negotiators for both countries were not wild free traders, but pragmatists responding to the new opportunities offered by a globalising world. They were perfectly well aware of Rabin's Law, that some people would be worse off. They judged, rightly or wrongly, that some sacrifices had to be made. Frequently they tried to minimise the damage. This holds true for most international trade negotiators.

Second, whatever the intricacies of the technical economics, the real problem in such negotiations is finding a political coalition strong enough to support the outcome and not be defeated by groups concerned only with protecting their self-interests. Because CER involved a broad agenda, there was limited scope for individual lobbyists. Under NAFTA, each new candidate for liberalisation had a pre-existing local pressure group ready to resist the detailed proposal. (Goodness knows who supported the protection of seawater, but they were successful for a decade.) When changes are made across a broad front, some interests will benefit from them and others will not be significantly affected. Here the power of particular interests to thwart the whole package is much reduced.

The point is nicely illustrated by the US arrangements for trade negotiations. The constitution delegates responsibility to the Senate, which in practice cannot negotiate a trade deal. Instead it passes a Trade Promotion Authority bill which gives the President this power, subject to any deal being agreed to by both the Senate and House before it is implemented. Both agree to accept or reject the deal without amendment. That means that no senator or representative can propose a change in the interests of a local lobby group. But the trade negotiators, aware that a coalition of politicians could reject the deal, take care to work closely with Congress. In contrast special deals are so numerous in domestic tax legislation that these are sometimes called 'leave no lobbyist behind' bills. The EU trade negotiators face a similar situation, in that they require the approval of the EU's member states, any of which can in principle veto a deal.

Most Favoured Nations and Free Trade Agreements

When Britain negotiated a free trade agreement with China following the nineteenth-century Opium Wars, it knew that other European powers would soon negotiate these too. The British faced the danger that the subsequent deals would be more favourable than their own. So their agreement required that any tariff concession given in a later agreement would automatically be given to Britain too. This is an example of 'most favoured nation' (MFN) status, in which a trade advantage accorded by one nation is given automatically to those with prior agreements. Those without MFN status – an automatic benefit of World Trade Organization membership – usually face higher tariffs.

Free Trade Agreements (FTAs) allow for exceptions to the MFN principle. An FTA involves the elimination (or reduction) of tariffs, quotas and the like on all (or some) products among a select group of countries. These concessions need not apply to any MFN outside the group. So in principle, concluding an FTA may be contrary to the interests of one of the countries involved if, instead of sourcing from low-cost economies which face a tariff, it goes to a high-cost FTA partner benefiting from a zero tariff

FTAs may go well beyond reducing protection. CER does not involve a common external tariff, monetary or fiscal union, or alignment of commercial law. In principle, each could be a part of the deal.

The World Trade Organization

Unlike more familiar international institutions such as the United Nations and the International Monetary Fund, the World Trade Organization (WTO) is not a supra-national organisation. Its 'small' bureaucracy (500 people based in Geneva) exists primarily to provide an environment for its members to operate within. It does not act as an independent agent. The WTO supervises three major international agreements: the General Agreement on Tariffs and Trade (GATT), established in 1947 (which covers goods), the General Agreement on Trade in Services, and the Agreement on Trade-Related Aspects of Intellectual Property Rights (TRIPs), both of which came into force in 1995.[2]

The WTO is governed by its members' trade ministers, who meet at least every two years, accompanied by lobbyists and protesters. It describes its ten benefits as:

1. The system helps promote peace.
2. Disputes are handled constructively.
3. Rules make life easier for all.
4. Freer trade cuts the costs of living.
5. It provides more choice of products and qualities.
6. Trade raises incomes.
7. Trade stimulates economic growth.
8. The basic principles make life more efficient.
9. Governments are shielded from lobbying.
10. The system encourages good government.[3]

This list does not distinguish between a general world trading system and the specific one regulated by the WTO. Nor, understandably, does it mention any downsides. The Friends of the Earth have countered with two lists of their own, one for world trading arrangements generally and the other for the WTO.

Ten reasons why the world trade system harms people and the planet:
1. The principles on which the trade system is based are fundamentally flawed.
2. The trade system is increasing economic instability.
3. The trade system is increasing inequality between the 'haves' and 'have-nots'.
4. The trade system does not respect the environment.
5. The trade system is increasing inequality between the 'knows' and 'know-nots'.
6. The trade system is increasing employment insecurity.
7. The trade system is bad for your health and safety.
8. The trade system pits the weak against the strong.
9. The trade system has not advanced human development.
10. The trade system has not relieved poverty.

Ten reasons why the WTO harms people and the planet:
1. The WTO is undemocratic.

2. The WTO is untransparent and unaccountable.
3. The WTO is increasing inequality and food insecurity.
4. WTO rules regard development and social issues as barriers to trade.
5. WTO rules regard environmental and health issues as barriers to trade.
6. WTO rules regard labels and certification systems as potential barriers to trade.
7. The WTO is eroding cultural diversity.
8. The WTO could undermine multilateral environmental agreements.
9. The 'all or nothing' approach of the WTO.
10. Influence at the WTO can be 'bought'.[4]

To which one might add, 'Rabin Rules, OK?'

Accession to the WTO

Rather than evaluate directly the arguments for and against the WTO, we ask, 'Why should an economy join the WTO?' Accession is not easy. Saudi Arabia applied in 1993 and was not admitted until 2005. Any new member must have a foreign trade regime acceptable to existing members. While a successful application requires the support of a substantial majority of members, in practice not every member negotiates bilaterally with the applicant.

As conditions for supporting its entry, the US insisted that Saudi Arabia reform its trade regime (including reducing and eliminating some tariffs); revise its legislation (in areas such as intellectual property protection, import licensing, customs valuation and fees, and standards and technical regulations) and its sanitary and phytosanitary measures; lift onerous non-tariff measures and health and safety inspection requirements and introduce a WTO-compatible system of inspection; and commit itself to reforms in the distribution, insurance, banking and telecommunications sectors, among others. (Ironically, some of the original members of the WTO, who as signatories to the GATT had their membership automatically carried over, would have to change radically aspects of their domestic economic practice were they to join anew.)

Many of Saudi Arabia's changes were administrative measures which its pragmatists might have supported even had they not been interested in joining the WTO. Here the application overcame bureaucratic inertia. But some will cause hardship to politically important groups. An obvious advantage is that Saudi exporters now get MFN tariffs. Yet the country does not export much more than oil and services to pilgrims visiting Mecca on the Haj.

The Saudis may also have judged it better to be inside than outside the WTO, a point nicely illustrated by the example of Russia, which also applied in 1993 and had not got in by 2007. Suppose the Ukraine was admitted first. It could then vote against any Russian application. No doubt it would be sorely tempted to do so, at least until the Russians offered better terms for its energy supplies. The insider has greater powers than those left outside.

Lessons from the Doha (Development) Round
In 2001, at the Arabian/Persian Gulf city of Doha, the WTO launched a 'development round', aiming to enable the poor countries of the world to experience 'growth, development and prosperity' through a reduction of trade barriers and distortions. The unanimity of the agreement disguised the fact that there were at least two different theories as to how this might happen.

The rich economies saw the high levels of protection and other government interventions in the poor economies as holding back their development. They thought the poor economies would develop if these interventions were reduced, a process the Doha Round could assist. On the other hand, the poor economies felt frustrated by such rich economy practices as restricting the access of their products (especially the more processed ones) to domestic markets and dumping subsidised agricultural surpluses on third-country markets.

These two distinct paradigms gave little room for compromise. The exact reasons for the July 2006 deadlock are too complex to summarise here. But one might see it as arising from the US belief that any deal would be unacceptable to its farm lobby, which wanted better access to other markets; the EU's expectation that the French would veto the deal in order to protect their farmers from increased outside competition; and an Indian judgement that the Rich Club's demands would compromise the living standards of their poor farmers (which number as many as 650 million – almost the population of the EU and the USA combined).

There were those who welcomed the deadlock on the basis that the demise of the Doha Round would see the end of 'globalisation'. That involves a very narrow meaning of the term. There will still be international trade and investment long after any collapse of these negotiations. Their growth rate may slow, but as long as the costs of distance continue to fall, globalisation will continue (as it did for 150 years when there was no GATT/WTO).

At issue, then, is not whether there will be a continuation of globalisation, but what sort of globalisation will continue. The alternative might be bilateral deals between countries. However, this option increases the power of the bigger economies. The US, for instance, has signalled its wish for concessions outside the normal WTO framework. The line between commercial and political policy can be an ambiguous one. The

US required Saudi Arabia to abandon its boycott of Israel (a member since 1995) as a condition for its approval of Saudi accession to the WTO. Was that because it was considered wrong that US businesses trading with Israel should be discriminated against? Or was it a part of the US's political support for Israel? Of course there is bullying in the WTO's multilateral negotiations too, but here small economies can support one another to reduce its effectiveness.

A fatal flaw in bilateralism today reflects the changing nature of international trade. Now that many finished products contain components sourced from numerous economies, there is a need for a 'country-of-origin rule' to determine which are eligible for any concessions. Country A does not want to find that a deal with Country B is exploited by Country C exporting through B. But by how much must B alter C's product before A will accept that it qualifies for a concession?

This might suggest that trade deals should involve regions – collections of interdependent economies which agree that the country-of-origin rule applies to all of them. But might not the world then divide into trading blocs, as it did in the 1930s, with acrimonious relations between them? What about poor Africa? Which trading bloc would it belong to? An African one would have little of the dynamism needed for development, yet who else might be interested? In today's world there are no natural trading blocs. Both the US and the EU would want to be part of any Asian regional free-trade area. Even more importantly, each is the other's greatest trading partner. In the end, multilateralism makes more sense than either bilateralism or autarchy (economic self-sufficiency).

The Rule of Law

What about trade disputes? Even with the best of intentions there are going to be problems. The existing WTO framework for their resolution involves principles, procedures, and a growing body of case law. Admittedly there are no comprehensive powers to enforce the rules, and no international police to jail offenders. But so far the countries involved have – often reluctantly – usually agreed to remedy any failures. However, it remains possible that a large economic power may simply walk out of the system, trampling over the interests of small economies.

The WTO's rule-of-law approach involves the regulation of public conduct by a set of rules (laws) and (independent) judicial interpretations of them, which bind everyone, including the powerful. The notion is central to the good governance of democratic nation-states, and there has been a parallel strand in international politics since the 1648 Treaty of Westphalia. The WTO treaties, and the decisions to settle various disputes taken under them, are creating a legal framework for international commerce. Better that than trade wars.

When Saudi Arabia joined the WTO it accepted the rule of law in international trading arrangements – in effect abandoning an 'outlaw' status – in return for having some opportunity to influence its development. That was its primary reason for joining. Compared to the law of the jungle, rule-of-law systems shift the balance of power a little towards the small and the weak. The big 'predators' limit their powers, not least when relating to other predators. Their multinational corporations also benefit from the increased certainty. Meanwhile, by forming coalitions with others, a weak member may gain a leverage it did not previously have.

The existing system is certainly neither comprehensive nor fair. One point of trade negotiations such as the Doha Round is to make the system more comprehensive, and also to 'disarm' some of the weapons which WTO members have carried over from the past. As for fairness, the critics remind us that the larger economies still exert an influence out of proportion to their size. That held true during the evolution of the domestic rule of law. When the English and Welsh barons set out in the 1215 Magna Carta that they were to be judged by their peers, they were not particularly concerned with the rights of their serfs. Their concern was that the king was not to arbitrarily judge them. Eight hundred years later, this principle extends to the entire population.

Today's anti-globalisers, aside from those whose interest is to protect their own interests, face the same quandary. Do they resist the forces of globalisation, seeking an (often vague) Arcadia which has never existed? Or do they see the prospect of a better deal for mankind (and even the environment) if the forces of globalisation can be harnessed? If they take the latter course, they may find that any harnessing will come from a long slow process of incremental change, with painful reversals and collateral damage. Crucial in that progress will be the further development of the rule of law for international commerce. The WTO system is as yet neither comprehensive nor fair, but it may be on the way there.

Eighteen | The International Financial System • The IMF

Does the international financial system compromise the sovereignty of nation-states? Yes, insofar as states borrow, and YES if the borrowing is imprudent.

Effective trade – be it domestic or international – requires a medium of exchange. If there is none, trade is reduced to barter, the exchange of one commodity for another. But it is unlikely that there will be a convenient coincidence of wants, with each trader involved in the exchange wanting the other's commodity. Instead traders exchange their commodities for money, then find the desired commodity for which the money can be exchanged. Karl Marx represented this by $C \rightarrow M \rightarrow C'$, where C is the commodity the trader begins with, C' is the commodity the trader ends up with, and M is the medium of exchange, or money.

Money has two other functions. First, it is a unit of account, used to record the value of commodities (so we value GDP in dollars, euros or whatever). And second, it is a store of value – one's wealth includes the money one holds.[1] Nowadays almost all money is held for transactional purposes. A better store of value is deposits or bonds which pay interest, and which can be purchased (exchanged) with the money which does not pay interest.

This book is about the global economy. Where once the pound sterling dominated international trade, this chapter is mainly written around the US dollar, today's most common medium of exchange. We will also discuss the increasing significance of the euro.

Marx observed a fundamental change in the role of money. Instead of facilitating a transaction, it became an end in itself, a phenomenon he characterised by $M \rightarrow C \rightarrow M'$, where M is the money the trader begins with, M' is the money the trader ends with, and C is the commodity which enables M' to be greater than M. This task of making money is so common today that we barely think it unusual. But it changes the nature of the economy, inverting the importance of production and finance. We still need food, clothing, accommodation . . . , but the pre-eminent role of the financial system is taken for granted.

The issue is further sharpened by the introduction of almost costless 'commodities' with extraordinarily large market values, which I shall call 'financial paper'. Money is an example, although sometimes it is useful to distinguish it from other forms of financial paper. (Maybe one day the 'paper' – or polymer – will be redundant, being replaced by silicon.) It is almost a mystery why a hundred-dollar bill, which costs less than ten cents to make, trades at over a thousand times its production cost. Once money was fully backed – a gold sovereign was worth its face value in gold.[2] At first notes had to have their equivalent value in gold in a bank. But why bother to tie up valuable metal if traders are willing to accept cheaper-to-make coins and notes at their face value?

The short answer is that we trust that others will also treat the currency at its face value. The most important agent to trust is the issuer, typically (in one way or another) a government, which will, we expect, accept the currency in payment of taxes and fines. As long as that happens, and we believe that it will continue to happen, we will treat the currency as worth its face value, rather than only what it cost to make.

There is a parallel with respect to financial paper. A bond with a face value of many millions of dollars may be near costless to produce, but because people trust that its issuer will redeem it for money in due course, they treat it as that valuable. While this seems to create something out of nothing, the asset which is the financial paper is offset by a liability in the issuer's balance sheet. (Other forms of financial paper are equities and financial derivatives.)

So the Marxian characterisation can be elaborated one stage further as $M \rightarrow FP \rightarrow M'$, where FP is financial paper. Note, however, that somewhere in the process someone has had to give up the difference between M' and M, the profit on the transaction, which they may do voluntarily or unwillingly (as when – usually later – the institution involved in the financial transaction crashes and the lender loses some or all of what they advanced).

In the modern international economy, the transactions associated with financial paper exceed the transactions associated with production by many times. If the financial transactions go badly awry they can damage the financing of international trade, given that money acts as a medium of exchange. That can cause a depression.

So although the international payments system is required for international trade, it is driven by capital markets. When they go wrong it becomes necessary to bail out the financial creditors to protect the trading system. Between 1994 and 2001 there were threats of possible major financial defaults by Mexico (in 1994–5), Thailand, Indonesia and South Korea (1997), Russia (1998), Brazil (1999), Turkey (2000) and Argentina (2000–1). Occasionally, defaults by giant financial corporations pose a similar threat.

The IMF and South Korea[3]

At the heart of each country bail-out was the International Monetary Fund, a sort of international central bank (we explain below what that means). This is popularly thought to be some over-powerful agency, combining as it does money and supra-nationalism, *bêtes noires* of many people.[4] The reality is that its powers are limited.

This was well demonstrated during South Korea's 1997 financial crisis. Every such crisis is unique in detail, but they all have the same general feature: the banking system runs out of foreign currency.[5] This can happen because somewhere in the balance sheet of the banking system (say the trading banks) there are deposits (liabilities) valued in the international currency (US dollars) matching assets valued in the local currency ('won' in the case of South Korea). When the financial institutions which own these liabilities withdraw their deposits, they want to be paid in US dollars. If too many make these demands at the same time, the banks run out of foreign dollars. That is called a 'run' on the bank.

The banks also supply the foreign currency used for international trade. When there is a run on their funds, banks no longer have the cash needed for trade either. Exporters and importers become stranded. Many will be trading with other economies, whose activities will also be compromised if their cash flow is affected by a run elsewhere.

Meanwhile, international investors will become nervous, identify banks in other countries which they do not trust, and withdraw their funds. (Many will need the cash they cannot get out of the initial country, and will have to raid those other banks anyway.) As this distrust spreads fewer and fewer banks will be able to finance trade, and payments will dry up. It is not difficult to envision a run on a significant central bank triggering a collapse of the international financial payments system, causing an implosion of the world trading system and, hence, of all economic activity.

The South Korea crisis was caused by a combination of nervousness arising from the difficulties other East Asian banking systems had experienced (including major IMF bail-outs of Thailand and Indonesia) with some unsound lending by Korean banks to associated chaebols (large oligopolistic companies active in many parts of the economy, usually holding shares in the banks lending to them), which meant that they were carrying a high proportion of bad debts in their balance sheets. South Korea is the tenth largest economy in the world (treating the EU as a unity),[6] so a default there could have been very serious. (Additionally there was a political dimension: would North Korea take advantage of the situation were there sufficient chaos?)

The core of any rescue package is a loan made in the international currency (US dollars) which enables the banking system to meet its obligations to depositors. Typically this comes with some policy requirements, to which we will return. When the IMF came to bail out South Korea it found it did not have enough money (US dollars) to do so. Unusually, this central bank – the world's central bank – does not issue the world's international currency. That is the role of the US. The IMF obtains its currency from the deposits of domestic central banks and has, at the maximum, only the total amount they have subscribed. Some of these funds had already been used for other rescues, and some needed to be kept in reserve in case a further rescue became necessary.

The IMF advanced US$21 billion to South Korea, the largest loan it had ever made to a central bank. Even when the World Bank and the Asian Development Bank chipped in, the total of $35 billion was still not enough, and a further $20–25 billion had to be advanced by country's central banks and treasuries, the biggest of which were those of the US and Japan. Even that was not enough (in part because of the reluctance of the US Treasury to over-commit itself) and eventually and reluctantly the financial institutions which had made advances to the Korean banks agreed to convert their short-term deposits into government-guaranteed long-term bonds (at generous rates of interest).

The Korean people did not fare so well. Following the financial crisis output fell by 7 per cent and real wages by 10 per cent. Unemployment rose, with 1.5 million finding themselves out of work in a country where previously there had been life-long employment. This contrast between the relative protection afforded the foreign financial institutions and the suffering of the Korean people is not unusual. Given the IMF's concern to protect the world financial system – to prevent the widespread bankruptcy which would undermine the integrity of the system of international payments – the institutions often get off lightly rather than losing a proportion of the advances they have (perhaps irresponsibly) made to problematic banks. As the Korean experience shows, faced with a run on their banks, politicians have little power to protect their constituents (and, in any case, powerful interests are likely to be given precedence).

The Future of the Euro

One player which does not appear in the account of the South Korean rescue is the European Central Bank, for the euro was not introduced until 1999. It will feature in future financial rescues. The extent of its role will depend on whether those withdrawing their funds from crisis-ridden banks have deposited them in US dollars or euros. It is inevitable that as time passes portfolios will hold a larger share of their assets in euros.

Recently, the US government has been running huge fiscal deficits, which have the potential to generate huge quantities of dollars. These injections were offset by the selling of US bonds, and so interest rates rose. Some Asian countries (which have strong savings records) purchased these bonds, but they may get a poorer return than had they invested in euro-denominated deposits.

The likely scenario then, is not too different from what happened initially to sterling when it began its retreat from being the premier international medium of exchange. If the US government remains in severe fiscal deficit, investors will turn to other currencies, especially the euro. This is already a major medium of exchange in the international payments system (even ignoring trade between countries in the European Monetary Union). But it seems likely – the usual caveats holding – that the world will move to a two-currency basis for international trade, rather than the euro replacing the dollar.

Among the caveats is that the US does not have the equivalent of a financial crisis. Because it issues the world currency, the US can not have a crisis like those we are about to describe. There are many possible scenarios and it is unnecessary to go through them all here. We need merely remind ourselves that the permanent monetary hegemony of the US is no more guaranteed today than was sterling's in the nineteenth century.

Responding to a Run on the Banks

Runs on banks (or banking systems) occur for many reasons. For example, suppose there was a whispering campaign to the effect that a domestic bank was bankrupt. Even if it was not, there could still be a run on the bank as cautious investors withdrew their deposits, as the bank would be unable to quickly call in its loans. The standard response is that, having checked that there is nothing fundamentally wrong, the central bank makes available the cash the withdrawing depositors want, secured by loans on the bank's assets that can be liquidated (turned into money) in due course. (If confidence returns quickly they may not have to be liquidated.)

But suppose there *is* something fundamentally wrong with a bank's balance sheet. Perhaps it has too many bad debts – loans which will never be repaid – and is technically bankrupt.[7] A central bank providing cash to cover a run on this bank would be throwing good money after bad.

So any package offered by a central bank is likely to require some changes in the management of the rescued bank. The central bank has no obligation to make an advance to a bank in need, just as a bank has no obligation to make an advance to a customer. Money is likely to be advanced only if the borrower is willing to accept the conditions the lender requires. Thus the principle of a central bank requiring policy changes when it is assisting a trading bank is neither new nor unreasonable. For 'distressed' lending, as when there is a run on the bank, it is harder to judge what requirements are reasonable. But undoubtedly there should be, and often will be, some strings attached.

The same general principles apply to international banking rescues.

The IMF's Response to a Financial Crisis

There is an implicit assumption that whenever the IMF is called in to cover a run on a country's banking system, poor management has contributed to the problem. Perhaps the logic, at the very minimum, is that international investors – far more sophisticated than the depositors who withdraw savings from a good bank – have reason to believe the country's banking system is unsound. And since no economy is perfectly managed (but then again, neither is any bank), there has to be some truth in the perception. So whenever the IMF (possibly in a consortium) assists a banking system, it is likely to require some policy changes, changes of greater scope than a domestic central bank would require of a trading bank. However, many would say that the IMF's demands are unnecessarily wide in scope. The Indonesian rescue of 1997 is a case in point.

During the crisis, Paul Volcker, the chairman of the American Federal Reserve Bank from 1979 to 1987, was invited by the Indonesian government to advise them on their financial system. It is a long flight from Washington to Jakarta and, as he relates, 'I'm half asleep and I get to page 46 or something [of the IMF proposals] and there I see [a provision for dismantling the monopoly on cloves].'[8] Is it the function of the IMF to require changes at this level, changes which are unlikely to have any significant impact on the stability of the financial system?

The IMF staff were not always experts on the countries involved. Often they seemed to demand economic reforms that would bring the country closer to the idealised models understood by the officials. Since these are based on competitive supply in markets, the IMF staff reasoned, Indonesia should have a competitive supply in cloves. (Perhaps it should, but is this the business of the IMF?) But economies are more complex than these models, which in any case are designed to be more relevant to rich economies than to poor ones.

It requires a messianic arrogance to impose one's model on an economy which one barely understands. In this case, an even more arrogant approach was contemplated. As it happens, the clove monopolist was a son of President Suharto, and Paul Blustein reports that consideration was given to toppling the president. Whatever one thinks of this unpleasant kleptocratic dictator, who promoted graft, corruption and cronyism, it is surely not the function of a supranational authority to decide who should be running a country. Fortunately, wiser heads within the IMF prevailed, and the Indonesians replaced him of their own accord (although the effects of the austerity measures that were a condition of the rescue package were one reason for the popular uprising).

Tough measures are almost always necessary. The most common 'ultimate' precipitant of the run on the banking system is that there has been domestic overspending which has in part been covered by borrowing the US dollars to pay for the resulting imports, so the banking system is short of the dollars needed when there is a run on the bank. Any central or trading banker called on for emergency finance knows that spending cuts are likely.[9] These may involve public outlays, but they may also impact directly on private spending if subsidies (common in poor countries) are ended, or controls on prices and interest rates are removed.

The cuts will affect many people's standard of living, for they will be deep and widespread. As it happens, the easiest measures to introduce tend to impact most on the poor and, sometimes, the middle class. Removing tax loopholes on the rich, or even enforcing the tax regime, is much more demanding. In any case, the IMF advisers' frame of reference is not to pay much attention to the distributional impacts of the cuts (just as trade liberalisers tend to ignore the distributional impacts of reducing protection).

Of course the IMF measures can impact on the rich – as in the case of the desire to eliminate the cloves monopoly. But often it is the poor who suffer most. They protest in the streets, which hardly contributes to political stability. (The main beneficiaries from the cuts are future generations, who will not have to service a debt generated by overspending. They are not able to cheer.)

So the IMF is associated with two popular images: it is powerful, and it is anti-poor. We have seen that it has some of the powers of a central bank, and as the world's central bank it is powerful, especially when a country is short of international currency. But as the 1997 South Korean crisis shows, it does not have unlimited power, but must work with the central banks of individual countries, especially the US. With a focus on monetary rectitude, its policy framework is not poverty-sensitive. So while the popular images have some validity, the reality is more nuanced.

For our purposes we are concerned about whether the IMF, or the international banking system more generally, undermines the sovereignty of the nation-state. The short answer is that once a nation-state (or the corporations in it) starts borrowing, it gives up some of its sovereignty. This is yet another example of the book's theme: to engage in international commerce reduces sovereignty. The reduction becomes all the greater if the country (or individual or business) mismanages its borrowing. Once the bankers have been called in, there is even less independence. But the loss is a consequence of the contractual arrangements which began with the borrowing. The power of the banker begins at that point, even if it is exercised later – and more rarely.

Should we look at the IMF in isolation? As the rescue of South Korea shows, it is part of the international banking system. Is that powerful? The answer is broadly the same – yes. The power comes from the contractual borrowing. Poor management of borrowing enhances the banks' power, but does not generate it. It is borrowing, not banks, that compromises sovereignty.

Taming the Electronic Herd?
The financial institutions are sometimes called the 'electronic herd' because of the way they react together. (Former New Zealand Prime Minister David Lange memorably described then as 'reef fish', swimming together in one direction, then suddenly all switching direction in formation.) The herd both contributes to each financial crisis by its actions and benefits from any rescue package, even though the purpose of the latter is to maintain the integrity of the international payments system. This situation seems imbalanced.

The editor of the *Economist*, a bastion of Manchester School economic liberalism, wrote on 1 May 2003:

> If any cause commands the unswerving support of *The Economist*, it is that of liberal trade. For as long as it has existed, this newspaper has championed freedom of commerce across borders. Liberal trade, we have always argued, advances prosperity, encourages peace among nations and is an indispensable part of individual liberty. It seems natural to suppose that what goes for trade in goods must go for trade in capital, in which case capital controls would offend us as violently as, say, an import quota on bananas. The issues have much in common, but they are not the same. Untidy as it may be, economic liberals should acknowledge that capital controls – of a certain restricted sort, and in certain cases – have a role. . . .
>
> Why is trade in capital different from trade in goods? For two main reasons. First, international markets in capital are prone to error, whereas international markets in goods are not. Second, the punishment for big financial mistakes can be draconian, and tends to hurt innocent bystanders as much as borrowers and lenders.

The *Economist* argues for restrictions on short-term capital flows into domestic financial systems, because such flows are destabilising. It cites Chile's imposing of taxes on such inflows, with the rate varying according to the holding period. It opposes controls on outflows, despite the Malaysian government successfully using them during the Asian crisis. However, in a globally connected economy, any controls are likely to have only a temporary effect.

Observing that the wheels of international finance spin faster than the wheels of international trade, Nobel economic prize laureate James Tobin proposed a more radical solution. The balance would be better with some 'grit' in the faster spinning wheel. Tobin suggested a very low tax on financial transactions, which would penalise the fast spinners much more than the slow ones.

As attractive as this solution may seem – some also support it because they hope that the tax can be used to fund aid to poor countries – it is a bit like belling the cat.[10] There is no international monetary agency with the power to impose the tax. Were there one, its constituents would be reluctant to allow it to use this power. It is the same as with global warming: solving a global problem requires a global institution which does not exist.

In the interim, countries prone to receiving volatile short-term deposits from overseas may be wise to adopt a solution similar to Chile's, or even direct capital controls. They are unlikely to – at least until after the next round of financial crises. Policy responses are notoriously a matter of shutting the stable door after the horse has bolted. But the fact that countries can still implement such measures demonstrates that they still have some sovereignty in the international payments system.

Nineteen | Foreign Direct Investment • McDonald's

Capital mobility and increased managerial reach have created multinational firms. Are these inherently different from domestic firms, or just bigger? Is their size a benefit or a burden to the countries in which they invest?

Falling costs of distance make it easier to invest outside the local market and for managerial control to extend around the world. Thus a local company can become a global company. So is there anything distinctive about a multinational company, other than its size and its reach? This chapter explores the issue by considering McDonald's Corporation.

The phrase 'McGlobalisation' is a part of the rhetoric of anti-globalisers. Certainly the McDonald's chain of fast-food restaurants is global – the company says it operates in around 120 countries and territories – and it is big, employing nearly half a million people, feeding 50 million people a day, and generating annual revenues of over US$20 billion. It is not the biggest multinational, a status which belongs to a bank, an oil company or a car manufacturer, depending on definitions. But McDonald's has a certain pervasiveness – not just from its ubiquitous golden arches, but because we all have to eat.

Critics abound. Any large company is going to be involved in misdemeanours (even crimes) and public relations disasters – of which for McDonald's the 'McLibel' case, in which a couple of Greenies were prosecuted with astonishing ferocity, was perhaps the worst. Sometimes ruthless competition seems unfair – McDonald's Corporation under Ray Kroc, having bought the business from the founders, Dick and Mac McDonald, then drove the one (original) restaurant they retained out of business by putting a competitor nearby. In a world which has been casual about the environment, McDonald's has almost certainly contributed to the despoliation, the best-known example being its use of soya beans grown in Brazilian fields which were once Amazon rainforest.

The list could go on. No vigorous corporate expansion is pure, no matter how many public relations agents are hired to clean the image.

We like to distance ourselves from such squalor, although it is impossible to live a life of total independence from it, so pervasive are such economic and environmental injustices, and the large and small businesses involved in them. But is there something special about the multinationals, or are the injustices and benefits greater merely because they are bigger?

The Impact of Multinationals

The term 'investment' is commonly used for two distinct kinds of activity, each of which gives a return. (The confusion is such that one may 'invest' in a lottery or on the horses.) To simplify, one sort of investment involves the purchase of financial paper such as bonds or shares in the expectation of being rewarded. That was the concern of the previous chapter. The other sort involves directly enhancing productive capacity, say by adding tangible capital such as plant and machinery, again in the expectation of reward. When such investment is in one country and the investor is in another, this is called 'foreign direct investment' (FDI), the concern of this chapter. Almost all FDI is carried out by multinational corporations, which are businesses having operations in more than one country.

Insofar as a multinational adds to a country's productive capacity it is widely welcomed, although with some hesitation, for reasons reviewed below. McDonald's, for instance, would claim that it is providing a new good and/or service, a supply of fast food not previously available. (It would add that the requirements of freshness mean that its restaurants mainly source ingredients from local suppliers, and that they employ locals.)[1] However, frequently – and this is not uncharacteristic of much multinational investment – local businesses such as Mom and Pop cafes are forced to close.

But suppose McDonald's was a local chain which displaced smaller restaurants. We might see the redundancies as part of the normal process of economic development, with its winners and losers. Perhaps Mom and Pop were soon to retire; perhaps their workers were reabsorbed elsewhere in the economy – even in the local McDonald's. Their new jobs may pay less, but the offset is that the majority of consumers get a cheaper or better – or, at least, preferred – product. Why should it make a difference if the new entrant is overseas-owned?

Multinationals in an Economy

A common concern is that overseas businesses repatriate their profits and interest overseas.[2] But this is the reward for the investment, for risking one's savings. Were there no such reward, few would invest and we would all be the poorer. The complaint that multinationals' profits go offshore – to pay for the foreign investments – is an expression of the natural habit of mankind to resent servicing debt. There are few anticipatory grumbles when the loans are taken up.[3] Nor do we complain when corporations use foreign exchange to purchase imports for use in the production process. So why do so when foreign exchange is used to pay for the foreign savings that financed the FDI?

The net outflow of profits and interest from an economy is evidence of a local savings deficit, not of the wickedness of multinationals. Had locals enough savings, they could purchase sufficient shares in the multinational for the dividends to offset the outward flow. If a country over-consumes and under-saves, it is going to have to borrow from outside, and in due course add to the economy's debt-servicing and foreign dividend payments.

A related grumble is that multinationals avoid paying tax. Tax avoidance is a normal (and legal) feature of the behaviour of both local and multinational corporations. Perhaps the multinationals have more opportunities for avoidance because they can shift income between jurisdictions. (One method is transfer pricing – over-charging for products sourced from low-tax countries.) It comes back in part to the strength of the tax authorities and the law in the local jurisdiction, but again the tax loss will be less if the country has the savings to hold shares in the multinational.

Multinational FDI not only brings savings to the economy, it usually brings the new technologies which can be central to economic growth. While we may not think of fast food as a cutting edge, McDonald's brings to each new site both hard technologies of food preparation and soft technologies of management.

The benefits to the national economy of a foreign direct investment would be limited if the value the technology generated was retained by the firm and the locals only got jobs (including those from the multinational's purchases of inputs). In such a case, all the technology benefits are repatriated in profits (and royalties). However, it is difficult to confine a technology to its owners (or creators). McDonald's' biggest rival, Burger King, originated when one of its founders, James McLamore, observing a McDonald brothers hamburger stand, sensed the potential in their innovative assembly-line-based production system. Neither can the arriving technology be insulated from the local economy. Every youth who has worked in a McDonald's and set up a business of her or his own learned some management techniques from their earlier employer.

Nor need multinationals pay low wages. Despite the frequent criticism that multinationals exploit their workers, the empirical evidence suggests that they pay higher wages than similar domestic industries.[4] So yes, multinationals pay much lower wages in poor countries than for the same jobs in rich ones – and their products are accordingly less expensive – but they usually pay higher wages than the local going rate. One reason for this is that some of the multinational's technologies become embodied in its workers.

To summarise a long and complicated debate: not all multinational investment has been economically beneficial, and some has been disastrous. But that is also true for local investment. While there are exceptions, the benefits from foreign direct investment often outweigh the damage. Most countries welcome FDI, some more cautiously than others.

Multinationals and the Nation-State

Are some multinationals so large that they overwhelm small countries? Frequently the total annual revenue of a multinational is contrasted with the GDP of a country. But GDP does not measure a country's total revenue (it is not even clear what that might mean), but its value added – which involves deducting the sales of suppliers from revenue. Ranked by value added, only two corporations are up with the top 48 countries.[5] That comparison is also unfair. Most corporations have a raft of dependent suppliers whose output contributes to the corporation's power, so ranking by added value underestimates their market influence.

But all this is to miss the inherent differences between the two kinds of organisation. Structurally, a corporation is a focused hierarchical bureaucracy, whereas power is much more dispersed in a state, even a dictatorship. The corporation's influence arises from its relations with the market, whereas a state's power is its ability to make and enforce laws (including laws which regulate markets). They need each other. Without a stable legal and civil framework, a corporation will operate so inefficiently that it will be very reluctant to become involved. It is no accident that McDonald's expanded first into economies similar to the United States. Even today it does not franchise in African, Middle Eastern or Caribbean countries which it considers insufficiently commercially stable. (It is said that no two countries with McDonald's franchises have ever gone to war against one another However, the United States invaded Panama in 1989, NATO bombed Serbia in 1999, and Israel was involved with Lebanon in 2006.)

McDonald's sells to consumers. But internal stability is also usually necessary for firms which export. (Multinationals based on resources are an exception, for they will accept considerable risks if the resource they are exploiting is sufficiently valuable.) As much as the multinational requires stability, it will exploit any defects in the law within a country, and will try to influence legislation in its favour. Obviously they take particular interest in the legal framework which sets conditions for work and the remuneration of labour. But then, so do national corporations.

On occasions, multinationals have been involved in destabilising governments. Most famously, ITT and Pepsi played a role in the coup which toppled Salvador Allende, the democratically elected president of Chile, and replaced his regime with the repressive one led by Augusto Pinochet. Both corporations supplied local consumers. Oil and mining companies have been equally ruthless elsewhere. But they do not always succeed. And usually, as in Chile, an external government has also been involved (the US in this case).

So are multinationals more powerful than nation-states? There are two circumstances where they may be. The first arises if they are backed by another nation-state, as in the case of the Chilean coup. A more common instance is where, say, US trade negotiatiors pursue the commercial objectives of some US corporations. It may be perfectly appropriate for the US to insist that other countries respect intellectual property rights, which prevents them 'copying' (stealing) ideas from US CD, video, software and similar producers. However, in the negotiations between the US and Australia which led to a free trade agreement in 2004, US pharmaceutical interests got Australia's pharmaceutical arrangements – the public sector is a sole purchaser for many drugs – on the agenda. Many might consider this excessive involvement. Pharma (integrated pharmaceutical firms) might argue that the power of the Australian government was being offset, which suggests that pharmaceutical companies alone are not as powerful as a nation-state. Even so, there may be a case for a future Multilateral Agreement on Investment to include a clause requiring other nation-states to 'butt out' of multinational–nation-state relations in exchange for a proper disputes process.

The second situation in which multinationals seem powerful is where the nation-state is weak. Insofar as its law and institutions are not comprehensive or allow (formally or informally) excessive intervention by corporations in its political process, multinational (as well as national) corporations will exploit opportunities when it suits them. Conversely, a nation-state often has considerable power where it has an effective governance, especially when multinationals are competing for its favours.

So while we may rail against the power of multinationals, the fault, dear reader, as Shakespeare almost remarked, lies not in the offshore stars but in ourselves, that we are underlings. This is not to deny the existence of considerable tension between governance by the market, of which corporations are prime practitioners, and the democratic governance of a nation-state. But in this respect there is nothing distinctive about the role of multinationals.

McDonald's and Culture

Eating practices are central to culture. McDonald's impacts on eating practices. Does it change culture?

McDonald's has certainly played a part in changing eating practices. Many more meals are consumed outside homes because of increasing affluence, the rise of a youth culture, and the increasing employment of women in the market economy. But this change would have occurred anyway. McDonald's is but one of many businesses which meet this demand. By systemisation it has been able to operate at the low-cost end of the market. Having found a successful formula, it franchised its operation, first in the US and then throughout the world. That it met a need is evident from the response by consumers.

It is true that McDonald's replaces indigenous food with an international menu, apparently homogenising the local culture. But it has been sensitive to local needs. In 1963 the Filet-O-Fish was introduced in Cincinnati, Ohio, in a restaurant located in a neighbourhood dominated by Roman Catholics who abstained from meat on Fridays. In Saudi Arabia, 'hamburgers' are called 'beefburgers' to distance the product, named after the German port, from pork. McDonald's India is 'proud' to announce that it offers no beef or pork products but concentrates on chicken and fish ones, including Chicken Maharaja Mac and Chicken McCurry Pan. US McDonald's got into difficulties with its Islamic, Jewish and Hindu customers when it was discovered that its french fries were cooked in non-kosher beef tallow. Such variations remind us that McDonald's is not selling a product, but a production process aimed at consumer demands.

That consumers are not trapped into eating what McDonald's supplies was seen in the early 2000s, when sales fell as consumers turned to what they considered healthier and more varied foods. The corporation responded by changing its menu, emphasising salads, fruit drinks and nutritional information. While McDonald's is a low-cost provider of fast food for children, customers do move on to higher-quality, more expensive food providers that are harder to franchise. As for McDonald's' apparent domination by American culture, people outside France do not grumble if a local restaurant offers expensive French cuisine. Why do those outside America resent the option of cheap American food?

Culture evolves. It is not sensible to blame this evolution entirely upon multinationals, although like every innovating business they do have some effect. Those who shed a nostalgic tear for the old eating ways did not patronise Mom and Pop sufficiently to keep them commercially viable. Do many women still long to cook every meal, every day of the week?

Are Multinationals Inherently Bad?

The theme of this chapter is that multinationals are but global extensions of local companies. Both their sins and their strengths are similar to those which the local companies provide. So why do we grumble more about the multinationals?

It is partly that their size gives them greater power than local companies as against the nation-state. Undoubtedly multinationals use their power, sometimes in ways that are not in the interests of others. The multinational (or local) company is much more focused on its immediate interests (profit) than is a nation-state trying to meet a diverse and often poorly articulated national interest. Indeed it is remarkable how often nation-states constrain (foreign and local) corporate pressures in some wider national interest. Perhaps the corporates should be grateful. Too much success might cause a revolution.

But the fact that they are bigger and, therefore, potentially bigger bullies is part of a trade-off. We want the benefits of economies of scale which corporations reap, and multinationals reap even more, but many people do not like the industrial organisations that go with this. In the end we tend to compromise by regulating corporations through the nation-state. Those who think the balance is still too much in favour of the corporations need to offer an alternative form of industrial organisation. (Higher-priced but similar or lower-quality Mom and Pop restaurants are hardly an alternative.) But that is an issue relating to all corporations, not just multinationals; it is about all commercial investment, not just foreign direct investment. Increasingly, in a globalising world, the distinction is irrelevant.

Part Three • Economic Development

Twenty | How Economies Develop • Smith to Solow and Beyond

Like much of economics, the theory of economic growth is extensive, complex and sometimes confusing, with much still unresolved. To attempt to encapsulate it in a few pages would seem unwise. But some remarks are necessary, if only to convey to the reader the account of the theory which underlies this book, with its central thesis that economic growth is accelerated by falling costs of distance.

Adam Smith's Pin Factory

In Adam Smith's famous account of a pin factory, increased productivity arose through specialisation and the division of labour. Rather than each worker producing the whole pin:

> One man draws out the wire, another straightens it, a third cuts it, a fourth points it, a fifth grinds it at the top for receiving the head: to make the head requires two or three distinct operations to put it on, [it] is a peculiar business, to whiten the pins another; it is even a trade by itself to put them into paper; and the important business of making a pin is, in this manner, divided into about eighteen distinct operations, which, in some manufactories, are all performed by distinct hands, though in others the same man will sometimes perform two or three of them.[1]

This specialisation is only possible if the market for the product is large enough. Smith could have added that this can happen when the costs of distributing pins are so low that one factory can supply a large area. Conversely, when the costs of distance are high, so that the potential market is small, specialisation is not practical and the productivity gains are not made. Although Smith's principle is often illustrated by the example that reducing a tariff enables the producer to extend into other markets, it is almost certain that falling costs of transport have been more influential in enabling the use of specialist production technology.

The Meaning of Technology

The previous sentence used the term 'technology', which – like 'globalisation' – is commonly used without definition. In this book we define a 'technology' as a method of producing a good or service. It is the plan or 'blueprint' of how to do something. Note that technology is a concept, part of what Karl Popper calls the 'third world' of ideas, but typically it is embodied in a 'first world' artefact. It is easiest to think of the blueprint as a diagram or manual, but it may exist only in a person's head, or in a product – when a firm strips down (reverse-engineers) a competitor's machine to find out how to copy its underlying ideas, it is seeking its blueprint.

In practice we can think of technology as the totality of blueprints which describe all the production possibilities – all the ways to do things. Many of these production possibilities are not (yet) known. Discussions of technology usually refer to known technologies (sometimes including those which may soon be known).

As we observed in Smith's pin factory, there may be a number of ways – blueprints – to do the same thing, even to produce a pin. So typically there are many relevant technologies. In a market economy, the producer usually chooses the one which gives the greatest surplus of revenue over costs. If the prices of inputs and outputs change, the technology used may change.

Since in different circumstances a different technology may be used, there is no unique superior technology. Rather there is a best one for each circumstance. That was the insight of E. F. Schumacher – famous for his book *Small is Beautiful* – who saw the relevance of 'intermediate technologies'.

The next few sections explain the role of technology in the theory of economic growth.

Karl Marx and the End of Capitalism: Classical Growth Theory

Both Adam Smith and Karl Marx were great economists whose contributions to economics are frequently misrepresented for ideological purposes. While Smith is upgraded to make him more significant, Marx is downgraded. It may be a matter of one's followers: Marx wrote that he was no Marxist; Smith would not have joined the Adam Smith Club.

Great economists are judged to have progressed the discipline in their era. Subsequent progress may overtake them, and their theories may with hindsight have been too simple. Smith's account of prices is rudimentary. Marx predicted that profits would fall and capitalism would collapse. Insofar as he was an orthodox 'classical' economist, his conclusion was explicit or implicit in the work of most economists of his era. Marx was just a little better known for arriving at it.

The classical economists implicitly assumed that all technologies were known. Businesses accumulated capital to invest in production. Because the amount of capital was increasing, it was invested in more capital-intensive technologies with lower rates of return – lower profit. When profits became too low, capitalism could no longer function.

The account is rigorously logical. But is it right? We know that – thus far – it has not been. How did the classical economists get it so wrong? Suppose that new and unanticipated technologies kept coming on stream, bringing higher productivity which offset the falling rate of return on capital. If that were to happen, there need be no falling rate of profit. Marx was not unaware of this phenomenon, but undervalued its significance.

Robert Solow and Technological Change: Neo-Classical Growth Theory

Classical economists focused on the role of capital in economic growth. The more capital per worker, the higher would be each worker's productivity, and national incomes would rise. I will not detail all the developments which flow from this, but jump forward almost a century to just 50 years ago, when another great economist, Robert (Bob) Solow, published what became the foundation of the 'neo-classical' theory of growth.

When Solow tried to measure the contribution of capital to economic growth, he obtained a result which was at first disturbing and later enlightening. He concluded that only an eighth of the growth of output per worker could be explained by the additional capital per worker. The remaining seven-eighths – the residual – he attributed to 'technical change', which he defined as follows:

> I am using the phrase 'technical change' as a shorthand expression for *any kind of shift* in the production function. Thus slowdowns, speedups, improvements in the education of the labour force, and all sorts of things will appear as 'technical change'.[2]

Here we have a simple explanation of why Marx was wrong. The stream of new technologies and the profits they create have more than compensated for the tendency of additional capital to depress the rate of profit.

Solow did not actually explain what this residual is. He named it 'technical change', and conjectured about some of the things which might be involved. Two British economists, Tommy Balogh and Paul Streeten, went as far as describing it as a 'coefficient of ignorance'.[3]

Over the years, attempts have been made to explain the residual – for example, as changes in the quality (skill) of the labour force. These have always left a significant portion unexplained. Those with policy agendas are quick to claim the gap for their cause: scientists say it demonstrates the importance of research and development; teachers, the importance of education and training; businesspeople, the importance of management and entrepreneurialism . . . . They offer little evidence. One could say that they are in effect trying to increase the coefficient of ignorance; some rhetoricians may have exactly the right skills to do so. This is not to say that science, worker skills and management are irrelevant. Rather, we know little about how important each is, nor the precise causal mechanisms, nor how the various effects are interrelated. Each is almost certainly less important than its rhetoric claims.

Solow's central insight was that production functions change over time, so that the amount of output for a given quantity of labour and capital increases. That is equivalent to saying that new technologies, in the sense I defined earlier, are being used. This is only replacing one definition by another, but it does explain why it is so hard to track down exactly what is going on.

The Solow analysis is based on an aggregate production function, with which the economy produces a single product. It is a very simple account of reality. As Solow himself remarked, 'Either this kind of aggregate economics appeals or it doesn't. Personally I belong to both schools.' Even if his analysis is applied at a more disaggregated – sector, say – level, the residual still exists.

Where do these new technologies come from? In the crudest form of the Solow model – one which Solow himself would be appalled to be associated with – the technologies turn up exogenously as manna from heaven. I sometimes imagine a warehouse of technologies which hand out at their front door a steady stream of new blueprints each day. But reality must have a better story to tell than that . . . .

The 'Knowledge' Economy

A generation later economists, led by Paul Romer, 'endogenised' technical change. That is, they began to explain where it came from rather than assuming it was exogenous – given from outside the economy. It was like changing what was going on in the technology warehouse. Now people rummaged in it to find the blueprints. Because this took resources and time, there had to be investment to identify the new productive blueprints. Hence the need for spending on research and development.

There is an odd economic feature about a technology. Possession of it does not exclude anyone else from possessing it. The same applies to knowledge, although despite the expression 'knowledge economy', not all knowledge contributes to economic – the knowledge of the colour of your shirt contributes little.

Your shirt is a very conventional economic product. If you are wearing it, then no one else can. If someone takes it, then you cannot use it. If they take it without your permission they are 'stealing' it, depriving you of its use. However, knowledge of the shirt's colour is quite different. If I also know its colour I do not diminish your knowledge, and I certainly do not prevent you using that knowledge. Both of us can use it without interfering with each other.

This is generally true for knowledge, including, of course, technology. The possession of knowledge or technology by one person or business does not exclude another from also possessing it. That it is why economists call knowledge 'non-excludable', in contrast to most goods and services, which are 'excludable'. It is true that use of the knowledge by others may make it less valuable to you – even the colour of your shirt may be valuable, say, for answering a quiz question. Sometimes the fact that knowledge is widespread increases its value. That you and I have a similar knowledge of the English language makes this book more valuable.

It is common at this stage in an exposition of non-excludables to discuss policy consequences. 'Rummaging in the warehouse' may be costly, but those who do not do it also benefit from any discoveries. So why should anyone spend their own money on research and development if everyone is to benefit from what is found? Perhaps there has to be some public funding so that, in effect, the other beneficiaries contribute to the cost of the research and development. This is easier said than done. What R&D to fund (since some of it is wasteful)? Who to fund (since the beneficiaries may be foreigners)?

These really important – and perplexing – policy issues are discussed further in Chapter 22. For this chapter's purposes, the point is that technology is critical to economic growth and development, even though it does not behave like conventional factors of production such as capital and labour.

Capitalism and Technology

If technology seems more important than capital, does that mean that capitalism is going to die out – albeit in a different way from what Marx envisaged? There would still be a reasonable rate of return on capital, but the organisation of the economy would no longer be based on the ability of businesses to accumulate and organise capital.

Such a conclusion may be premature. First, the alternative is not obvious. As long as economies of scale remain significant, large organisations are necessary. Even where the firm's blueprints are protected by, say, patents, the enterprise is likely to remain an essentially capitalist one, with the technologies shown as items in its balance sheet. Today's pharmaceutical firms are an example.

Even so, it would be idle to expect the organisational structures of the economy to remain unchanged. In future, while the ownership of capital will continue to dominate economic organisation, this will take more diverse forms. There may be a proliferation of smaller – even one-person – organisations as the large capitalist organisations outsource specialist services. There will be organisations based on human rather than physical or intangible capital – on individuals' mastery of valuable technologies. Universities and professional firms in law and accounting are examples. But even these may have to be glued together by non-human capital.

So Marx seems to have been broadly correct. Capitalism will continue as long as there is a reasonable return on capital, which has two components: a payment for waiting – forgoing consumption – and a payment for risk. Innovation is a major source of risk. As long as there is technological innovation, there will be a return from taking that risk.

Growth, Resources and Technology

To round off this short survey, we need to acknowledge another sort of economic growth – that arising from resource depletion. Thus Saudi Arabia's economic boom is a result of its use of the world's largest and cheapest-to-exploit oil reserves. Indeed there are those who think that all economic growth comes from such depletion. It is certainly true that some does. But as best as can be measured, most economic growth comes not from resource depletion, but from technological innovation. The role of resources in economic growth is the focus of the next chapter.

Twenty-one | **Resources • Oil**

> *Technology is likely to provide substitutes for depleting resources, albeit at higher costs. The consequence is that as the cheap oil (or whatever) runs out, there could be a period of productivity deterioration and even economic stagnation until the world economy has made the adjustment to the new long-run price level. The chapter also looks at sea-fish, water and changes to the atmosphere because of global warming. In each case the prognosis is more gloomy than it is for oil. Because these resources are not properly owned, the market processes which will ease the transition from oil will not work as well.*

At the beginning of the globalisation era, the world's first professor of political economy, Thomas Robert Malthus, argued that population would outstrip food supplies, leading to widespread famine and early death. Thus far he has been wrong. He did not foresee that the opening up of the Americas and Australasia would dramatically increase the supply of land on which to grow food for the burgeoning nineteenth-century population. Nor did he predict that new agricultural technologies would dramatically increase the amount of food produced on each unit of land, or that improved systems of distribution would get more of it to the public.

Malthus was not unique in underestimating the impact of technological progress. He was joined by twentieth-century economists of the eminence of John Maynard Keynes and Joseph Schumpeter, among others. The failure to forecast technological progress by some of the greatest members of their profession may be a major reason why today's economists are more sanguine about the prospects for the world economy as resources run out. Technology will save the day again – perhaps.

Peak Oil

Economists are certainly not denying that resources will run out: the cheap reserves of liquid hydrocarbons on which so much of the world's transport is based are being depleted. One day the world's total oil production will reach a peak, then start to decline. Some experts think this point is imminent, others that it is decades away. In 1979, experts in British Petroleum predicted it would happen in 1985. Forecasting the year involves a complicated assessment of future oil demands, recovery costs from depleting fields, the discovery of new fields, and the extent to which alternative fuels will be adequate substitutes.

Probably in the lifetime of most of this book's readers, total oil production will peak. The world as we know it will not end the following day. The peak will have been signalled by rising oil prices, which will encourage further production from old fields and the tapping of known fields that have been too expensive to use (such as Canada's enormous tar sand reserves). It seems unlikely that any major new oil fields will be discovered, but you never know. More important, substitutes – from biofuels, coal, electricity, gas, nuclear energy, wind, solar energy – will become commercially viable, and users will become more fuel-efficient.[1]

The world's ways will steadily – but probably slowly – change. Higher prices will force motorists to drive less, in smaller, more fuel-efficient cars, and walk, bike, and use public transport more. Houses on city outskirts should become less attractive. Inner-city accommodation may boom. Businesses will seek more efficient ways to ship their goods.

New technologies will, as they have done in the past, moderate the impact of any resource depletion. Once the products of whales – oil for lamps and bone for corsets – were a crucial part of the world economy. Regrettably, they were fished out. But substitutes were found. Once the world's commercial transactions were backed by gold. Total stocks proved insufficient. In 1971 the link was broken under the Smithsonian Agreement, and new ways were found to underpin the integrity of monetary systems.

Estimates of the future costs of the substitutes made with new technologies are fraught with disagreement, perhaps inevitably because predictions about technology are so difficult. They may be further complicated when those making the predictions have an ideological or corporate interest. My expectation is that the price of oil will typically settle in the US$70 to US$80 a barrel range in the long run (ignoring inflation). This is not too different from its level during much of 2005, and slightly more than double what had seemed to be the 'normal' level, around which the world built its investment in transport and the location of home and business. In the long run transport and buildings will have to accommodate themselves to the higher cost of liquid fuels.[2]

On occasions the oil price may jump above this range. Perhaps there will be disruption to supply, perhaps the world economy will surge and demand will temporarily outstrip available supply. But in the long run there will be a range within which the world price will typically hover. The range suggested here is on the basis of the forecast cost of their production in a decade or so.[3] The most likely alternatives are biofuels, the Canadian tar sands (which seem viable if oil prices exceed US$45 a barrel), perhaps hydrogen (which is promising but has yet to deliver), and the use of standing energies (typically electricity) for transport, as for railways and second-generation hybrid cars.

It should be noted that the future of biofuels is confused by the heavy American subsidy to convert corn (maize) into ethanol. This process has a low energy return (output to input ratio) but does convert crops into transport fuels. More promising options for such conversion are sugar cane and wood. Yet the US restricts imports of cane-based biofuels from Brazil.

That there is a plethora of increasingly commercially viable alternatives gives some confidence that the depletion of the oil reserves will not be too disruptive to economic activity. But there will be some disturbance, especially if the depletion happens faster than we are prepared for.

Reductions in energy use per unit of output will not reduce the long-run price, but will put off the day of peak oil reckoning. The main effect will be an effective reduction in the cost of fuel. When fuel prices double, energy costs for a hybrid car which is twice as fuel-efficient as a conventional one will be the same as for the conventional car at the old price.

This is not to imply that the transition will be simple or painless. In the short run the costs of distance may rise, especially for shipping and flying, where there appear to be fewer alternative fuel options. Even so, such have been the efficiency gains in fuel economy in planes that a doubling of the price of avgas would merely return flying costs to about what they were fifteen years ago. Nor should we underestimate the ingenuity of other possible solutions. A bigger Panama Canal would cut shipping costs from East Asia to the eastern US.[4] Would electrified rail offer a cheap high-speed direct link between East Asia and Europe?

During the transition the world may experience a period of little growth in output, as the main investment effort goes into adapting to the higher oil (equivalent) price. Continued productivity growth in most sectors will be obscured by the productivity deterioration resulting from the ending of easily recoverable liquid fuels.

A reconfiguration of living, recreational and business locations will further reduce demand. However, the pattern of change will not be uniform. A hike in the price of oil will not impact greatly on electronic communication. That means that ICT-based activities in, say, India are likely to be less affected than manufacturing activities in, say, China. Globalisation may intensify in some locations and for some activities, while it stagnates or even retreats elsewhere. Some offshore production may return to sites closer to consumers.

As far as I can see – although as mentioned, economists are not renowned for their foresight – providing the world economy remains orderly, technologically driven economic growth will continue after the period of adjustment. (We should not ignore possibilities of disorder, such as from global warfare.) The view which attributes the growth of the world economy entirely to the unsustainable depletion of resources is as limited as Malthus's.

Malthus thought that food was the primary limitation on population and, so he thought, on economic growth. Today we focus on energy, using much the same underlying theory. As best we can assess, though, sufficient alternative energies will be available at costs not so high as to put a permanent brake on economic development. However, in the very long run, it seems unlikely that technologies will be able to offset all the resource depletions – although to repeat, economists do not have a good record of predicting technological change.

Does this hold true for all resources? Three of the many possibilities – seafish, water, and the use of the atmosphere as a dump for carbon emissions – will be explored here to illustrate some general propositions.

The Sea-Fish Resource

The world is rapidly depleting the fish in the sea. As the more attractive fish (in culinary or catching terms) disappear, the fishers move on to less attractive ones. Typically there is little or no attempt to limit fishing to the biologically sustainable catch.

The problem is that nobody owns the fish until they are caught. Imagine a farm where sheep grazed but no one owned them until they were captured. There would be no incentive to sustain the flock. Each hunter would try to capture as many sheep as possible to prevent other hunters taking them first. When the livestock on one farm was hunted out, the hunters would move onto the next. This is the 'tragedy of the commons', where land owned in common is over-grazed because, with no economic mechanism to enable best-practice management, each person with grazing rights puts on another sheep until there is no grass left.[5]

Fishing is a more complicated example than hunting or grazing, but the same logic applies. Whalers cleaned out the whales in the North Atlantic, moved on to the South Atlantic, then further afield to the Indian and Pacific Oceans. Nobody owned the whales; nobody looked after them. Fish species such as North Atlantic cod have experienced the same fate, and others are now experiencing it.

Where fish are confined to a country's Exclusive Economic Zone (EEZ) – 320 kilometres (200 miles) offshore – the country can regulate the catch. Australasia uses systems of Individual Transferable Quotas (ITQs) under which the total catch is limited to what is judged to be biologically sustainable. Individual quota are tradeable between fishers, so that more efficient fishers (those who use fewer resources to catch fish) acquire more quota. The catch limit requires both sophisticated knowledge of the fishes' ecology and an effective enforcement regime. In effect the fish in its waters belong to the nation, which sells the ITQ as the right to catch them. The nation has an interest in a sustainable catch, in a way that the fishers do not, although they do get sustainable employment from such an arrangement.

Other countries have less effective EEZ-policing regimes; and deep-sea and migratory fish cannot be so regulated. So the total stock of sea-fish is being depleted. (Some nations even subsidise fishing, to a total of US$20 billion a year.) As economic theory predicts, the price of fish is rising faster than inflation. Proper ownership – public or private – does not solve the problem of the depletion of sea-fish and other resources. But in a market-driven industry, it is a step on the way.

The Water Resource[6]
It is rare for water to be owned by anyone before it is taken for private use. In this respect water contrasts with oil. Every known drop of oil in the world has owners by the time it is pumped to the surface. Usually they are a combination of the country under which the reservoir exists and the discoverer (or whoever the right has been on-sold to).[7]

Because water is not properly owned, market forces accelerate its depletion. All over the world vast (and usually ancient) underground reservoirs are being utilised faster than they are replenished. Effluent, wastewater and hot water are being flushed into natural watercourses, ruining the supply for those downstream. Complicated systems of (non-tradeable) water rights may limit the use of water for the most socially valuable purpose.

However, unlike oil, there is no international problem with water, water being more expensive to transport relative to its cost. (The fact that icebergs melt in the tropics eliminates any commercial return from transporting them very far.) There are a number of acute regional problems, some involving more than one country. China wants to tap into Russian rivers which flow into seas as far away as the Arctic (although heaven knows that Russia has its own water problems). It is even more difficult to see any amicable solution to the sharing of two Middle East river systems – the Tigris-Euphrates (Turkey, Syria, Iraq, Iran) and the Jordan (Syria, Lebanon, Israel, Jordan) – which flow through countries without histories of cooperation.

Desalination appears to be a simple solution, for there is more water than fish in the sea. Desalinating water using nuclear power is currently estimated to cost about US 4 cents a litre (US$6.50 a barrel), a figure which should perhaps be doubled to allow for the expected rise in the price of energy. In any event, this is well below the likely long-term price of oil.

Today many consumers pay nothing for their water. This will have to change if desalination ever becomes a normal source of water. That is likely to generate considerable local tensions.

Resource Wars?
We could even see wars over water. The economic theory which says that proper ownership of a resource is the first step to its efficient management does not say who should own which resource.[8] War is one way to settle the question – albeit often generating long-term grievances.

The two world wars were, in part, about countries trying to obtain control of resources. That was the idea behind Japan's Co-prosperity Sphere and the resource dimension of Germany's quest for *Lebensraum*. The contrast was with America, with enormous resources in its interior, and Britain, with its resource-rich empire. But the empire has fallen away, and America is increasingly dependent upon others for its resource requirements. Wars with a resource dimension did not end in 1945.

Today Japan, Germany and Britain meet their resource deficits commercially rather than militarily, by purchasing in open markets rather than through conquest. So does the US, although it sometimes seems that its corporations are more willing to use military means. The requirements of multinational (oil) corporations are different from those of the country in which they are based – unless the corporations are so powerful that they can align the country's interest with their own. Britain's oil supply is no more secure or cheaper because British Petroleum and Shell are based in London.[9] Britain is still dependent upon the effectiveness of the international market in oil.

But what will happen if supply is severely reduced during an oil crisis? Perhaps Britain might be able to twist the arms of its corporates to divert a little more oil its way. Recognising such a possibility, 26 rich countries who are net oil importers (aside from Norway) established the International Energy Association, which has arrangements for sharing scarce supplies in an emergency (including the reserves required in normal times). The important lesson here – one which Germany and Japan have learned well – is that for most of the time the market meets the needs of the resource-hungry, with less disruption and more cheaply than military intervention. However in times of severe market stress, the lesson is less clear: large countries may use force (military or other) to meet their immediate needs.

The water story is different. Conflict will be region-wide – although alarmingly, the rest of the world could get drawn in. Without ruling out future military conflict over oil, which certainly happened in Iraq/Kuwait in 1991 and arguably happened again in 2003, water looks likely to be a much greater problem in some areas, where adequate supplies may run out long before oil does.

Global Warming

Nobody owns the atmosphere, which is used – like many watercourses – as a dump for waste, especially carbon dioxide, chlorofluorocarbons, methane and sulphur dioxide. The mechanisms by which these wastes affect global climate – especially by increasing average temperatures – are not fully understood. Until recently there was much dispute over the extent to which they generate global warming. But, unquestionably, significant warming is occurring. Because no one owns the atmosphere, no individual or country has the right to sue or charge any polluter or enforce any restrictions against others to stop the pollution. So it is proving difficult to deal with the pollution and the warming it generates. Currently, two different strategies are being pursued by two groups of countries.

One group, led by the US and concerned with energy security, is hopeful that new technologies will continue to enable them to use coal, while reducing pollution sufficiently. These may (or may not) be related to those that will ameliorate the transition from oil. There is no certainty that the alternative fuels will be less carbon-polluting. Coal will not, unless new coal-burning technologies (together with carbon sinks) are developed. It may be that it will be harder to find technologies that reduce carbon-pollution than ones which replace oil. However, the response to oil depletion is not simply new technologies, but also a raising of the price, which will reduce demand.

So a second group of countries, led by the EU, is setting aggregate carbon output caps for each country, with the expectation that the price signals that the targets generate will both induce technological innovation and reduce demand, in a manner similar to what is happening for oil. However, whereas oil is commercially traded, carbon-emission caps are voluntary and penalties for failure are not enforceable.

While the world can probably survive without sea-fish (Malthus might disagree), a prolonged transition to a warmer world would prove much more difficult. In both cases, the creation of an international regime to own and guard the resource would be a major step forward. In neither case does such a regime seem likely in the near future. Despite some success in limiting the emission of chlorofluorocarbons to reduce the damage to the ozone layer, one is left deeply pessimistic that – as for sea-fish, but not for oil – the world's response to global warming will be ineffective. We shall explore one possible solution in a later chapter on the future of world governance (Chapter 29).

Conclusion

Malthus worried about a potential food shortage. Technology (and new lands) has proved him wrong – thus far. Today we worry greatly about oil, but while the transition to high-cost energy will be difficult, it is not impossible. The bigger problems may be the more mundane medieval elements, air and water (the other two were earth – land for food – and fire – energy). In the meantime we shall probably almost eliminate the edible fish in the sea.

With no ownership of these resources, the market pressures on them cannot be resolved by conventional regulation. Where water is confined to a single jurisdiction, creating ownership rights may be possible. Any solution to the pollution of the upper atmosphere will require a higher (pun noted) level of world government than we currently have. This will not come easily.

Twenty-two | Information • The World Wide Web

This chapter looks at the implications of a set of propositions:
1. *The creation and distribution of, and access to, information uses resources.*
2. *Not all information is accessible; there are various mechanisms to restrict access.*
3. *Information is not the same as knowledge.*
4. *Knowledge is not the same as technology.*
5. *In principle, technology is internationally mobile. (That it is not in practice is the focus of the next chapter, and the consequence underpins the following chapters.)*

By bringing down the cost of reproduction, Johannes Gutenberg's printing innovations made information widely available. There would have been no Reformation in the fifteenth century without the printing press, which enabled Martin Luther's writings to be quickly distributed throughout Europe. As with many technical innovations, there were feedback loops. Cheap books were an incentive to learn to read, especially the Bible. In parts of Europe literacy soon became the norm, even among women. It was not unknown for seventeenth-century Puritans to correct their poorly educated ministers – access to cheap Bibles had given them superior knowledge.

On the other hand, printing in Arabic scarcely existed until the nineteenth century.[1] There was a rich scholarly tradition based on madrasas – centres of learning first established in the ninth century. But as written knowledge was found only in individually transcribed manuscripts, it was largely unavailable to the masses, and so was essentially esoteric. In medieval times the Arab realm was more technologically advanced than Western Europe. While the reasons for its relative decline are vigorously debated, the inability to transmit knowledge cheaply and to the masses must surely have held back Arab thinking and science, as it would have done in the West had the use of printing been delayed for four hundred years.

Yet compared to today's methods, the printed word is a clumsy means of disseminating information. (I hasten to add that I love books, and am glad you are reading this one – hopefully not online.) Over the years improved methods for conveying information were developed. (London's 'penny post' for letters, dating back to 1680, was extended throughout Britain in 1840.) Today, because of the internet, information is extraordinarily globalised – it is accessible virtually anywhere.

The Consequences of the Costs of Information

As a general rule, the production of information requires resources – including the time of the gatherer or writer. (The main exception is when the information is spun off from another activity, such as a bureaucratic procedure.) Disseminating the information also takes resources. (An author commonly gets a royalty from a book, of only – say – 10 per cent of the cover price, the other 90 per cent going to the production of the artefact and its distribution.) Why then should anyone bother to create or disseminate information? Some do it because they have non-commercial objectives, in effect providing a subsidy from their own resources. Most famously, hotel rooms often have Gideon Bibles provided free.

Access through the World Wide Web is also largely free. Consider Wikipedia, the online encyclopedia written collaboratively by volunteers.[2] Access to the entries is free, but their delivery and maintenance is funded by donations. Most of today's writers with online access requiring factual information have used it or an equivalent. The quality of entries varies considerably: one is reminded of Douglas Adams' *Hitchhiker's Guide to the Galaxy*, which 'has many omissions and contains much that is apocryphal, or at least wildly inaccurate, . . . [but] it is slightly cheaper; and second, it has the words "Don't Panic" inscribed in large friendly letters on its cover.'[3]

Yet not everything can be delivered by volunteers and donations. The more sophisticated reference directories on the web are accessible by subscription, just as once there were subscription lending libraries. In some cases, such as the *Oxford English Dictionary*, one can get a free subscription to the web resource by purchasing the book (or one can subscribe to the web resource alone). The same applies to many newspapers and magazines.

Such periodicals are also funded in part (often the larger part) by advertisements. So too are search engines and other websites. It is not necessary here to discuss the efficiency of such funding, nor the possibility that it distorts what is available. Once again, the cost of distance for information has been falling. It is likely to fall further, not just because the means of delivery will become cheaper, but because the mass of available information is increasing.

It is less clear whether the cost of creating the information in the first place is falling. Certainly technology has reduced the cost of some means of generating information – collecting worldwide news for a television channel, for example – but others may be getting more expensive – the living costs of those who wrote the Bible were much less than the salaries of those who write exegeses of it today. Similarly, it is much more expensive to develop a pharmaceutical today than it was a couple of decades ago. Estimates of typical cost range between US$250 million and US$1000 million. What incentive is there, other than altruism, to undertake such investments if there is not the possibility of commercial reward?

Restricting Access to Information

The obvious response is to keep the information secret wherever possible, and sell it at a profit. That is what Coca-Cola does with the recipe for Coke. However for much information that is impractical – a novelist wants to be read. Moreover, it is often possible to reverse-engineer a product – take it apart to find its underlying principles. That may apply even for Coke.[4]

In order to provide incentives for the production of information, there evolved a system of intellectual property rights – such as copyright and patents – which enables the producer to charge users of the information. The outcome is not always very efficient or even equitable. But in some fields it shapes the way information is created and utilised.

A particularly fraught case is that of pharmaceuticals. The cost of production of most drugs subject to patent protection is a fraction of the price charged for them. Why should the patient (or whoever is financing the treatment) pay that price, especially when many (especially those in poor countries) cannot afford it?

The pharmaceutical companies rightly point out that they have investigated numerous molecules, most of which were discarded on the way, to identify a particular drug. They need a return for their substantial investment outlays. Moreover, pharmaceuticals to treat many of the scourges of poor countries are not being developed because the return on investment is thought likely to be too small. On the other hand there is the argument that the return on the companies' investment is too high. Profit is all very well, but there are people dying of, say, HIV-AIDS in Africa because they do not have access to the expensive drugs, which are much cheaper to produce.

There are no easy solutions. The pharmaceutical companies fear that if they provide their drugs at low expense to the poor, the unscrupulous will recycle them to rich countries at a profit. This already happens. The companies do not charge exactly the same price in each rich country; so some Americans go to Canada to obtain cheaper drugs.

Falling costs of distance increase the difficulties of internationally policing property rights. Music can be downloaded from the web at a trivial cost. How to protect the interests of those who create and distribute music? Computer software can easily be replicated, but how is its development to be paid for? (Companies build up brands. What is to prevent another company replicating the product and even falsely labelling it with the reputable brand name?)

Intellectual property rights need to be enforced. A rogue economy which does not do so – perhaps it has no laws, or cannot enforce them – can easily act as a source of copies and fakes for international distribution. Countries joining the World Trade Organization are required to have suitable laws and enforcement mechanisms. Even so, there remains a private incentive to evade the law. Moreover, not all property rights are, or can be, covered by the law; and some laws seem irrational. What is the justification for giving copyright in a work to the author for up to 70 years after her or his death? Surely few people write on the basis of that financial incentive.

Falling costs of distance, particularly as a result of the Internet, have complicated intellectual property rights. The wider market that globalisation creates has increased potential royalties but made the rights harder to enforce. It is not impossible that the long-run effect will be that almost all information becomes costless. There may be a lag in getting access, but even that may be getting shorter.

Information, Knowledge and Technology
This chapter uses 'information' to mean data to which meaning can be assigned. Search engines and even online dictionaries require us to discriminate between high-quality and low-quality information. Those who praise the development of online access to information (perhaps as an educational tool) ignore the real issue of how to process it.

If you have any doubts, do a web-search for 'cancer cure'. When I did one the 800,000-odd entries were dominated by 'alternative' therapies, with surprisingly little on conventional therapies. An experienced oncologist of my acquaintance was distinctly unimpressed by the top site, and even less by the second, which advocated a particular therapy for which there was no positive evidence and some damning negatives. The third website on the list he thought helpful; the (American) National Cancer Institute appeared only fifth. Without the knowledge needed to discriminate among the mass of information, one could be poorly informed. (My oncologist friend is not opposed to the use of safe 'alternative' medicines – not all those proposed are safe – to complement scientifically proven therapies.)

We need to be able to distinguish high-quality information from the rest. One is tempted to call the former 'knowledge', but perhaps this term is better used to describe the process by which we discern its quality. (Another term for this knowledge is 'intelligence'.) The notion of a 'knowledge society' does not refer to a society based on piles of high-quality information – a society of super quiz-kids – but to one which values the ability to discriminate between high- and low-quality information, and make use of the conclusions.

Sometimes the 'knowledge society' is transmuted into the 'knowledge economy'. For either meaning of the term knowledge, that is wrong. The modern economy is based on the knowledge society, but much high-quality information is irrelevant to it. A knowledge of Sanskrit is hardly of significant commercial value, even though it may be valued in the knowledge society. What is important to an economy is the subset of high-quality information we call 'technology'.

Introducing Technology

As we saw in Chapter 20, a 'technology' can be defined as a method of producing a good or service that is perhaps embodied in a plan or blueprint. As such it is information, and successful technologies are high-quality information. The totality of technology is the totality of the blueprints which describe all production possibilities – how to do things. Many of these are not yet (fully, or even partly) known.

Only some of the many available ways to do things are efficient. Economists call this subset the 'frontier' technologies. If circumstances change – different prices, different availability of resources – another frontier technology may be used. In certain circumstances the best way to obtain water from a distant well may be by water tanker, but in others it may be by a woman carrying a jug on her head. Both are frontier technologies, although they have different productivities.

Frontier technologies have higher 'productivity' than the alternatives which are not used. Productivity is a 'good' thing, because more can be produced with the same resources – or fewer resources can be used to make the same output. (The production is 'technically efficient'.) New technologies move the frontier by replacing old technologies. Productivity increases. It is unnecessary to detail here the process of innovation by which the discoveries are made. We focus on the extent to which new technologies are made available to the entire world.

The Mobility of Technology

Is this frontier subset – of the best technologies available at any time – available to all countries? In practice different countries may use different ones – a rich country may truck water while women carry it in a poor country. While we tend to call the former 'advanced', both may be frontier technology in that the one chosen depends upon on the costs faced by the producer. (So a frontier technology need not be an advanced technology, and an advanced technology need not be a frontier technology: a water tanker with flat tyres is more advanced than the woman water carrier, but is unlikely to be used.)

As an economy becomes richer it tends to shed the 'less advanced' technology and adopt the more advanced one. But will the more advanced technology be available when the need arises? Generally, yes. There are numerous ways to obtain it even when it is 'owned'. The technology may be purchased embodied in equipment. On the above definition, a truck has a technology blueprint embedded in it. Or perhaps the right to use a proprietary blueprint may be purchased from its owner. Paying for particular technologies is part of ordinary market behaviour. We expect to pay for the labour and capital others provide. Why not pay for a technology, especially as the possibility of financial reward will encourage the discovery of better ones?

We have seen that information is becoming increasingly globalised. Technology, a subset of all information, is globalised too. While it may have to be acquired by purchasing a product or paying a royalty, generally it is available. It is often not possible to prevent a new technology being used by competitors anywhere in the world. If it were, having a competitive advantage would not be so stressful, since competitors could not copy the innovation (perhaps after reverse-engineering it) and undermine the firm's technological advantage.

Technology is more mobile – more globalised – than capital, and much more mobile than labour. Yet it cannot always be applied. Why this is so is the focus of the next chapter.

Twenty-three | Technology Transfer • Japan

Even though technology is more mobile than capital or labour, poor countries may be unable to adopt the most productive ones because they may not have suitable meta-technologies – the formal and informal institutional arrangements which facilitate their implementation. Japan did. A combination of international technology transfer and wage restraint caused its post-war economic miracle. When its technologies caught up with other rich economies in about 1990, its economic growth slowed down. In a sense, however, Japan's growth centres relocated offshore to the 'Asian Tiger' economies.

The Technology Problem: Meta-technologies

If every economy has access to the same technologies, what is the technology problem? It cannot be just a matter of timing. Economies may take a few years to introduce new technologies, because it takes time to find out what works. But some economies seem to be centuries behind others.

The logic might seem to be that all the poor countries should introduce the advanced technologies of the rich countries as quickly as possible, and they too will soon be rich. Why don't they? The simple answer is that having access to blueprints does not mean that one can use them. That requires 'meta-technologies', the institutional arrangements which enable the implementation of technologies. ('Meta' here means 'transcending'.)[1]

Meta-technologies are central to economic and social development, encompassing a wide variety of phenomena associated with the institutions which govern and regulate the economy. However, they are much harder to analyse than the objects of standard economic analysis. Douglass North, who was awarded an Economics Prize in honour of Alfred Nobel for his studies of the role of institutions in economic development, has remarked on the 'vast gap between the relatively clean, precise and simple world of game theory [which underpins much formal economic analysis] and the complex, imprecise and fumbling way in which human beings have gone about structuring human interaction'.[2]

What is clear is that it involves not merely the formal institutions of a society, but also the informal ones of how people behave. North nicely illustrates this by pointing out that while many Latin American countries adopted constitutions based on the US model, they did so with much less success. Russia's experience also supports North's insight. When the Soviet Union collapsed in the early 1990s, many anticipated economic prosperity. These expectations have not been fulfilled. Russia may have abandoned (some of the) Soviet institutions, but it did not have the alternatives necessary for economic success.

Markets are systems of decentralised economic decision-making where centralised political processes have a limited role. They allow experimentation, rewarding the use of advancing technologies and punishing bad choices. A successful market economy is underpinned by institutions, including stable property rights, which ensure that experimenters are rewarded with profits which in turn determine the choice of technology. Stability of personal and property rights is critical. (Instructively, as we saw earlier, environmental difficulties are often related to ambiguous property rights.) Economic transactions – especially those involving technological innovation – involve players who have to make judgements about uncertain outcomes. Sound institutions remove unnecessary uncertainty.

Perhaps even 'democracy' – whatever that means – is not a precondition for high economic performance. Such a conclusion can be drawn from the post-war experiences of Hong Kong, Singapore and even Japan, which has largely been ruled by one party.

Among the important questions relevant to assessing – or designing – an economy are:

1. Is there sufficient civil stability and integrity of social relations (trust)?
2. Do the economic incentives encourage technological innovation (and introduction)?
3. Are there social blocks to technological innovation (and introduction)?
4. Has the labour force got the abilities – the skills, the attitudes – to enable the new technologies to be implemented effectively?
5. Have the managers got these abilities?

Perhaps a question about capital and financial investment could be added, but if the responses to the questions on this list – especially the first one – are positive, this should be well taken care of.

Ultimately, as the economist William Baumol emphasises, an economy which wants to grow must reward innovation and productive activity rather than destructive activity (such as the plundering of warlords), rent-seeking (patronage or deriving benefits from legal anomalies and loopholes), or even – dare one say it – financial speculation (as against risk-taking with a productive outcome).

A review of successful economies shows there is no unique institutional configuration, although there are clearly things not to do. As there is no ideal, this chapter looks at Japan, which had one of the most extraordinary post-war economic performances.

Japan and Technology

As Table 23.1 summarises, Japan's per capita output today is a little above that of the twelve countries in Western Europe. Yet as recently as 1950, it was less than two-fifths of the West European Twelve.

TABLE 23.1: PER CAPITA OUTPUT AS A PERCENTAGE OF WEST EUROPEAN TWELVE

	1950	1970	1990	2004
West European 12	100	100	100	100
Japan	38	89	111	104
Asian Tiger 6	20	20	44	64
United States	191	137	137	142

Source: Maddison Data Base.[3]

The extraordinary growth performance of the post-war Japanese economy is shown in Table 23.2.[4] In the first two decades after 1950 Japan grew at an annual per capita rate of 8.4 per cent, more than twice that of the West Europeans and nearly four times the US rate. In the next two decades, to 1990, Japan continued to grow much faster than Western Europe and the US.

TABLE 23.2: PER CAPITA OUTPUT: GROWTH RATE (PER CENT PER ANNUM)

	1950–70	1970–90	1990–2004	1950–2004
West European 12	4.0	2.2	1.3	2.6
Japan	8.4	3.4	0.9	4.5
Asian Tiger 6	4.2	6.2	4.2	4.9
United States	2.3	2.2	1.6	2.1

Source: Maddison Data Base.

One factor in the initial rapid growth was that in the early 1950s much of Japan was still suffering from wartime devastation. Post-war reconstruction brought big gains, not only because the survivors were willing to make big sacrifices, but because many of the key requirements for growth – the meta-technologies and the human capital – were still in place despite the destruction of physical capital during the war. A lack of physical capital may not always be the handicap it might seem. More important were the institutions and people who survived the war.[5]

Japanese industry was particular skilful at assimilating Western-created technologies. The usual put-down is that Japanese manufacturers were excellent copiers, obtaining state of the art machinery, stripping it down to its individual components, and then developing their own model based on what they learned. That is to overlook the excellence of Japanese meta-technologies. The Japanese have proved particularly adept at introducing and managing technology generated elsewhere. Their practices became the core of modern management: kaizen (continuous improvement), total quality management, outsourcing, just-in-time inventory management, on-the-job training....

It would be easy to attribute this to the advice of W. Edwards Deming to Japanese managers after the war.[6] But it does not matter that it was an American's advice: it was Japanese culture which adopted it. They did not 'copy' Deming's advice: there was nowhere to copy it from. It was America and Europe which copied the Japanese management practices. The Japanese meta-technologies extended beyond a willingness to adopt management strategies favourable to the introduction of technologies. There was considerable civil stability – almost a one-party state – but this was offset by the decentralisation of industry.

For while a degree of political stability is necessary for technological transfer, political sclerosis is not. The economist Mancur Olson has a thought-provoking thesis that a society can be *too* stable, with political decision-making weighted to the past.[7] That produces a tendency to legislate in favour of existing technologies, since new ones will devalue the old, reducing the incomes of the existing political elite. Olson argued that a major political upheaval – in the case of Japan, the Second World War – tends to wipe out backward-looking political interest groups.

Olson's thesis has the uncomfortable implication that perhaps Mao Zedong was correct when he advocated a permanent revolution. What Mao did not appreciate was that a competitive capitalist market tends to be in such a state, although its permanent revolution is more creative than the 'Great Leap Forward' and underpinned by stability of personal and property rights.

An associated requirement is that there is the labour to implement and run the technology. As Deming argued – and Japan demonstrated – this is not just a matter of having expert engineers. It involves the entire workforce having both a broad general education and specific (and ongoing) on-the-job training. Without this, continuous improvement and total quality management don't work.

Thus Japan had the institutions – the meta-technologies – it needed to adopt the technologies created by North America and Western Europe. And so it caught up with the other high-income countries. (Capital was also needed. Much of it came from Japanese savings. Today capital is highly internationally mobile, seeking out the most profitable opportunities, typically where labour is cheap and the meta-technologies are favourable.)

Completeness requires mention of other factors which contributed to Japan's growth, as well as some which inhibited it. It was important that Japan had an export-oriented (rather than import-substituting) strategy.[8] For much of the post-war era, there was a tendency for the yen to be undervalued, thus making exporting relatively profitable. This was possible because the Japanese economy had both wage restraint (in return for high long-run wage growth and job security), which meant relatively low wages compared to other economies using the same technology, and large savings (and so a current account surplus in the balance of payments, which tended to depress the exchange rate).

Once Japan had caught up to Europe and North America, and was using top-of-the-line technology just as effectively as they were, the process of growth through technology transfer no longer worked, and the Japanese 'economic miracle' came to an end. From 1990 Japan began to grow at roughly the same rate as the other rich countries. Initially the economy had considerable difficulties adapting to slower growth. The experience was reminiscent of those a rapidly expanding business faces when it has saturated its market. The culture which facilitates an upswing may not work as well in the slower-growth environment of maturity.

Today Japan faces the challenge of contributing to the creation of and implementing new frontier technologies, a much more daunting task than borrowing well-established ones. All rich countries borrow technologies from one another – competitive advantage applies to them too. But for Japan there are no more easy gains to be made by adopting well-tried technologies.[9]

Lessons from the Japanese Economic Miracle

Japan's growth, based on international technology transfer and consumption restraint, may be a model for other poor countries with the required meta-technologies. Ireland and Spain have had a similar growth pattern (from a higher base than Japan's). In due course, so may the ex-Soviet economies which have just joined the EU (if their skilled labour does not migrate to Western Europe). But, as the example of Japan shows, the beneficiaries of a strategy of technology transfer need not be economies with Western-based cultures.

The six Asian Tiger economies of Hong Kong, Malaysia, Singapore,

South Korea, Taiwan and Thailand also illustrate the success of growth by technology transfer. Their 'tiger growth' began in the 1980s. Despite the Asian financial crisis of 1998, their post-war growth rate now exceeds Japan's, albeit from a lower base.

Hong Kong and Singapore, which today have per capita outputs similar to those of Japan and Western Europe, are beginning to show the same slower growth as Japan.[10] South Korea and Taiwan have about three-quarters of Japan's output per capita, and may soon reach it. Malaysia and Thailand, at about one-third the Japanese level, presumably have considerable opportunities for further growth. Other Asian economies – including the potentially huge ones of China, India and Indonesia, may join them.

One way of interpreting the experience of the Japanese and Asian Tiger economies is that as the benefits to Japan from technology transfer ran out, Japanese investors turned to other (nearby) countries, such as South Korea and Taiwan, which had economies with good meta-technologies but lower wages and higher returns. At the same time, Japanese businesses began to outsource production to offshore plants with advanced technologies but lower wages. In effect they are all a part of a Greater East Asia region, illustrating that the boundaries between economies may not be as important as the conventional wisdom assumes.

From this perspective, the Asian Tiger experience is no different from that of the post-war US, where investors and business shifted their focus from the North-east and Midwest to the South and the Pacific Coast. But because the US regions are in the same jurisdiction – and under the same statistical authority – the regional shift is disguised by national averages. Because the Asian region is a plethora of countries under different jurisdictions and with separate statistics, we see the shift and fail to observe that if Greater East Asia is treated as a single entity, the growth 'miracle' in the Japanese economy continued offshore after Japan slowed down to the same pace as other rich economies.

The process of relocation will continue. We are already seeing Hong Kong struggling as it offshores to the Chinese mainland; Singapore may increasingly do so as Malaysia and Indonesia become more attractive.

The lesson we learn from this chapter is the importance of advancing technology in the growth process, the relative cheapness of acquiring it, and its effectiveness in an economy with appropriate meta-technologies. In principle, any economy can join the Rich Club – if it has high-quality meta-technologies. Many do, and will. Sadly, others don't, and won't.

Twenty-four | The Rich Club • Argentina

Membership of the Rich Club has been largely stable. However, new members such as Japan have joined, and in the mid-twentieth century the primary produce exporters Argentina and Uruguay left. The international transfer of primary production technology is more difficult than that of manufacturing technology, and farm product exporters have faced severe protection against their exports, especially from the Rich Club. Argentina's industrialisation strategy was inward-looking – unlike the export orientation of Japan and the Asian Tigers – and did not arrest its relative decline.

One of the central features of world economic development is the existence of a group of rich countries that persistently remain rich. A century ago Western Europe, the US, Canada and Australasia had markedly higher incomes than most of the rest of the world.[1] That was broadly true even two centuries ago, and it remains true today. I call this group the 'Rich Club'. The economics literature calls them the 'convergence club'.[2] I'll explain shortly why this term is used. The club is not exclusive. In recent decades its membership has been extended to include Japan, Ireland, Spain, Hong Kong and Singapore.[3] Perhaps South Korea and Taiwan will join soon – or have already. So, in a decade or so, may some of the economies which recently joined the EU.

The persistence of membership of the Rich Club contrasts with the transience of the great corporations. Lists comparing the top 30 international corporations today with those 100 or even 50 years ago would have little in common. As the New Zealand Māori say, 'Only the land remains, constant and enduring'.[4]

There is some variation of income levels between the members of the Rich Club, the result of differences in both the possession of resources and their intensity of use, and in productivity. Hourly productivity of workers seems higher in some parts of Western Europe than in the United States, but their annual per capita output is lower because they work fewer hours. While rankings within the Rich Club change from decade to decade, the US has always been near the top. But compared to the rest of the world, Rich Club incomes bunch together.

Economists have identified a 'convergence' process. Laggard members of the club tend to catch up with those at the top, it being easier to do this than to get out in front. Once an economy has caught up, it strains (along with the rest) to stay there. That requires different policies. Japan from about 1990 and Ireland from about 2000 are examples of this struggle.

Why don't poorer countries with lower wages attract capital and technology and grow faster than the rich ones? Some do – like the new members of the Rich Club. But generally it is very much a matter of, 'for unto every one that hath shall be given, and he shall have abundance: but from him that hath not shall be taken away even that which he hath.' What is the mechanism by which the rich keep getting richer?

The previous chapter's description of the process of international transfer of technology explains this clustering and convergence. Rich Club members have meta-technologies which enable the rapid adoption of the most productive technologies. The limited membership of the club indicates that this is no mean feat. While in principle such economies need not create new technologies, it seems likely that local innovation complements the process of adoption. Convergence occurs because it is easier to adopt established technologies than to create the new ones which the Rich Club's leaders are already implementing.

The strain is articulated publicly in the ongoing rhetoric for 'reform'. The term has two different meanings. It can mean 'to improve by alteration, correction of error, or removal of defects', as in, 'to reform a corrupt government'. This ought to be a one-off endeavour: once the reforms are implemented, the situation can go back to non-reformist normality. But the word also means 'to change for the better'. New technologies (and meta-technologies) create opportunities for improvement, but frequently require some other adjustment. Thus the Rich Club faces the need for reforms – 'changes for the better' – as long as innovations generate opportunities for improvement.[5] Being in a well-off country has a number of advantages, but a quiet life is not one of them.

While persistence of membership is characteristic of a Rich Club of nations based on high and advancing technology, with new members joining by adopting these technologies, a couple of countries – Argentina and Uruguay – have left the club.[6] Once economically up with the leaders, they fell behind.

The Experience of Argentina
According to the available statistics, in 1913 Argentinean income per capita

exceeded the average of the West European Twelve. (While this section focuses on Argentina, the story it tells also applies broadly to Uruguay. In 1913 Uruguay's per capita income was a little below that of the West European Twelve, but above Finland, Italy, Norway and Sweden, and close to Austria, France and Germany.) Argentina had not been a member of the Rich Club 40 years earlier. The refrigeration revolution described in Chapter 3 enabled the exporting of frozen meat that began soon afterwards. Between 1870 and 1913 its population doubled and per capita incomes trebled. Yet by 1998 Argentinean income per capita was just half that of the West European Twelve.[7]

A country does not wake up one morning to find itself excluded from the Rich Club. It is more a matter of increasingly failing to turn up than a barring of membership. It slips away, each year growing a little slower, until it finds itself so far behind that it cannot call itself a member any longer. This process takes longer than the rapid growth which shifted some economies, such as Japan, from the Poor Club into the rich one.

Argentina seems to have begun its slide shortly after the First World War, with a broad downward trend superimposed over fluctuations. Argentina's GDP has been growing on average about 1 per cent per annum slower than the West European Twelve ever since. The substantial literature which seeks to explain why often compares Argentina with the more successful Australian economy. However, many of the explanations describe the internal mechanism which external events triggered, rather than identifying the critical drivers. Some possible external explanations pertinent to this book's theme can be rejected. It cannot be a matter of size: Argentina's population is about twice that of Australia. Nor can it be the tyranny of distance: Australia is further away from both Europe and North America. It would be easy to blame Spanish heritage, but there are substantial groups of British and German origin in the Argentinean population, and in any case Spain recently joined the Rich Club.[8]

While Argentina and Uruguay are the only countries to have left the Rich Club, others have struggled to stay there. The next slowest growth in the last century was in Australia and New Zealand. At the beginning of the twentieth century they had markedly higher incomes than the West European Twelve, and as they have lagged behind less than the Latin American pair, they remain members of the Rich Club.[9] These four countries were all settler colonies – but so were Canada and the US, which have grown more quickly. What the four have in common is that they were all (and are all, except in the case of Australia recently) very dependent upon farm product exports in the twentieth century.

The international transfer of technology is less easy with respect to primary production. It is not difficult to replicate a factory, providing the general conditions – the meta-technologies – are favourable. However, a farming, fishing or forestry technique has to be adapted for local conditions. It is not merely a matter of bringing a prize flock from overseas and grazing it on a local farm. Getting the right grasses for it to feed on will depend on the land, the climate and the seasons, and almost certainly require changes in animal husbandry and even in the animals themselves.

Sometimes local conditions can add to the difficulties. Foot and mouth disease (*Aphtae epizooticae*) is a highly contagious and sometimes fatal viral disease of cattle and pigs that can also infect deer, goats, sheep, and other animals with cloven hooves (as well as elephants, rats, and hedgehogs). On the whole it is not a threat to humans, but it is devastating to animal productivity. The disease arrived in Argentina in 1870 and became endemic early in the twentieth century. Argentina did not follow the lead of the US Department of Agriculture, which embarked on an expensive programme combining education, the slaughter of infected animals, and financial compensation for affected ranchers that eliminated the disease by 1929.

The US and other disease-free countries – including Canada, Australia and New Zealand – then put restrictions on the import of meat products from those countries which were not disease-free. They had no reason – or commercial incentive – to find solutions to the disease. So there was no readily available treatment or technology for Argentina to import, once it had failed to go down the US path of slaughter to elimination.[10]

Protection Against Primary Product Exporters

This example of the specificity of the relevant technologies for some natural resources could be repeated many times, if not so spectacularly. But the restrictions against foot and mouth disease also illustrate a problem faced by primary product producers. Argentina thinks that some of the restrictions against its exports justified by phyto-sanitary provisions against foot and mouth disease are really excuses to protect domestic farmers from competition.

The Rich Countries' support of their agricultural producers has been more widespread, more generous and more persistent than their support of manufacturers. Although the difference is sometimes explained by the importance of farmers electorally, it matters that land is immobile. Capital, labour and technologies can go elsewhere, but land cannot. Thus the only profitable strategies available to a landowner are to increase productivity and, when that no longer suffices, to seek government support for the industry.

The effect of this support for domestic producers is to depress the prices received by their competitors. Excluded from the high-price markets reserved for inefficient but protected domestic farmers, exporters also find their returns in third markets undermined by the (subsidised) dumping of the surpluses produced by the same protected farmers. This has been the fate of Argentinean (and Uruguayan, Australian and New Zealand) farmers. In the nineteenth century they benefited from the huge British market being open to all-comers, but from 1932 there were restrictions on access. A decade later, British farmers began receiving subsidies.

The ratio of the prices for Argentina's exports to the prices it paid for its imports – its 'terms of trade' – declined for most of the twentieth century.[11] By the end of the century, Argentina's terms of trade were less than half what they had been at the beginning. That means Argentina had to export twice as much to import the same amount. In an average year a large chunk of a farmer's productivity gain benefited consumers – mainly overseas ones – in lower prices. Meanwhile Argentina had to work harder to purchase its imports, including capital goods and fuel necessary for production. Economic activity slowed down.[12]

Is there a long-term tendency for the export prices of primary products to decline relative to the price of manufactures? The truth of this proposition is not obvious. Oil prices tend to rise as reserves run down, as do fish prices as we exhaust the stock of the seas. What about more renewable products, such as the beef and wheat Argentina exported? The record shows that for much of the twentieth century their terms of trade – the quantity of manufactures a unit of them could purchase – fell. But that does not mean this is inevitable.

Of course, once things are going badly for an economy's key industries, and its rate of economic growth slows down, political management becomes more difficult. This usually leads to policies aimed at protecting interest groups which further damage the economy. The unintended effect is to undermine key meta-technologies. Foreign investors seeking political stability find coups very unattractive.

Import-Substituting Industrialisation versus Export-Oriented Industrialisation

When a leading sector suffers such difficulties, the obvious strategy is to diversify into industries with better price trajectories. Argentina was one of many struggling economies which tried to increase the size of its manufacturing sector, especially in the decades after the Second World War. How it got it wrong, and others got it right, is instructive. The strategy is obvious enough. If technologies for manufacturing are cheap and internationally available, why not import them and implement them domestically? The difficulties are twofold.

First, the economy may not possess the necessary meta-technologies – even if the country thinks it has them. Setting up a factory according to the intentional blueprint does not guarantee that it will produce efficiently. Second, manufacturing subject to economies of scale requires a large market. The problem seemed to be resolved by protecting the domestic market from imports, reserving it entirely for one or a few domestic producers (which may be multinational companies). That did not work in Argentina. Its domestic market was too cosy and local producers did not compete sufficiently, seeking the most efficient and advancing technologies. It was not simply a matter of comparative advantage. Manufacturing subject to economies of scale needs the pressure of competitive advantage.

One can see this in the success of those who have joined, or shortly will join, the Rich Club. Japan and the bigger Asian Tigers fiercely protected their local markets, privileging the domestic suppliers. They did so directly through tariffs and import controls, and by various formal regulations or informal practices. Where they differed from Argentina was that local companies used the home market as a platform for exporting. Prices in the protected local market were high enough to cover the fixed costs of production, so that any exports at a price above the marginal cost of production were lucrative. Price is not the only factor in export markets. Quality matters too. Pressures to meet the quality required by overseas markets drive competitive advantage in domestic production. Argentina's manufacturers missed out.

Under such pressures, Asian manufacturers developed to be among the best exporters in the world. Their export-oriented industrialisation enabled them to join the Rich Club, whereas Argentina's import-substituting industrialisation did little to slow its leaving.[13]

Of course, if everyone practised export-oriented industrialisation with a protected home base, there would be no prospective export markets. Today no Rich Club member has fearsome protection against manufactures (although most should be ashamed of their protection against farm products). The Asian Tigers were able to prosper in part because Japan dismantled its protection and practised offshoring – as have the US and the EU.

What are the prospects for Argentina (and Uruguay) to return to the Rich Club? It missed the export-oriented industrialisation strategy, and its farm exports continue to face both restrictions on market access and dumping. The same challenge applies to many other farm-exporting countries, including Australia, New Zealand and many poor countries. We shall see in Chapter 27 that the world terms of trade for food and resources may rise in the twenty-first century.

Twenty-five | Poor Countries • Africa

The two-thirds of the world's people who live in poor countries produce only a sixth of the world's output. The poorest region is Africa, although the majority of the poor are in Asia. The differences between rich and poor were not so great 200 years ago. The process of globalisation accelerated the growth of the economies of what is now the Rich Club, relative to the poor. Even so, the incomes of the poor countries have risen about threefold in this period (although some economies have had lengthy setbacks).

Two thousand years ago the average annual income of the world's population was around $450 (in 1990 international dollars), not far from today's poverty line of US$1 or US$2 a day. For the next 1800 years the average income grew slowly, increasing by about 1.2 per cent every 50 years.[1] This growth was uneven. Levels in Africa barely changed, and may even have fallen slightly. Meanwhile, Western European incomes, after falling during the first millennium following the collapse of the Roman Empire, grew faster and were about double the world average in 1800, as the globalisation of the world economy was getting under way. The income of other regions – North America excepted – hovered around $500 to $600 a year, still less than US$2 a day.

By contrast, in the last 200 years world per capita income has increased to more than nine times the 1800 level, at an average 1.2 per cent per year (instead of every 50 years). Before asking why, we need to explain the meaning of the data.

What is GDP per Capita?

Even today, making international comparisons is difficult. The most common economic one, GDP per capita, involves valuing the output of each economy using the same prices (the above used 1990 international dollars), adding up all the values and dividing this figure by the population. There are many steps in this process, and much can go wrong. We have to trust the statisticians to do the best job they can.

Even statisticians working with competence and integrity face almost insurmountable problems of comparison. If the product is internationally traded a comparison can be made, because it is valued in different economies. But many products are not traded. How does one compare the value of housing for a person living in the middle of the Kalahari Desert with that for somebody living in Johannesburg, let alone Tokyo or Buenos Aires? Differences in quality matter. Not all retailers, to take one of the largest service sectors, provide the same quality of service, even in the Rich Club.

Comparisons across time are even harder to make. According to the Maddison Data Base, world GDP per capita is around thirteen times higher now than it was two thousand years ago. That does not mean that on average we have thirteen times more of everything. Today's computers are much more than thirteen times more powerful than the abacuses of those days (or even the computers of twenty years ago). Many of the things we use today are new products that were unimaginable in earlier days (or even sometimes when older readers were young).

Statisticians will explain patiently that they use a chain linking method which allows year-on-year comparisons to accumulate into comparisons over longer periods. The theoretical justification for this approach misses the point. Economic development is about changes in the availability of goods and activities. To focus on increases in output – which is what GDP per capita, at best, measures – collapses kaleidoscopic variety into a single index. So GDP per capita, or whatever, provides at most a crude insight into the complexity of what has been happening.

Second, GDP per capita measures material output. It does not measure happiness. The statistics may show that people have become materially better off over the years, but they do not demonstrate that their psychological well-being has improved. Economists have tended to assume – albeit with various caveats – that the more goods and services one consumes the better off one is. People tell you they will be happier with more consumption. But are they? In recent years surveys have asked people how happy they are. US surveys go back to 1950, since when the consumption of material goods and services by the average American is three times higher. But Americans do not report that they are any happier (and certainly not three times as happy) than they said they were half a century ago.

Suppose we look at happiness and income among people living in the same country at the same time. While higher income does correlate with greater happiness, the effect is exceedingly small. Married people are happier than unmarried people – on average, of course. A Jane Austen character famously commented that 'happiness in marriage is entirely a matter of chance'. The surveys suggest that being married generates on average as much additional happiness as an additional US$100,000 of income a year. (What would Austen have made of that?)

Perhaps the most revealing finding comes when happiness is surveyed across many countries. Among Rich Club countries, average happiness is much the same, independent of the exact material standard of living. However, in poor countries, those with higher GDP per capita tend to report higher average happiness. As best we understand it, raising the material prosperity of poor countries will raise their population's happiness. But above a certain threshold, that effect ceases.

More important may be some concomitant benefits of higher material consumption. Health is better and life expectancy greater (so one is happy longer). Greater literacy gives individuals greater knowledge. (John Stuart Mill thought it better to be an unhappy philosopher than a happy pig.) More generally, high-output economies offer individuals more choice in terms of work, leisure and consumption (which is not to be confused with how much they consume). Recognising this complexity, the United Nations Development Program has gone as far as constructing a 'human development indicator' based on longevity and educational attainment, as well as income, with its ability to purchase material consumption.

So while the research on happiness challenges the conventional assumption that more consumption is necessarily better, it certainly does not say that poor countries should not try to raise their incomes along with their health status and educational levels. So GDP per capita may be a useful measure for assessing the well-being of the poor (but less useful for the rich).

Finally, the figures used here are averages of the incomes of all the people in a country. In practice there is considerable variation of income within every country, and even the poorest have very wealthy citizens. India may have more millionaires than the entire population of more than 80 states and micro-states.[2] Similarly, members of the Rich Club have many poor (although proportionally not as many, and not as destitute, as the Poor Club).

Poor Countries

Defining exactly what is a poor country involves drawing a more ambiguous line than is needed for the Rich Club. Here we are looking at the very poorest nations of the world. We shall use a GDP threshold of $3500 per capita in 1990 international dollars, a quarter of the minimum for membership the Rich Club. (The choice of this figure is explained in the next chapter.)

Aside from micro-states, 75 countries had an average annual income of less than $3500 per person in 1998: 33 were in Africa, 15 in East Asia, 14 in West Asia, 10 in Latin America, and 3 in Europe (Albania, Moldova and Romania).[3]

Their total population is nearly 4 billion, some two-thirds of the world's total, but they produce only a sixth of the world's output (GDP).

The numbers of countries may mislead, because the poor countries are dominated by a few large states: China (1.3 billion), India (1.0 billion), Indonesia (210 million), Pakistan (140 million), Bangladesh (130 million), and Nigeria (110 million). So the bulk of the poor are located in Asia. Nevertheless, Asia also has some Rich Club members, while Africa has none. Only five African states – Gabon, Namibia, South Africa, Tunisia and Mauritius – are above the $3500 threshold, and the first four are not far above it.[4] So Africa is the poor continent. It has been for the last 500 years, although in 1500 the income gap to the rest of the world was much smaller.

The Great Divergence

While average incomes have increased to nine and a bit times the previous level in the last 200 years (after increasing about 50 per cent in the previous 1800 years), not all countries fared similarly. Table 25.1 summarises the regional pattern.

TABLE 25.1: INCOME CHANGES IN THE LAST 200 YEARS

REGION	2000 income relative to 1800	GDP per capita (in 1990 $)		Percentage of world population	
		1820	1998	1820	1998
Other Western Offshoots	45.9	753	20,082	0.1	0.9
United States	38.5	1,257	27,331	1.0	4.6
Japan	33.4	669	20,413	3.0	2.1
Western Europe	17.1	1,232	17,921	12.8	6.6
Latin America	9.8	665	5,796	2.0	8.6
Eastern Europe	9.6	636	5,461	3.5	2.0
WORLD	**9.3**	**667**	**5,709**	**100.0**	**100.0**
Other Asia	6.6	565	3,734	8.6	19.8
Former USSR	6.3	689	3,893	5.3	4.9
China	5.0	600	3,117	36.6	21.0
Africa	3.4	400	1,368	7.1	12.9
India	3.2	550	1,746	20.1	16.5

Source: Maddison Data Base.

The greatest growth has occurred in the US and the Other Western Offshoots (Canada, Australia and New Zealand), in part because richer people migrated there. Add Japan and Western Europe, and the Rich Club sits at the top of the table, well above the average. At the bottom of the table are the poor regions. The gap between those at the top and the bottom opened up dramatically after globalisation. Because the data does not exist, we do not know the extent to which the income growth of African countries (perhaps 'regions' would be a better expression, for most hardly existed as countries in the nineteenth century) differed over the period of globalisation.

Of the (literally) handful of poor countries for which we have data going back to 1800, only China experienced a systemic fall in per capita income during the nineteenth century. Indeed it was not until the mid-1950s that it regained its level of 1800.[5] China aside – a big aside – we do not have much evidence that globalisation damaged the poor countries of the world in absolute terms. Rather, the benefits of globalisation did not accrue equally across all economies. Moreover, some poor countries benefited greatly. In the eighteenth century, before the process of globalisation began, Japan was probably one of the poor countries, as were some of the other countries which have recently joined, or will soon join, the Rich Club.[6]

Is There a Poor Club?
Tolstoy wrote that 'Happy families are all alike; every unhappy family is unhappy in its own way.' That may be an equally useful distinction between members of the Rich Club and poor countries. Members of the Rich Club have to adopt the top-of-the line technologies – the competitive pressures insist on this – and while their meta-technologies may reflect national differences, they have commonalities. Poor countries use different technologies and meta-technologies.

On the other hand, we observed in the previous chapter that membership of the Rich Club persists through time, with members rarely leaving. The same holds true for the poor countries. As the previous chapter observed, it has been rare for any member to leave that 'club'.

Given the efforts countries have made, often with the support of those who live outside their borders, to accelerate the economic growth of the poor countries, the results have been largely disappointing. In the last 50 years, average African incomes grew more slowly than those of the rest of the world. They have barely risen in the last 30 years, and in some countries they have fallen. Obviously African countries need better meta-technologies – easier said than done – to win a greater share of the capital and technology flows. But what else do they need?

Income transfers from aid and debt redemption may help, but the experience of the last half-century is that while these may lift immediate incomes, they may not accelerate development. It is a bit like giving the unemployed a social security benefit. They may be better off in the short term (and to that extent the benefit achieves something), but it does not address their long-term well-being, and it may keep them in permanent dependence. Something else is needed too.

Increasing access for a country's products to rich markets can be beneficial, especially if it lifts the returns, for often rich countries restrict access to their markets and dump their surpluses into third markets, depressing prices there (as we saw for foodstuffs in the previous chapters). There is also an innovation bias towards the Rich Club's technologies. They can afford to pay for their development, whereas poor countries cannot, as we saw in the example of the pharmaceutical industry's lack of interest in developing drugs for tropical diseases. As the 'small is beautiful' movement has shown, this is also true for more prosaic activities such as supplying water.

If we really want to address sub-Saharan African poverty in the long run, the experience of the Asian Tigers suggests that the best chance would be for Africa to have a dynamic growth node. The obvious candidate would be South Africa, whose per capita income is about three times the African average, and which has a population near 50 million. If it could boost its economy through an export-oriented industrialisation strategy, then in due course it would offshore business to lower-wage African economies which could then experience a growth boom parallel to that experienced by the Asian Tigers.

Sadly, though, for most of the latter half of the twentieth century South Africa's relations with the rest of the world were corrupted by apartheid, with its iniquitous race-based treatment of individuals. Today its GDP per capita is much the same as it was 30 years ago. (Whereas Western Europe's is up by more than half. It is ironic, isn't it? The rich countries where happiness may not be boosted by additional material output, have grown, while the poor countries, where GDP growth can contribute to welfare, have not grown to the same extent.)

Moreover, and even more sadly, sub-Saharan Africa is being ravaged by the scourge of HIV-AIDs.[7] The optimist might recall the impact of the bubonic plague which killed about a third of the population of Europe in the fourteenth century. The devastation changed social institutions and increased agricultural productivity (as there was more land per peasant), providing the base for the economic growth of Europe over the next few centuries, and thereby the platform for its globalisation boom. However, not only did it take many decades for the conditions created by the Black Death to bear fruit for those Europeans left, but the HIV-AIDs epidemic is more selective, impacting more upon those of working age, including those caring for children. Thus the collapse of output relative to the population is likely to be comparatively greater in Africa than it was in Europe, the course of events more agonising and more prolonged, and the recovery so much harder.

It may well be that such events will be overtaken by the West's demand for labour as its population ages. It is not inconceivable that in the very long run

Africa will be depopulated as much by out-migration to service the needs of the Rich Club's elderly as by the HIV-AIDs epidemic. That prospect may be some time off. In the immediate future, Africa's economies may be enhanced by aid, development assistance, better access to markets for their exports, and supporting the growth of South Africa. As much as better meta-technologies are crucial, their successful implementation will depend upon the internal politics of the individual countries.

Did Globalisation Increase Inequality?

There are two debates about whether globalisation has increased or decreased world inequality. One addresses the last quarter of a century, with some arguing that globalisation has lifted many or at least some of the poor out of poverty, while others argue that it has had little impact. The answer depends on the quality of the available data, which may not be always reliable.[8]

The second debate refers to the impact of globalisation in the last two centuries. In a comprehensive survey, the eminent economic historians Peter Lindert and Jeffrey Williamson argue that globalisation has reduced inequality by spreading the benefits of the industrialisation of the Rich Club to other countries.[9] They argue that while industrialisation may have raised the Rich Club's output per head some sixteen times, the threefold increase in even the poorest regions income is far more than would have occurred had the world economy continued along its pre-industrialisation path.

Such an analysis, however, assumes that we can separate industrialisation from globalisation. I argue that we cannot. The falling costs of distance which drove globalisation also released the resources and reaped the economies of scale which facilitated industrialisation. This is not to argue that industrialisation was caused solely by globalisation, only that enough of it has been to qualify the Lindert/Williamson analysis. If this is correct, globalisation has unquestionably contributed to the increasing inequality in world incomes.

But is that necessarily a bad thing? Incomes have generally risen, even among the poor. It is better to be poor today than it was 200 years ago – although of course there are caveats. What if it were inevitable that the economic growth which derived from globalisation would benefit some regions more than others? (I am inclined to think it was.) If so, would we want to have forgone the opportunities globalisation generated?

Suppose that two centuries ago you were given a choice between a continuation of the previous two millennia of stagnation, and the economic growth resulting from globalisation – but you did not know which region you would be living in. The philosopher John Rawls proposed a 'veil of ignorance' behind which one could chose the destiny of nations (or whatever) without knowing where one would be resident. My guess is that, given a choice in 1800 between globalisation, with its growing inequality but average incomes rising for all (albeit at different rates), and a continuation of the stagnation of the previous millennia, most people behind a veil of ignorance would have chosen globalisation. The worst that happened was to be in a region whose per capita output was 'only' three times higher 200 years later.

This is not to argue that the globalisation experience was the best of all possible worlds. Had we known 200 years ago what we know today, we may have modified its course. Nor is it to argue that no one was greatly disadvantaged by globalisation. But many more people would have been disadvantaged if stagnation had ruled. Even so, one is left with the lingering thought that some people – amongst whom Africans are most prominent – did relatively badly out of the last two centuries of globalisation, and perhaps unnecessarily so.

Twenty-six | The Insignificant Middle Club • The Bifurcation Model

> This chapter addresses two related features of the world economy: the M-shaped income distribution by country, with relatively few countries in between a Rich Club and a Poor Club; and the way in which manufacturing concentrated in the Rich Club of the upper part of the M. It argues that the most promising way to explain such phenomena is through an account of two development paths which international trade makes interdependent. The main drivers of the explanation for this bifurcation are the costs of distance and economies of scale in manufacturing.

In comparison with most income distributions, the world income distribution by country is peculiar. While the usual distributions are not necessarily symmetrical – the rich tend to be much further from the middle than the poor – they tend to have a single peak – a mode – in the middle, around which most cluster. The left-hand figure is typical:

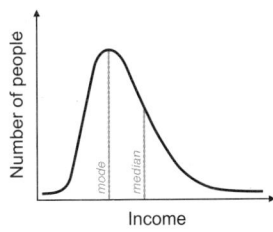 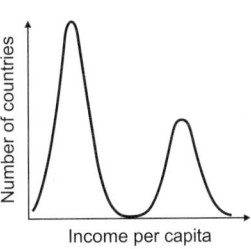

In contrast, the world income distribution by country has two modes, with a big peak at the lower mode, a smaller peak at the higher one, and not much in between, as in the right-hand figure.

We can see this shape in Table 26.1, where countries have been divided into groups. We have set the cut-off point for the Rich Club at an average income (GDP per capita) of $14,000 a year in 1990 international dollars. The richest in the club, the US, comes in at $28,000. The next group (the Middle Income Club) have average incomes of between $7000 and $14,000 per annum;

the 'Just Out Of Poor Club' has incomes between $3500 and $7000 per annum; and the Poor Club has incomes below $3500 per annum.[1] It could be argued that the lowest threshold is too low and should be raised, or that there should be a lower 'Very Poor Club'.[2] The M-shaped distribution is robust to such refinements.

TABLE 26.1: WORLD INCOME DISTRIBUTION BY COUNTRY: 1998

Income Range (1990 international prices)	Number of Countries	Percentage of World Population	GDP
$14,000–$28,000 (Rich Club)	23	14.5	54.6
$7000–$14,000 (Middle Income Club)	19	3.7	6.6
$3500–$7000 (Just Out Of Poor Club)	29	14.7	13.8
$3500 (Poor Club)	109	67.2	25.0

Adapted from Maddison Data Base. Micro-states are not included in the country count, and EU countries are counted separately.

What is instructive about this categorisation – other than just how many are in the lowest groups – is the size of the Middle Income Club. It has only 3.7 per cent of the world's population and 6.6 per cent of its GDP, less than either of the categories above and below it. It is this sparsity which gives the M-shaped distribution.

There are nineteen relatively small countries in this middle group. Seven are very dependent upon oil.[3] Six are on the fringes of the European Rich Club,[4] as is Puerto Rico in relation to the United States, and South Korea to Japan.[5] That leaves the three Southern Cone countries – Argentina, Chile, and Uruguay – Mauritius in the Indian Ocean, and Malaysia, which may be in transition to the Rich Club. Whichever way they are counted, the Middle Income Club is not a large community and its composition seems unusually heterogeneous.

The challenge is not to explain why country X or Y is in the Middle Income Club, but why so few are there. Why is there an M-shaped distribution and not a ∩ one? Answering that is going to take a little consideration of mathematical modelling – albeit with a minimum of mathematics.

Explanations of Bifurcation

We have two broad options to describe an outcome with an M-shaped distribution. One is to assume that two different mechanisms generate the two clusters. Swans and ducks belong to different cluster groups (biological families), with some variation within each cluster. Biologists tell us that a particular set of genes causes some life forms to be ducks, and another set generates swans.

The conventional economic analysis to explain why the Rich Club are rich and the rest are not tends to follow this line. One set of economies have a certain set of conditions which enable them to be rich, and another have another set of conditions that keep them poor. The difference is so strong that it is not unusual to treat the two clusters quite separately, as if the economics of developed countries is different from the economics of developing countries. (For many countries 'developing' is a euphemism: 'Less Developed Countries' is another term.)

But what are the key conditions? In the biological model the genes underly what happens. They have a major influence on the outcome (phenotype). It is not obvious what their economic equivalent is.

Many of the things which we use to explain poor economic performance are consequences of the performance rather than determinants of it. Perhaps Argentina's experience of the populism of Peronism and the later coup resulted from the deteriorating economic performance rather than causing it (although they made the performance worse). Had the economy performed better, the political disturbances may not have happened.

An even bigger problem is to explain how some poor countries become rich. It would be easy to claim that Japan was like an ugly duckling which in due course turned into a swan.[6] But that seems a bit ad hoc. Is Malaysia an ugly duckling; is Mauritius? The two-explanation account is deterministic, but not good at predicting what with hindsight appears unexpected.

A third problem of the account is that it ignores the interactions between the members of the Rich Club and the Poor Club. Throughout this study, and indeed throughout other conventional economic histories, references to such interactions are common. (The most recent here was to explain that some countries appear to be in the Middle Income Club because they are near Rich Club members.) But the theory of two development mechanisms ignores this interaction. Each follows its own development (or non-development) path, with the barest awareness of the other.

Instead of a two-mechanism approach we might seek a single mechanism which generates what mathematicians call a 'bifurcation', in which the elements of the system go down one of two paths. Such bifurcations are more common than we normally think. Put a bottle on the edge of a table and knock it. What happens remains under the same laws of physics, but the outcome will be very different if the bottle stays on the table than if it falls off.

Consider a couple of trampers on a ridge top, their view obscured by fog. One decides to go down on the north side, the other on the south. They may end up in different watersheds. Perhaps the northbound tramper strikes an easy track, wanders down to a hospitable farm and is made comfortable. Meanwhile, the southbound tramper has struggled through dreadful vegetation and an almost impassable gorge, and is cold, hungry and miserable.

The standard advice for lost trampers is not to separate. But suppose they had to. Suppose they chose which way to go on the toss of a coin. It would be so easy for the northbound tramper to think that her or his comfort reflected tramping skills, fitness, character, preparedness, equipment, and so on. But we know that luck was crucial.

Suppose, too, that the watersheds come together at some point and the two trampers meet up again. Suppose that they now have to sleep in the same room. The northern tramper may become worse off by sharing the facilities. He (or she) is unlikely to dwell on his previous good luck and may forget how easy his trip has been compared to that of his companion. Rather, he may grumble that their meeting has made him worse off.

The course of economies is more complicated, in that sending a tramper down one path forces the other to go down the second. Although their paths seem separate, they are interdependent. While the mathematics which underpins such phenomena is more complex than need trouble us here, we can use its intuitions to explain the development of the world economy.

Interlude: The Manufacturing Conundrum

The history of manufacturing poses a challenge to conventional accounts of economic development. Suppose that I ask you to name the two biggest manufacturing economies in the world in 1750 (we have data for that year). Between them they produced more than half of the world's total output. My friends usually nominate Britain and another European country.[7] They could not be more wrong. As Table 26.2 shows, the two biggest manufacturers in 1750 were China and India.

TABLE 26.2: MANUFACTURING OUTPUT (PERCENTAGE OF WORLD TOTAL), 1750–1938[8]

	1750	1800	1860	1913	1938
Britain	1.9	4.3	19.9	13.6	92.8
Other Europe	21.3	25.8	33.3	43.0	
US & Canada	0.1	0.8	7.5	32.9	
Japan	3.8	3.5	2.6	2.7	
China	32.8	33.3	19.7	3.6	3.1
India	24.5	19.7	8.6	1.4	2.4
Other	15.6	12.6	8.4	2.8	1.7

In the eighteenth century China and India had about 55 per cent of the world's population and produced about 55 per cent of the world's manufactures. That seems reasonable.

But we see the world differently today. In 1938 the 'developed core', roughly the Rich Club, produced more than 90 per cent of all manufactures, with hardly any production in China and India. Given the changes described in earlier chapters – offshoring and the arrival of new members in the Rich Club – the developed core's share is a little less today. As the bottom row of the Table 26.3 shows, the intensity of manufacturing in the developed world (even excluding recent recruits) was still higher in 1990 than it had been for most of the nineteenth century.

TABLE 26.3: DEVELOPED WORLD'S TOTAL PERCENTAGE SHARE[9]

	1750	1800	1860	1913	1938	1973	1990
Population	17.7	17.1	20.4	23.7	22.8	18.4	17.0
Manufacturing	26.8	32.2	63.3	92.5	92.7	90.1	83.0
Intensity	1.7	2.3	6.7	39.7	43.3	40.4	23.8

Intensity = ratio of developed countries' manufacturing per capita to that of the remaining countries.

Why this concentration in relatively few countries? Earlier chapters explained that where there are strong industry economies of scale, manufacturing ends up in particular locations if the costs of distance allow. But that does not explain which location. If economies of scale are so important, why has manufacturing not been located in the countries with the biggest and densest populations: China and India?

Of course one can think of special explanations; we will traverse some of these shortly. One which does not make sense is that manufacturing 250 years ago was very different from today, and so China and India acquired no special advantages from their dominance in traditional manufacturing. Manufacturing developed incrementally, with craft manufacturing evolving into factories. Those with more manufacturing ought to have had an advantage.

Two Development Paths

An economic model developed by Masahisa Fujita, Paul Krugman and Anthony Venables provides an explanation of how we can get two paths, one of manufacturing development (the Rich Club) and one of agricultural development (the Poor Club).[10] The model is not easy to understand, and even when I set it out in English it remains complicated. It goes like this.

Consider an entire world consisting of just two economies, which are identical in every way: the same population and labour force, the same capital and land, the same technologies and meta-technologies, and the same patterns of demand. They will therefore have the same levels of sectoral production and consumption, and there is no need for them to trade – or so it would seem.

Suppose both economies have just two sectors. Because the quantity of land is fixed, the agricultural sector has diminishing returns, so that average labour productivity falls as more workers work on farms. However, the manufacturing sector has increasing returns to scale, so that labour productivity rises as additional workers work in factories.

When there is no trade between the two economies the production level in each sector is the same, because they are mirror images of one another. Suppose the cost of distance falls, so that it is now possible to trade. For this to happen the two economies must specialise. One produces all the manufactures for both economies, drawing workers from its land, and trading its surplus manufactures for the farm products it needs from the other economy. However, the manufacturing economy also produces some farm products and its farmers are relatively productive. (This corresponds with the historical reality.) The other economy specialises in agricultural goods – it cannot compete with the other's manufacturers because it has not the economies of scale. Instead it sells its surplus agricultural products, using the proceeds to purchase manufactures.

The economy that specialises in manufacturing will have higher incomes than the one which specialises in agriculture. The manufacturing specialist has higher worker productivity, because its manufacturing is benefiting from the economies of scale, while its agriculture production has higher labour productivity, because there are fewer workers on the farms. The farm specialist economy, with all its workers on the land, has lower productivity. Even though they are identical in terms of resources and many other things, the two economies have now embarked upon different development paths.

The theory does not tell us which economy goes along which path. The manufacturing specialist is a member of the Rich Club, and the agricultural specialist is a member of the Poor Club. But in this model, it is an accident which is which.

The essence of this story is that when the costs of distance are low enough, there is international specialisation and trade, but when there are economies of scale the two economies do not benefit equally.

The next chapter extends the model to make it better fit the experience of history. However, two features of the explanation seem to contradict the conventional wisdom. One is that, as we shall see, the paths later come together. The second is that the two paths are not independent, but intimately linked. It is only possible for the Rich Club to exist by exporting manufactures to the Poor Club, which perforce cannot reap those economies of scale and hence the high productivity and incomes. There is a sense then, in which the Rich Club succeeds by climbing on the back of the Poor Club. Is this fair?

Fairness and the Two Paths
A curious feature of the two paths is that although the model assumes that the workers in each economy are identical, the Rich Club workers get paid more than Poor Club workers, because their productivity (in manufacturing) is higher than the productivity of the Poor Club's farming. The inequality could be eliminated were the poorly paid workers allowed to migrate to the Rich Club.

What about the fairness of the two paths? Generally the workers in the Rich Club are better off than if there were no trade, since their wages are higher.[11] The Poor Club's situation is less clear. Its workers receive a lower wage relative to farm product prices, but they get their manufactures cheaper. So whether they are better or worse off depends on the balance of purchases. Landowners are almost certainly better off because more workers are working the land and they get a bigger rent. Overall, the Poor Club's average incomes may rise or fall. It all depends. What is unquestionable is that its incomes will be below those of the Rich Club.

This conclusion may seem heresy, since it is widely assumed that an increase in trade benefits both economies (although not necessarily every person in each economy). Economies of scale are complicating the conventional story.

This analysis does not contradict the conclusion of the previous chapter that globalisation has been broadly beneficial. Thus far the bifurcation model has left out the technological innovation that those taking the Rich Club path generated. Without it, perhaps those in the Poor Club would have been worse off. But as we saw, their path experienced growth too – but markedly less than that of the Rich Club.

We will now bring the analysis of the last few chapters together by considering the example of China.

Twenty-seven | The Pattern of World Development • China

This chapter extends the previous chapter's analysis into the future. In particular, it asks if China will 'peel off' from the Poor Club and join the Rich Club over the next century? It may – or it may not. But given orderly world development, some countries will join the Rich Club. This will pose challenges for its current members and bring dramatic changes to the world economy.

The previous chapter described a simple model in which economies could go down one of two paths, into a Rich Club of manufacturing or a Poor Club of farming. This chapter applies the model to the real world. But how robust is it? We cannot examine all the many assumptions. Further detail adds to its complexity. But while much of the discussion that follows is – necessarily – a little vague, it comes to some useful, if cautious, conclusions.

What may seem to be the most important omission can be dismissed quickly. The model assumed no technological change, and therefore no economic growth other than from gains from economies of scale.[1] Technological change can be incorporated in the model without distorting the bifurcation and its two paths, so that assumption need not matter. In this chapter we will assume technological change, but not highlight it.

Does it matter that there are only two sectors? Probably not, for each represents an aggregation of various sub-sectors. Some sub-sectors may leave the Rich Club for the Poor Club earlier, depending on circumstances such as economies of scale and costs of distance. (Textile manufacturing has already gone.) Some of the new industries which the Rich Club sees as central to its prospects, such as design and innovation, are likely to move offshore eventually, although perhaps not for some generations.

How about adding more countries? This introduces additional possible paths. It seems that under certain circumstances an economy in the Poor Club can peel off and join the Rich Club, leaving the others behind. Since this is what has happened to Japan, and to some other regions and countries, it appears that the model generates behaviour not unlike the historical experience. However, each time this happens the gap between the rich and the poor closes, because the benefits of the industrial specialisation get shared across more economies.

But even with only two countries, there is a parallel outcome when the costs of distance are sufficiently low. The wages (labour costs) of those in the Poor Club are so low that its factories can undercut the Rich Club manufacturers despite the latter's advantage of economies of scale. The wages in the Rich Club fall and those in the Poor Club rise. The process continues until they are equal because the two economies are once again mirror images of one another. The two economies return to producing identical levels of manufactures and farm products. The bifurcation ends and the two development paths rejoin.

It is very unlikely that all the Rich Club and Poor Club members will merge onto the same path at the same time. Instead, there will be a steady peeling off of members from the Poor Club to join the Rich Club. We describe the practical implications of this towards the end of the chapter. But before looking to the future, let's review history.

The Great Nineteenth-Century Bifurcation

The differences between the economies of the world in 1800 were not great. A century later, the world had divided into a Rich Club and a Poor Club, with very few in between. It is tempting to see this period as one dominated by the sort of processes which underpin the bifurcation model. Here is the story written from this perspective.

Sure, there were differences between countries in 1800, but they were not large (and they may have been no larger than regional differences within countries). But the costs of distance were falling towards the bifurcation point where manufacturing tended to be concentrated in a few locations in order to benefit from economies of scale, with the rest of the world specialising in farming. Why did manufacturing concentrate in Western Europe and North America? The bifurcation model cannot explain why this occurred in one region rather than another, because it treats all regions as identical. There are two very different accounts of why 'the West' might have been favoured: an economic one and a political one.

The economic account argues that some countries were better placed to seize the opportunity presented by falling costs of distance. The West was already slightly richer and already had slightly more manufacturing than other countries. Moreover, it had better meta-technologies, in particular a stronger record of scientific research and application (although in earlier eras, other regions had dominated the scientific world, such as it was). After three centuries of exploration, the West was more open to new ideas and new challenges. Moreover, technology was not as mobile as it is today, so that its discoverers were able to benefit exclusively from it for longer. So manufacturing concentrated in the West. Once it began to do so, the cumulative causation implicit in the bifurcation model reinforced the concentration. However, the economic growth of the West spilled over through trade and technological transfer to other countries, whose incomes also rose as a result, but not by as much.

That is the benevolent story. Alternatively, one might see more politics in the West's supremacy. Exploration encouraged commercial outreach, and by 1800 the West's empires were beginning to encompass the world, giving it political dominance. It used this political and technological hegemony to shape the rest of the world's economies in its favour.

Perhaps the best-known example is provided by the Opium Wars. Opium had been used in China since the fifteenth century. The Chinese imperial government prohibited its smoking in 1729, and reaffirmed a ban on opium imports in 1799. Meanwhile Europeans, particularly the British, were purchasing porcelain, silk, spices and – especially – tea from China, which wanted little in return except silver. So the British sold the Chinese opium, creating a demand for the product through widespread addiction – by the 1830s it seems likely that virtually all Chinese men smoked opium – converting a Chinese trade surplus into a deficit. The emperor responded in 1838 by imposing extremely severe punishments, including death, for smoking or trading opium. Following the enforcement of the ban in Canton (Guangzhou) in 1839, a British fleet easily defeated the Chinese forces, took the city, and then sailed up the Yangtze River and captured the tax barges (strangling the revenue of the imperial court). In 1842, the authorities sued for peace, which was concluded in the Treaty of Nanjing, a so-called 'unequal treaty' which opened up China by giving Britain commercial access to its markets. Two years later, China, again against its will, signed similar treaties with France and the United States.

There was a Second Opium War between 1856 and 1860, followed by a settlement which further improved commercial access for Britain, France and the US (and Russia). Historians argue over the extent to which opium was the reason, or the excuse, for the wars. What is unquestionable is that the result was that China was opened up to Western trade on the West's terms. (It also led the Chinese to recognise that they were technologically backward and embark on a programme of modernisation.)

Ironically – or significantly – opium was banned in Britain at the time. Supplies for China were provided by the British East India Company. Not that India did very well from British rule. The tariff regime discouraged the manufacture of cotton goods in India to protect British manufactures. Not surprisingly, the British administration in India did not vigorously challenge the ban. On the other hand, Britain's policy of free trade in raw materials and food gave its colonies the incentive to specialise in their supply.

This account of Western imperialism inhibiting opportunities for the economic development of its colonies and neo-colonies is the malevolent story.

We have here two quite separate accounts of why manufacturing concentrated in the West in the nineteenth century. One says it was because of its better technological preparedness for the new industries, and the rest of the world benefited; the other says the rest of the world suffered because of the West's political dominance (together with its technological superiority). The reader can choose the balance between the two accounts. Either explains why manufacturing was located in the West following the bifurcation.

The bifurcation did not happen instantly. Throughout the nineteenth century, the powerful forces of agglomeration concentrated manufacturing into Western Europe and eastern North America. Regions on their periphery later became manufacturing centres too. Then Japan joined in, and nearby regions also began to grow. Thus was the Rich Club born.

Meanwhile, the rest of the world, aside from those with access to particular scarce resources or with low populations relative to their resource base, went down the Poor Club track. Their incomes generally rose, providing the country was not too disrupted (as China had been), as the Rich Club purchased raw materials from them and new technologies became available. The technologies used in the production processes of the Rich Club involved bigger productivity gains. Output on the high-income path of the bifurcation now grew even faster.

What Might the Bifurcation Model Say About the Future?

The bifurcation model predicts that more economies will peel off from the Poor Club, transitioning to join the Rich Club. While Malaysia, Thailand and some European countries which were once parts of the Soviet empire are possible candidates, the most spectacular new member could be China.

We need to be cautious. Certainly China is growing rapidly at the time of writing, albeit probably slower than its official statistics claim. Certainly it is going to be a big economy, measured by GDP, for whatever its GDP per capita, its fifth of the world's population is an awful lot of 'capita'. But that does not mean that the Chinese economy will shortly dominate the world.

In my lifetime there has been a constant rush from the promotion of one fashionable country to another. Each time the claim has been that it would join the Rich Club or overtake the US as the world's leading economy. My earliest memory is of Soviet premier Nikita Khrushchev's 1956 promise that 'we will bury you'. Since then the list has included at various times virtually every big country or region: Brazil, China, India, the Middle East, the East Asian Tigers.... In the early 1990s, airport bookshelves in America promised that the Japanese economy would soon dominate the American one. Making such claims, backed by anecdote and unreliable statistics, induces the hysteria which makes for attractive marketing when there is little content in the product. Soon a new claimant with equally spectacular promise appears as the old one fades.

The argument here is more complicated. First, note that most of the new joiners have taken two or three decades to catch up to the Rich Club. China is starting from a lower base, and there are further complications, discussed below. It will take longer, although some parts of China – the region around the Yellow River Delta – may arrive earlier.

Why China? Since the theory tells us little about preferred regions, we must guess. In the early 2000s the Chinese manufacturing sector certainly seemed to be expanding rapidly. It looks like a bigger Asian Tiger – an Asian Dragon? – well placed in relation to Japan and the United States to seize the benefits of the falling costs of distance and act as an offshore manufacturing centre. Because of its size, the agglomeration effects may be especially powerful. However, India is another possibility: almost as big, in a slightly inferior location that is offset by its much larger English-speaking population.

The Future of Wages

Chinese manufacturing is succeeding because its workers are doing the same job as Rich Club workers at a fraction of their labour cost. Despite the costs of distance, the product is more cheaply sourced offshore in China. In order to avoid unemployment, the Rich Club's workers in these sectors must either accept wage cuts or find new jobs. Many Rich Club wage rates have hardly changed in real terms (after adjusting for price changes) for up to 30 years. Many of the West's workers are taking major reductions in their fringe benefits. By 2005 established American automobile workers were losing pay, working conditions, health benefits and pension rights as their competitors turned to greenfield sites in America with lower labour costs. (That the plants are in the same country, albeit different regions, does not prevent this being interpreted as part of the process of globalisation.)

Cars are such an integral part of the manufacturing sector that this transformation is obvious, but it is also occurring for products such as personal computers, which are so recent that the Rich Club workers never got a chance to bed in generously paid jobs. Conversely the first great industry of the industrial era, textiles and clothing, has already relocated offshore.

This is not all bad news for Rich Club workers. Not all their jobs can be replicated in poor countries. Those in sectors which cannot be offshored benefit from cheaper clothes, computers, and other goods and services produced offshore. Even automobile workers protesting at their loss of pay and conditions benefit in terms of the other goods and services they purchase. They would argue that they are worse off overall. But many Rich Club workers are better off.

The Rich Club faces the challenge of generating enough jobs which the Poor Club cannot easily replicate. The Danish company Novo Nordisk makes a cartridge used by diabetics to inject themselves with insulin. It develops each new generation of its product and perfects the production process in Denmark. Only then – after three or four years – does the company ship the equipment to its plants in China and Brazil, while moving on to the next-generation product. (Similarly, Germany's Volkswagen assembled its last Beetle in Brazil long after its Rich Club factories had moved on.)

Development in the core and production in the periphery will become an increasingly common Rich Club survival strategy. But will this – together with the service industry – generate sufficient (high-paid) jobs in the Rich Club? Eventually China and other current Poor Club members can replicate that activity too, as Japan already does. The West has no exclusive ability to innovate and develop new products and processes.

Wages and incomes need not necessarily fall in the Rich Club. That depends on the new technologies. Most likely, the Rich Club will experience continuing wage stagnation while others catch it up.

Again, it may seem surprising that increased trade makes one of the participants (possibly) worse off. The standard international trade theory assumes that for everyone to benefit, the terms of trade – the price of exports relative to imports – do not change. But in this projection, the price of manufactures falls relative to the price of foodstuffs as wages are cut and peasants leave the land. Thus the key assumption of no change in the terms of trade may not apply, as Paul Samuelson has pointed out.[2] If so, food and resource producers – including some members of the Rich Club – will be better off. Argentina and Uruguay may rejoin the Rich Club. Meanwhile, Poor Club members which are net food importers may be worse off. The simplicity of the bifurcation model gets lost in a plethora of individual cases, although the broad trends remain. We may already be seeing the terms of trade turn around. China's rapid growth is sucking in raw materials and food, driving up their price relative to the manufactures it produces.

The challenge of industrial relocation is not peculiar to the Rich Club. A rapidly growing China is likely to undermine some of its competitors. Hong Kong already seems to be stagnating, and South-east Asian economies such as Cambodia and Vietnam are finding their recently established markets undermined by cheaper Chinese exports. It is a bit like a flotilla of boats moving down a narrow channel. The Chinese boat is so large that as it powers away, its bow and stern waves are severely rocking the boats nearby.

The Future of China

The long-term outcome may not be so favourable to China. Its current manufacturing boom could come to a choking end within a decade. Its manufacturing transformation is generating social tensions which could lead to a political disturbance that would set back economic progress. Its serious environmental problems – particularly lack of access to good-quality water – could do likewise. Its infrastructure – such as roads – probably cannot bear the pressures soon to be placed upon it. And given its size, China's ingestion of resources such as energy and minerals is going to strain the entire world economy. Because it is less efficient at using these resources, China will suffer more than average from the rising prices.

So it is not inevitable that China will join the Rich Club by the end of this century. What is surely inevitable is that, assuming the world develops in a reasonably orderly manner, the Rich Club will gain members. The newcomers may be European economies currently on the margin, East Asian economies, India (almost as big as China, its accelerated development would be almost as disruptive), Brazil, Chile, South Africa . . . as well as, or instead of, China. We just don't know. Who would have predicted in 1900 that Japan – with a per capita income below that of Russia and Latin America – would be a secure member of the Rich Club in 2000? We may be certain, though, that if China joins, fewer of the others will make it.

The best an economist can predict is that, given a peaceful twenty-first century, there will be new members of, and candidates for, the Rich Club, some of whom may be as large as China or India. That will make the world very different politically as well as economically. The Rich Club needs to start thinking about that now. We shall do so in the final chapter. Before that, we will think about the future of the nation-state.

Part Four • The Future

Twenty-eight | Options for Nations

This chapter explores the various relationships which nation-states may enter into in the future. While acknowledging that there may be particular reasons for merging with other nation-states or groupings such as the US and the EU, it argues that this option is not always an attractive one. Medium-sized and smaller nation-states will continue to have a place – although micro-states may need patrons.

What is the future of the nation-state in a globalised world? Its role is changing, and it is losing some policy autonomy. Previous chapters showed that jurisdictional boundaries are increasingly porous. Will they become irrelevant? Will the nation-state fade into nostalgia? Or will it still have a role for some time to come?

The five major economic powers currently provide almost two-thirds of the world's GDP (United States 21.3 per cent, EU 21.1 per cent, China 12.2 per cent, Japan 7.0 per cent, India 5.4 per cent)[1] and contain just over half the world's population (China 20.5 per cent, India 16.7 per cent, EU 7.2 per cent, United States 4.6 per cent, and Japan 2.0 per cent).[2] Where do the other 147 fit in? Explicitly or implicitly, many fear they may be too small to remain economically viable.

What are the options? Pro-fertility policies have not proved particularly successful at increasing population size, and in any case it takes a long time. Migration is a beggar-thy-neighbour option. A common solution to smallness has been a merger with a larger economy. This chapter looks at various possibilities while observing that there are also pressures for fragmentation.

Should Samoa Merge with New Zealand?
Samoa is an example of a micro-state (population 190,000) which might conclude that it is not large enough to be a viable economic and political entity and consider merging with a neighbour. It had that choice half a century ago, when, as a trust territory under a UN mandate, it might have joined New Zealand rather than becoming independent. In today's more

globalised world, it might reconsider this decision. The nub of the issue is that Samoans have no automatic right of entry to New Zealand. Each year a limited number are permitted to join the 120,000 Samoan New Zealanders. Were Samoa to merge with New Zealand, there would be no restrictions on movement and many more Samoans would go south.

A merger would also involve fiscal union. Samoa would raise its average standard of living as its inhabitants would receive the same social welfare support and tax concessions as other New Zealanders. But the impact on Samoan society and fa'a Samoa (the Samoan way) could be damaging, especially as it would be the young who would move to New Zealand. Samoans coming under New Zealand law would lose much of their local political autonomy in exchange for limited parliamentary representation (a handful of seats out of 120).

Though there is no enthusiasm for such a merger, there are parallels in the reunification of East Germany (the German Democratic Republic) with West Germany (the Federal Republic of Germany) in 1990. This has not always been a success for the eastern German regions, despite the two Germanys' claim to have a common culture. Fa'a Samoa is very different from the New Zealand way of life.

A merger has reverse parallels with various separatist movements which thrive around the world. Among the more prominent in the Rich Club are Québec in Canada and the Basques and Catalans in Spain. Britain has recently given greater autonomy to its Scots and Welsh (and many years earlier, to the Irish), while the Slovaks separated from the Czechs (and then the two countries joined the European Union) and Yugoslavia fragmented. In each case the differences in standards of living between the actual or putative countries were less than those between New Zealand and Samoa. But the Slovaks probably suffered a reduction in their standard of living following independence. That may apply for other separations too (although separatist movements play down such possibilities).

So local autonomy is valued in its own right, especially – but not uniquely – where there are cultural differences. Some are even willing to accept some reduction in their standard of living in exchange for greater autonomy.

Should New Zealand Merge with Australia?

The population and economic activity of Australia is about five times that of New Zealand, its neighbour across the Tasman Sea. Already there is considerable economic integration between the two countries, including a free trade agreement, little restriction on labour movements, and a range of measures to unify the two markets under the Closer Economic Relations Agreement (CER) discussed in Chapter 17.

CER is not a comprehensive commercial arrangement; there are restrictions on the flow of investment and differences in commercial law. There is no monetary union – the Australian and New Zealand dollars are distinct and have no fixed parity – and no fiscal union – each nation taxes and spends separately. Culturally the two countries claim to be close, although each emphasises its distinctiveness.

Despite considerable policy alignment, Australia and New Zealand are not integrated in trade terms. New Zealand is not generally a major export market for Australia, and while Australia is New Zealand's largest market, it takes only one-fifth of all exports (and one-sixteenth of total New Zealand output). Moreover, while both are commodity exporters, Australia exports more minerals, New Zealand proportionally more foodstuffs. Export destinations also differ, with Australia sending more to Asia.

In any case, a merger would not really resolve New Zealand's problems of size. Indeed it could lose out if the economies of agglomeration resulted in companies' headquarters moving from Auckland to Sydney. Nor is it clear how such a merger would enhance comparative and competitive advantages, supply chains, or the other drivers of economic development. Certainly exporters to Australia would benefit from a common currency – providing the exchange rate was a favourable one. (Yet fixing the rate has been mismanaged on many occasions, most notoriously when Britain joined the European Monetary System in 1990, only to crash out of it in 1992.) But exporters to other places could suffer.

Monetary Union?

If it is argued that the New Zealand dollar is too insignificant to survive in the increasingly dynamic international monetary system and should link itself to the Australian one, the same argument applies for the Australian dollar. Perhaps both countries should form a monetary union with the United States. Here the experience of Argentina is instructive. In 1999 its peso was 'dollarized'. In effect the US dollar became the Argentinian currency, with all financial contracts written in US dollars (although a 'currency board' meant that the peso stood in for the US dollar). Such an arrangement has the advantage of price stability if prices in the primary currency are stable.

When the US dollar appreciated relative to the rest of the world in the early 2000s, the peso rose with it. Argentina's exporters were priced out of their markets, while its domestic industries were destroyed by a flood of cheap imports. (Brazil began selling meat to Argentina.) Unemployment doubled. The obvious solution, devaluation of the peso, was no longer possible. The government imposed financial controls which had bizarre impacts: small businesses which traded in cash rather than credit found they had no customers. Eventually Argentina reneged on its international debt repayments, unhooked the peso from the US dollar, and devalued. Since people's debts – their home mortgages – were denominated in US dollars, devaluation increased their debt burden. People took to the streets; governments fell.

The Argentinian economy was more vulnerable to changes in the US exchange rate because only 10 per cent of its exports went to the US, compared to New Zealand's 20 per cent to Australia. The post-crisis mechanism would work differently too. Unlike the trans-Tasman labour market, there are restrictions on Argentinians moving to the US (although following the crisis, some Argentinians did move to Spain).

Fiscal union changes the nature of the relationship. Suppose that a US state (Kansas, say) was to suffer in a way similar to Argentina (although a higher proportion of its 'exports' go to the rest of the country). Not only would there be migration out of the state, there would be (net) fiscal transfers into the state. The latter would be both automatic (higher benefits, lower taxes) and discretionary (grants voted by federal politicians).

The implication is that countries should form a currency union with one another only if they are already sufficiently economically integrated, including through some elements of a fiscal union and a common labour market. Given that nowadays there is no taxation without representation, any fiscal union would involve some sort of political integration which would undermine local autonomy and cultural independence.

Joining the United States?

Puerto Ricans wrestle with the issue of becoming the fifty-first state of the United States. Their Caribbean island has been a 'Commonwealth' in association with the US since 1952. Puerto Ricans are US citizens (many live there, for there are no restrictions on access), use US dollar bills, and elect their own governor and legislature. But it is not a state of the US and so does not send voting members to the US Congress, or contribute to electing the US president, or to changing the US constitution. Yet neither is it a sovereign state, as its ability to participate in international relations is circumscribed by the US.

On the basis of referenda and surveys it appears that nearly half of Puerto Ricans support their island becoming the next state of the US, while a similar proportion support the status quo. The independence movement is very small. The pro-staters argue that the country would become economically better off. The alternative view was summarised by Sila Calderón, a recent governor of Puerto Rico: 'we are proud of our ties to the US and we are proud to be US citizens, but we value our cultural differences. Integration into the US would make us disappear.'

Joining the European Economic Association?

The European Economic Association (EEA) was formed in 1994 between the European Free Trade Association (EFTA) and the European Union (EU) to allow three EFTA countries – Iceland, Norway and Liechtenstein – to participate in the European Single Market without having to join the EU.[3] In principle, EFTA members have more autonomy than members of the EU.

The EEA is based on 'four (commercial) freedoms' – the free movement of goods, persons, services and capital between EEA countries – which already apply within the EU (with a few exceptions). The EFTA members also agreed to enact legislation similar to that in the EU in the areas of social policy, consumer protection, the environment, company law and statistics. As the Norwegians grumble, laws enacted in Brussels by the EU automatically become, in effect, the laws of the EFTA countries, even though they have played no part in their enactment. In Switzerland, another member of EFTA, a citizens' referendum rejected joining the EEA. Instead there are Swiss–EU bilateral agreements, with different content from EEA arrangements. Even so, the Swiss object to a 'faraway' place (Brussels) making laws over which they have no influence.

In principle, any interested country might contemplate joining the EEA or having a bilateral agreement like the Swiss. In practice, few have. Perhaps the EU has been too busy extending its membership to give much thought to lower-level associations . . . as yet.

Joining the European Union?

The EU currently consists of 27 'sovereign' states. The European Parliament is much weaker than the US Congress, so EU governance has much less input from electors and much more from the governments of the member states.

In principle, any European nation can be a member of the EU. Successful applicants must meet standards of civil liberty and democracy as well as accepting the four commercial freedoms. New members are also expected to eventually join the European Monetary Union, which involves adopting the euro as the local currency.

It was probably no accident that two of the richest European states (Norway and Switzerland) chose not to join the EU. On the other hand, there has been a stampede of poorer European states applying for membership. While there are political and defence considerations, they also assume that they will benefit from net fiscal transfers and that their economic performance will be enhanced as businesses invest in their low-cost locations. The Irish and Spanish economies did benefit substantially by joining the EU. But Greece has not, thus far; and the experience of the northern part of East Germany, after it merged with West Germany and hence joined the EU, suggests that some regions may lose population rather than gain industry.

The sharpest current debate is about whether Turkey should join the EU. It would be its poorest member, but also an exceptionally large one, increasing the EU's population by a quarter and growing much faster. Turkey applied for associate membership of the then European Economic Community in 1959 and submitted a formal application to join the EU in 1987. Because of the EU's budget cycle, the earliest it can now join is 2013.

EU members have been increasingly reluctant to allow Turkey to join, albeit for varied reasons. Although it is a secular state, the fact that its culture is founded on Islam (just as the EU's present secular states have Christian cultural foundations) does not help its chances. Some fear an inflow of Turkish workers that will undercut local jobs. Turkey's human rights record leaves much to be desired. Its military, while a force for secularisation and modernisation, remains more prominent in the governance of Turkey than is the case in existing EU members. There are various unhappy conflicts: with Armenia, Cyprus, Greece and the Kurds. Its population size could change the political balance: already larger than every EU member other than Germany, by the time it can join it may be the biggest.

While the attitudes of the existing EU members will be decisive in determining whether Turkey joins, Turkish attitudes are of greater interest for our purposes. The initial application reflected a judgement that EU membership would boost the economy by attracting capital and skills to combine with the cheap, but reasonably well-educated, Turkish workers to supply the European market. There would be financial transfers from the EU, and Turkish migrants to the rest of Europe would increase the home population's spending power through both remittances and visits home.

Moreover, while the Ottoman Empire was Islamic, although tolerant of Christians and Jews, it had a substantial European component in the Balkans. Istanbul is a European city, rather than only an Asian one. Similarly, the almost worshipped founder of modern Turkey, Mustafa Kemal Atatürk, had a vision of a secular state that was more modern European than traditional Middle Eastern.

However, the prolonged application process and the apparently increasing resistance of some of the existing EU population has triggered doubts within Turkey. It is easy to say that the fox thinks the grapes are sour, but the doubts also reflect a view that Turkey would have to give up too much to join the EU. Not all Turks are committed to a secular state (nor are all Europeans), while some of the required concessions over human rights and conflicts are seen to undermine national identity.

In any case, Rabin's Law says that some Turks will be economically worse off. The loss of skilled people to the rest of Europe may not be compensated for by their remittances. It also seems likely that only the west of Turkey, around the Aegean Sea – pre-eminently Istanbul – will benefit economically, and that the Asian east could suffer as north-east Germany has done.

Many of the countries that joined the EU in 2004 and 2007 did so for the economic benefits, but also because this would protect them from reverting to being satellites of Russia. Turkey, on the other hand, has never been under Russian hegemony, and has been a member of the Western military alliance (NATO) since 1952. The defence benefits are not as evident.

For Turkey, then, the case for joining the EU is not clear-cut (as it has not been for Norway or Switzerland). And it will be decades before most of the other potential candidates join an EU. By then it will be very different from what it is today.

The EU currently faces difficulties arising from its recent enlargement. (The kindest thing to say about governance by 27 members is that it is clumsy.) That is a far stronger reason for deferring further enlargement than the claim that Turkey is not 'sufficiently European'. It seems likely that in the meantime a variety of different economic and political relationships will develop, with the EEA and the Swiss bilateral arrangements as precursors.

It's Not Easy Being Small
Are small states viable in the long run, or are they condemned to be (reluctantly) merged with bigger states, as the five or so big economies take over the world by growth and acquisition? I want to argue a very cautious 'no'. It is likely that Rich Countries outside the big economies will get increasingly involved in Closer Economic Relations-type arrangements on a bilateral and multilateral basis. These will involve free trade in goods and services, and increasing mutual recognition of goods and occupations. But, unlike the Australia–New Zealand, US and EU arrangements, there will not generally be free movement of labour.

There are three reasons why small economies may not disintegrate, despite the force of economies of scale.

First, small countries may have a comparative advantage in governance. Economists have tended to focus on the advantages enjoyed by large economies in the market sector.[4] But smaller countries may be better able to deliver non-market products such as the administrative services of government, police and justice, and – more arguably – education, health, social welfare and cultural services. These make up around a fifth of a Rich

Country's production, giving small countries with good governance a significant advantage. There are two important implications if this be true. Small countries should not look to large countries for guidance on the size and organisation of their non-market sectors. The US, in particular, does not have a good record of delivering such services, and so has had to use 'more-market' solutions more than small economies need do. Moreover, this better delivery may attract some immigrants to smaller economies, despite the additional tax they will have to pay.

It may not be easy being small, but the advantages are nicely illustrated by the Danish Government's *Progress, Innovation and Cohesion: Strategy for Denmark in a Global Economy*. The details of the report, and its 350 recommendations – most of which have already been adopted – need not detain us. What is significant is that a country of 5.5 million people has been able to evolve a common, bi-partisan response to globalisation. Denmark sees globalisation as an opportunity, but its aim is that 'everyone participates in the renewal process . . . everyone shares in progress and cohesion'. The key element of social cohesion would be much more difficult in a larger society. Even obtaining a common approach in the way the Danes had would be more difficult.

Second, some small countries may survive because their economies are resource-based, especially if, as has been argued, resource prices rise relative to manufacturing prices during the twenty-first century. However, resource-based economies may need to be smaller than they are today. For instance, it is said that the ecology of Australia can sustain only about 8 million people. While this figure is contentious, it is much smaller than the 21 million who live on the continent today, and very much smaller than the numbers favoured by those who vigorously promote the expansion of Australia's industrial sector.

Third, if a small country faces issues of economies of scale across all its activities, it can reap some by specialising in a small range of tradeable products for export, while importing those it does not make. Such a country will be very dependent on the world trading system. It will have little practical control over the movement of goods, services or products across its borders. It will be especially dependent on an international rule of law, and will need to form multilateral alliances within which to pursue its ends.

Thus small economies may be able to survive and maintain some sovereignty (albeit with little independence over their international trading relations) by paying close attention to social cohesion and the culture that goes with it, and managing well their non-market activities (including dealing with pollution and urban congestion).

Twenty-nine | A Confederation of Nations?

> *The future for world governance is a confederation like the European Union, not a federation like the United States. Confederations may be less efficient than federations, but they need not fail.*

Despite ongoing globalisation, the nation-state is likely to remain an integral feature of the world economy, providing a framework within which local economic activity can flourish, expressing the cultural aspirations of its peoples, and implementing distinctive domestic policies. While it seems likely that nation-states will have less scope than in the past to pursue independent commercial policies, there will be opportunities in non-commercial areas for policies which reflect local needs. Some independence of action may also remain in some economic areas. (Those who regret the loss of independence in commercial policy may take some comfort that there will also be less scope for unilateral military action.)

How, then, will relations between states be organised?

The European Union as a Model of Confederation?
States are unlikely to commit suicide and create a supra-national agency. International institutions are more likely to be based on confederations of states, along the lines of the EU, the IMF and the WTO, than on federations. The best example of the latter is the United States, which governs a 'globalised' (economically integrated) region. Whatever the merits of US federal government, its foundations were laid before the consolidation of the nation-state, so that the powers of the original thirteen states were quickly lost to the federal government.

When, some 200 years later, a similar merger began to evolve on the other side of the Atlantic, nation-states were powerful and reluctant to give up those powers. Thus while there are those who favour a federal 'United States of Europe', their vision is unlikely to be achieved in the foreseeable future. The European Union will remain a confederation of nation-states which are central to the governance of the entity in a way that the states of the US are not, with the European Council (the heads of the member nation-states) and the Council of Ministers considerably more important than the European Parliament.

In many ways this structure has made the governance of the EU difficult and clumsy, since policy has to be negotiated among all 27 members. Unanimity may not be required, but a (sometimes grudging) consensus is.

The advocates of further integration favour wider objectives which include offsetting the power of the United States and the notion of an 'idea of Europe'. There is nostalgia at work here, yet it may be a forward-looking nostalgia. A world in which the US dominates the international economy and is the one markedly strong military and political state is arguably not a healthy world, nor ultimately healthy for the US. The EU could be a second world power (although in the longer run there will be Asian world powers). However, while the EU is already a world economic power with a GDP similar to that of the US (and a larger population), it is yet to show the political cohesion and sense of purpose that the US exhibits in international affairs.

EU member states have been very reluctant to delegate foreign policy authority to the centre. Despite the desire for a common foreign policy, there is still considerable divergence between members (as was shown by the varied responses to the American invasion of Iraq in 2003). That each member of the EU has a foreign minister contrasts with the US, whose states' lack of interest or involvement in foreign affairs is demonstrated by the fact that state governors running for president are generally ill-prepared to deal with foreign policy issues.

In one critical respect the EU is not a model for a confederated world. Nation-states are unlikely to give up their sovereign power to determine who, and under what conditions, can reside in them – even though migration will rise. Members of the EU have, in principle, abandoned this power, although the majority response to restrict labour movement from the new members who have joined since 2005 suggests that they are having second thoughts.

A Return to the Local?

The 'idea of Europe' usually involves culture. It is sometimes vague, but generally refers to a common European heritage, a set of common values which developed from this, and a commitment to nurture and promote those values in a common European enterprise represented by the EU. It expects that each person will be able to maintain a specific culture within a wider context – to be, say, French and yet a European – in a culture of tolerance which will avoid conflict. Such tolerance implies devolution and the EU objective of 'subsidiarity', the principle that every problem must be treated at the most efficient or appropriate, and as far as possible the lowest, level (EU, national, regional or local).

Subsidiarity has its EU origins in Catholic social teaching, but is central to liberal political philosophy. The notion is found in several constitutions around the world, including implicitly the Tenth Amendment to the United States Constitution: 'powers not delegated to the United States by the Constitution, nor prohibited by it to the States, are reserved for the States respectively, or to the people.'

By its very nature, subsidiarity can apply to lower political levels than the state, including the family and the individual. Demands for regional autonomy and separation pose particular difficulties. They have resulted in the fragmentation of Yugoslavia, with its appalling conflict and genocide, and the intriguing, but more benign, separation of Czechoslovakia into the Czech Republic and Slovakia. Not only did the Slovaks make themselves fiscally worse off, but both nation-states then joined the European Union, apparently judging that their independence was compromised less by being members of the Confederation of Europe than it was by being parts of a federated Czechoslovakia.

A recent European practice has been to give greater regional autonomy. Britain has given Scotland and Wales different degrees of autonomy, while Spain is made up of seventeen autonomous communities (including Andalusia, the Basque Country, Catalonia and Galicia), again with different degrees of autonomy. In each case there are historical and political reasons for the devolution, but the decision may be facilitated by membership of the EU. Because this effectively proscribes full independence, devolution is not a step towards total separation, demands by regions notwithstanding. (Québécois demands face no such check.)

But what does this autonomy mean? Europe-wide standards of civil liberties constrain national and local policies, while EU law and practices limit the commercial autonomy of both nation-state and autonomous region. There is some freedom over social, educational and health policy, cultural policy, the local environment and infrastructure, although, as described in the next section, this cannot be unlimited because commercial sovereignty is restricted once transactions cross jurisdictional boundaries.

The other serious constraint is the need to have sufficient public revenue to pursue regional objectives. (It is instructive that the member states of the EU have not given up their powers to tax.) A nation's tax revenue is constrained by the ability of businesses and individuals to operate offshore. A region is constrained similarly, and also by the willingness of the national authority to either share revenue or allow the locality the means to raise effective revenue on its own account.

Thus while subsidiarity is a prized principle of the EU, it may be whittled away in a globalised world. A member state giving increased local autonomy to a region may, in the long run, be offering less than at first appears. And yet, be it nation-state or autonomous region, there will be a fierce demand for cultural and policy independence.

Commercial Sovereignty in a Confederation

Commercial intercourse has some analogies with marriage. The sovereign individual takes on a relationship which reduces her or his sovereignty. The partners do so because they judge that they will be better off despite that reduction.

Commercial intercourse between nations is not a one-off affair. Each sovereign country is continually entering into arrangements which limit its de facto sovereignty. Unlike Christian marriage, there is the possibility of unilateral divorce. In principle, the nation-state retains the de jure sovereignty to withdraw from an international commercial arrangement, even where there may be no explicit provision to do so. In practice, such withdrawals are rare.

The Treaty of Westphalia created a notion of political sovereignty – legislative, judicial, and/or executive authority over a geographic region – for Europe which was elaborated and later extended outside the continent. Usually such sovereignty is treated as 'supreme', but in practice nation-states – even those outside a confederation such as the EU – do not have supreme political authority. Today civil liberties are widely treated as so inherent that they may be imposed – in various ways – on a nation-state from outside. Even more problematic is the issue of sovereignty over commerce.

Globalisation has increasingly circumscribed the power of a nation-state to regulate commerce within its own boundaries. That was not a major issue in 1648, when a state's commercial reach barely crossed its borders. (Recall that trade was largely based on products made under conditions of 'absolute advantage' – unable to be produced in the jurisdiction being supplied – and amounted to a small proportion of total consumption.)

As commerce extended its reach, various measures were developed to deal with trade between nations. These ranged from tariffs and quotas to discourage imports, to treaties of mutual cooperation, to wars for economic ends (such as the Opium Wars). For the last 50 years the measures have generally occurred, by mutual agreement of the parties involved, within the framework of the WTO and its predecessors. In principle, then, nation-states have voluntarily forgone some of their commercial sovereignty, although in practice any agreement may have been reached grudgingly or under duress by one of the parties.

The difficulty, as we saw with the UNESCO Convention on Cultural Diversity, is that there is no clean boundary between commerce and other activities over which the nation-state is likely to demand considerable policy discretion. However, because information, products, capital and people cross jurisdictional boundaries, it is very difficult to isolate a particular activity. Any positive list of what are primarily national responsibilities would include the promotion of local culture and language. But this may conflict with the first EU freedom (mobility of goods) were the Basques, say, to require all products to be labelled in the local language, or the fourth freedom (mobility of capital) if the Catalans were to restrict ownership of local broadcasting to those with an authentic commitment to their culture and aspirations.

While there is no ready resolution to this tension between political sovereignty and commercial sovereignty, it is inevitable that in a globalised world the nation-state will have less commercial sovereignty than recent generations have taken for granted.

A Confederation of Nations?
A federal government of the world is not an option, because nation-states are unwilling to forgo so much of their sovereignty. The United Nations is not a world government. Whatever its institutional defects – which may be substantial – the unwillingness of countries to empower it blocks off this possibility. It is perhaps ironic that the desire of the world's most successful federal state – the United States of America – to protect its national sovereignty is one of the major obstacles to a federal world.

A kind of confederation of nations has evolved through a series of ad hoc decisions and arrangements. Just as the EU has a 'constitution' arising out of various treaties, agreements, practices and decisions, even though it has no code (in the way that the US has), so has the world as a whole. The world's federal constitution is constantly evolving. Like the EU, it has created institutions to enable federalism, including the UN and its agencies, and the IMF and the WTO. As we saw, despite public perception, the IMF and the WTO (and the UN itself) are not autonomous agencies but dependent upon the nation-states involved. Inevitably, the large ones have more influence.

As with the EU, the governance of this federation is not notably efficient. Sometimes it can be frustratingly inept, as the inability to deal with political challenges such as Bosnia in the 1990s and Darfur in the 2000s illustrates. The economic record is little better. It is hard to provide a rational justification for the current world trading arrangements for farm products, while the treatment of international resources such as sea-fish is likely to lead to further widespread extinction.

The practical issue is the degree of world confederation. Will the world divide into trading blocs? A less stressful variant of this would be a collapse of the international multilateral economy brought about by economic nationalism and special domestic interests. It would be foolish to rule out such possibilities, but a regime of bilateral and plurilateral (involving more than two countries) trading is likely to be unstable. Today, every country contributes to value chains and has a wide range of trading partners on which it depends for products which it cannot produce itself, or only at a very high cost. It will probably have substantial foreign investments or foreign investors (and often both), and will receive or pay income for royalties and patents. In order to improve its economic performance its industries will need the competitive pressures imposed by foreign markets.

So each country seeking economic progress is driven towards participating in an international multilateral economy. That does not rule out the possibility that things could go horribly wrong, with the world economy stagnating or even retrenching for a period. But it seems likely that in the long run multilateralism will prevail.

The Market-State Option?

Aristotle's vision of civic nationalism, described in Chapter 12, may be more than two thousand years old, but it is thriving today. For some decades at least, the nation-state is likely to remain a key element in the affairs of the world, encouraging some commonality of national identity and culture, exercising some policy discretion in domestic affairs, and representing its peoples' interests in international affairs.

However, Philip Bobbitt predicts in *The Shield of Achilles* that the nation-state, concerned for the welfare of its peoples, will transform into a 'market-state' whose primary purpose is to give people choice.[1] The difficulties with this thesis are two-fold.

First, it projects American trends. It would be unwise to apply the particularities of America to the generalities of the entire world. Perhaps the hegemonic power can ignore its people's welfare yet bind them to the nation by taking an aggressive economic, military and political stance towards the rest of the world. Other countries do not have that option. In any case, as the US becomes but one of a number of powerful countries, would Americans be satisfied with a polity both unable to impose itself on the world and uninterested in their domestic welfare?

It is also pious to say all Americans have choice. Certainly many do, beyond the wildest dreams of their ancestors and much of the rest of today's world. But America has a large disenfranchised underclass which lacks access to decent health care, among other things. It seems unlikely they will remain quiescent forever. It is possible that Bobbitt's market-state, unconcerned for the welfare of its people, may descend into fractious class warfare. And will America's new immigrants make a commitment to a market-state rather than a nation-state?

Nevertheless, Bobbitt is touching on a very real issue. Probably more than any other peoples, Americans are going to have to adjust to the changing world – uncomfortably. The outcome may well be the opposite to Bobbitt's prediction. The market is a means of coping with the US's extraordinary heterogeneity. Perhaps there needs to be more heterogeneity of government among the US states, with them taking up more of the responsibilities of nation-states. California, with its environmental initiatives, may be a leader in this trend.

This is not to argue that the US federation will be replaced by a confederation – foreign policy is likely to remain federal (which will force on the EU greater federalism in its foreign policy). But we are likely to see a more conscious differentiation of domestic policy between states, and perhaps some renegotiation of state–federal relations – although not necessarily via explicit changes to the constitution. Perhaps Catalonia is a guide to the US's domestic future.

The Functioning of a Confederation of Nations: Responding to Global Warming

A confederation of nations is likely to resolve significant problems on the basis of a series of ad hoc actions. It is therefore impractical to give much guidance as to the principles underpinning conflict-resolution strategies, other than very high-level and vague ones, such as that states should not infringe one another's political sovereignty if they can help it.

To illustrate how international problems might be resolved, consider the challenge of global warming. Chapter 21 argued that since there were no property rights in the air, everybody has the temptation to inject waste – such as greenhouse gases – into the atmosphere, at the expense of others in general and global warming in particular. Of course nations can sign treaties such as the Kyoto Protocol of 1997, under which industrialised countries undertook to reduce their collective emissions of greenhouse gases in the 2008–12 period by an annual average 5.2 per cent compared to the volume in 1990. At the time of writing the United States and Australia had refused to ratify the treaty (although it is not unusual for the US president to sign a treaty using presidential executive power, and in effect implement it even though Congress fails to ratify it). The greater threat is that some of the signatories/ratifiers will make little effort to fulfil their commitments, there being no significant sanctions for failure.[2]

Consider the dilemma of the Pacific nation of Tuvalu. With about 10,000 inhabitants, it is the second-least populated independent country in the world. (Only the Vatican City is smaller.) Its 26 square kilometres (10 square miles) are scattered across nine islands which rise to just 5 metres (16 feet) above the sea. Insofar as global warming will melt ice and raise sea levels, Tuvalu is likely to be wiped out as a geographical entity as world temperatures rise. (Perhaps it would still exist as a sea-based exclusive economic zone and in cyberspace as .tv in a web address.)

What can Tuvalu do to avoid this fate? Becoming carbon-neutral itself would have a negligible effect on global temperatures. Perhaps all it has is a moral claim for consideration, although the powerful are more likely to be swayed by pragmatic self-interest than by international morality.

At the other end of the scale is the European Union, one of the world's largest emitters of greenhouse gases and a ratifier of the Kyoto Protocol. It is large enough to have some impact on the path of global warming if it reduces its emissions – although the rest of the world will derive more benefit. Moreover, it has a strong popular lobby favouring taking action for reasons of both self-preservation and morality.

Suppose the EU were to reduce its carbon emissions. Some of the measures would be costly, and raise the price of output. In some cases the higher-priced products could be undercut by imports from countries which were not reducing their emissions. In response, a joint EU lobby of those concerned with global warming and those whose costs had been forced up to a level at which they were internationally uncompetitive would demand action, the former pointing out that it was useless reducing carbon emissions in one country if they increased in others, the latter railing against the losses of jobs and profits.

We can only speculate what measures the EU would take to correct these anomalies. They might put a general levy on the imports of high carbon-emitting nations or prohibit imports from high-emitting industries (as they may be permitted to do under WTO protocols for environmental ends). Whatever the measures, their effect would be to provide an incentive for those countries with significant EU markets to reduce their carbon emissions. In turn they would adopt similar border measures against other carbon emitters. Given the interdependence of world trade, there would be pressure on the whole world to reduce their carbon emissions.

All this would take place with much negotiation, litigation and threats of counter-measures. How the US responded would be crucial. The point here is not to detail the likely course of events, but to emphasise that a large economy may have enough power in a confederated world to initiate a solution which at first seems to require a federated world. Of course this would be a clumsy process (and almost certainly inefficient compared to a federal solution), but it may be more viable than seeking to federate first.

And that is the painful conclusion of this chapter. Nation-states will operate in a confederated world. They are doing so already. But how efficient the various confederations' decision-making processes will be is yet to be seen.

Thirty | A Multipolar World

The future will see a multipolar world dominated by five economies, none of them individually dominant. While this will involve considerable adjustment by all countries, it will be particularly difficult for the United States to accept this new configuration, given its current status as the hegemonic economy.

Will Globalisation Continue?

Globalisation will continue for as long as the costs of distance continue to fall. Protest or denial will not stop the globalisation process, although they will lead to poor responses to it. But after more than two centuries of falling costs of distance, can we expect the trend to continue? There are three obvious reasons why it might not.

First, the depletion of resources may offset any technological gains. Chapter 21 argued that the higher cost of alternative fuels may slow down or even stagnate the globalisation process – but only for a period. While technology will often overcome a resource shortage, a greater challenge arises where political action is necessary because markets are incomplete and the resources not properly owned. Failure to address such instances as sea-fish and water may reduce overall consumption in the long run. It is unlikely to reverse long-term economic growth, except in particular regions. Global warming, we suggested, may be dealt with in a confederation of nations with a lead player, although it may be addressed clumsily and belatedly.

Second, globalisation may be compromised by terrorism. Surveillance at airports for persons and seaports for goods have already slowed down the fall in the costs of distance. However, it seems unlikely that these measures will become so onerous as to stop or reverse globalisation.

The third possibility is a generalisation of the second. Perhaps there could be a substantial breakdown of world cooperation, as happened from the beginning of the First World War in 1914 to the end of the Second in 1945. Technology continued to reduce the costs of distance, but politics limited the ability to benefit from it. One would like to think that the world has learned from this instance, but as Hegel reminds us, 'The only thing we learn from history is that we learn nothing from history.'

Will technology continue to reduce the costs of distance? Not all the current opportunities to do so have been exploited – particularly those arising from the cheap transmission of digital information (which would be hardly touched by rising fuel prices). So there would still be considerable changes to the world economy during a decade or two of stagnation as the world adjusted to higher prices of transport fuels.

Consider the book you are reading. It was printed in one place and transported to another where you obtained it – probably from a shop, although you may have purchased it online and received it by courier from a warehouse. A book is information encoded in print on the physical artefact of the page. What I write goes into a file in my computer. It will go through a series of transformations to reach the page you are reading. (In principle, one can read from a screen – virtually cutting out the physical artefact all together – but thus far reading lengthy texts on screen has not proved attractive.) Does a book need to be printed at one central site and transported to shops? There already exist technologies by which every bookshop could have its own printery. The purchaser identifies the required book, the bookseller downloads a digital record, presses a button, and the book is printed in the shop. Currently the end product is not particularly physically attractive, and short-run production is too expensive to offset the saved transport costs of distance. But the technology is being developed. How long will it be before it becomes competitive?

Music and videos are already distributed in this way. The story is similar for newspapers and magazines: because of time zones, Australasians can now read American and British newspapers while the locals are still in their beds. Content is different from the artefact which embodies it. Increasingly, content can be transported digitally without the artefact.

While there may be a minimum level below which costs cannot fall, this may be some way off. It is unlikely that all the technologies which might reduce the costs of distance have yet been invented. Transport fuels aside, the costs of distance in one hundred years' time will probably be significantly lower than they are today – and higher costs of fuel may be offset by more efficient use. Globalisation seems likely to continue, albeit with occasional – even decadal – stagnation.

The Future Pattern of World Development

It is commonplace to predict that the relative size of the world's economies will change, with today's Rich Club making up a smaller share of world output. This conclusion can be derived from a mechanical extrapolation of existing trends. This book's analysis, based on the falling costs of distance and the increased mobility of factors of production and technology, provides a more subtle understanding of the underlying processes.

Its basic insight was that in a world of high costs of distance, the pattern of economic activity corresponded broadly to where people lived. That correspondence also largely applies when the costs of distance are very low. However, between these scenarios, economic activity concentrates in a few economic centres – the Rich Club – which benefit far more from economies of scale and agglomeration, so that there is little correspondence between economic activity and population.

The phase of high international inequality may be a transition, albeit one which has already taken two centuries. The transition will not end with a snapping together of the paths of the rich and poor countries. More likely poor economies peel off, passing through a phase of rapid growth to join the Rich Club, at which point, having exhausted the gains from technology catch-up, they grow at a similar pace to the Rich Club as a whole. Then more poor economies go through the same transition.

We cannot predict the sequence of poor countries peeling off. The next may be China, but it faces severe challenges from its aging population, its environmental pollution, and its size, which may drive up the world costs of the resources it needs. (Nor is it certain that its political system is robust enough to cope with the social changes.) Perhaps smaller poor economies will overtake China's economic growth in the medium term. They need not be East or South-east Asian. It is possible that the economic strength of North America will stimulate growth in Latin American economies. India is another possibility, with its advantage of having a growing – and English-speaking – workforce.

But while other economies will have joined the Rich Club by the end of the twenty-first century, it is unlikely that all the poor economies – especially, and sadly, those in Africa – will have gone through the transition. If it has taken two centuries for the world to get to its current level of inequality, it seems unlikely that the dispersion will unwind in only one.

The Future of Today's Rich Club

By the end of this century the membership of the Rich Club may be wider than it is today. The ethnic composition of the current Rich Club members will also be more diverse as a result of emigration from the poor countries. (Despite this migration, and regional differences in population structure, fertility, and mortality, the pattern of population in a hundred years will be more like today's distribution than will the pattern of economic activity.) But the Rich Club cannot expect its incomes to be substantially higher than they are today; certainly not by the eightfold increase in real per capita incomes which happened over the last century.

Suppose that technological change continues at its past rate, and innovation offsets resource depletion. World production may rise to 4.7 times the level it was at the beginning of the century, as it did in the twentieth century (or to 2.4 times, as in the nineteenth century). But even if its productivity grows rapidly, the Rich Club's incomes may not. Income is derived from production multiplied by price. The products which have been central to lifting the incomes of the rich – general manufactures and relocatable services – are likely to experience falls in their prices relative to those for depletable resources and farm products. Those who provide these manufactures may not get comparably rising incomes because their market value relative to other products seems likely to fall. That won't matter for new suppliers, whose incomes will rise. It will matter for current producers, whose incomes may not.

The trend may already be evident in the rise in relative prices for depletable resources and farm products in recent years. This is usually attributed to the demands of the expanding Chinese economy, whose lower-paid workers also make products more cheaply for export. That is precisely the mechanism which the bifurcation model predicts. If the trend continues, some of the resource-supplying countries may flourish as they did not in the twentieth century. Argentina and Uruguay may rejoin the Rich Club.

In recent years the fall in the price of manufactures sourced from East Asia has made a major contribution to low inflation (relative price stability) throughout the world. While Rich Club consumers have benefited, not all their workers have, with median real wages stagnant for some decades. However, insofar as there is downward pressure on unskilled workers not in the manufacturing industry, this is coming from the opposite process of migrants from poor countries moving to rich ones. Nor does it seem to affect remuneration at the upper end of the labour market, where offshore workers are not yet competitive.

How the Rich Club can deal with this hollowing out of middle incomes is not obvious. Income redistribution policies would require higher taxes. Currently the main response, insofar as there has been a coherent one, has been to try to create more jobs at the upper end, and shift domestic workers into these jobs by such means as upskilling.

The bifurcation model described earlier in the book assumes only two sectors and products. Adding a domestic-supply service sector does not alter the model's behaviour, and tradeable services may also be treated as 'manufactures'. However, ignoring the heterogeneity of manufacturing products and processes is more problematic. At the very least, we need to distinguish routine manufacturing from innovative manufacturing. The distinction is not simply a matter of low and high levels of technology. Routine production may involve very sophisticated (imported) machinery, albeit largely operated with routine skills. Creativity can occur with the simplest technology – the writer with a pen.

Routine 'manufacturing' (including some services) is likely to be offshored, moving to wherever costs are lowest. Innovative 'manufacturing', crucial for technological development, depends more on the agglomeration of technical and creative skills. Initially, at least, these are likely to be found in the urban centres of the established Rich Club.

This is a further reason why a Rich Club member cannot rely on barriers to protect itself against cheap imports. That would be to cut its innovative industries off from both the pressures which generate competitive advantage and the opportunities to produce their products cheaply offshore. In any case, Rich Club members will need to import resources. It will be difficult to opt out of a multilateral world.

Insofar as it can keep its competitive edge in technologically advanced activities (and its stronger agglomeration of skills), the established Rich Club will maintain higher average incomes than most of the new entrants. But those of European origin have no inherent biological superiority in innovation and creativity. It may be that culture and experience will inhibit Asian and other countries' achievements, but eventually they are likely to catch up. (Japan's record suggests that this need not take long.)

The Changing Balance of Economies

The world faces the prospect of four, possibly five, super-economies: the US, the EU, China, Japan, and possibly India, favoured by existing economic performance or by population size, which becomes more important as the costs of distance continue to fall.

The EU is likely to grow in both population and GDP as it accepts new members. But it will probably be hamstrung in foreign policy by the aspirations of its member nation-states.

With minor exceptions, there appear to be few prospects for the extension of the boundaries of the other four major economic powers, whose immediate neighbours are typically robust nation-states. The shares of the world economy supplied by China and India may be expected to grow, and those of the US and Japan to fall.[1] Together, the five are likely to continue to produce around two-thirds of the world's GDP.

What will happen to the other third, produced by the remaining nation-states? Could the world be divided into five spheres of influence – the modern equivalent of empires? Some areas such as Africa do not fit naturally into any sphere, while others such as East Asia and the Middle East will be bitterly contested by all five super-economies. In any case, how can any of the five privilege any sphere of influence when its main trading partners will be the other four, which together will import more than the rest of the world?

There may be scope for bilateral arrangements like the Closer Economic Relations (CER) discussed in Chapter 17 to be made between each of the five and some satellite nations. (The European Economic Association is an example.) These are unlikely to involve fiscal or labour market union or, consequently, monetary union. They will be useful adjuncts rather than central to world economic relations. Similarly, confederations of smaller countries may form plurilateral commercial arrangements, although as like as not the great economic powers will want to get involved.

This may be a niche for 'medium-sized' economies, even though these are small compared with the big five. The largest have GDPs less than half that of India. Any list is likely to be invidious, but it would probably include Australia, Brazil, Canada, Russia, and South Korea. For the sake of Africa, it should also include South Africa (currently 24th in GDP terms if the EU countries are combined). The medium-sized countries will have influence as regional powers, and perhaps as brokers between the great ones. Members of the EU of a similar size will retain the ambitions of medium powers.

What is the future for smaller states? Some may try to form an exclusive alliance with a great economic power, perhaps because of proximity or complementarity. Most will try not to depend too much on a single patron. (Patrons may be more necessary for micro-economies.) Yet bilateral relationships are not enough. All have an interest in a multilateral world. So they will work with like-minded nation-states in multilateral fora, pursuing common objectives with the implicit agenda of minimising the dominance of the big five.

Inevitably that will involve a loss of autonomy in those aspects of economic policy where they interact with their trading partners. But for as long as a nation-state has a cultural centre, and some power over its domestic policy and foreign circumstances, it will continue to exist – and even thrive.

A New World Order?

Given the relative growth of China and India from productivity gains and the European Union from enlargement, it is hard to see the United States retaining its political and economic hegemony.

The US is dominant today because it is able to focus its economic power for purposes it judges to be in its (and perhaps the world's) interest. It is easy to decry the abuse of that power – the invasion of Iraq is a ready target. But sometimes the US has used its power with considerable generosity.

Europe has reason to be grateful for the Marshall Plan, through which the US contributed to its reconstruction after the Second World War. China and Japan have much to be grateful for today, for it is the US Navy which patrols the sea lanes on which their shipping – not least that carrying oil – depends.

But the US is able to display such power only because of its relative economic superiority. Even then it is limited. Its military forces are struggling to find sufficient resources to maintain order in Iraq and Afghanistan as well as meeting other US strategic needs. As its relative economic superiority diminishes and other economies catch up, the US will be able to devote proportionately fewer resources to military purposes.

It might be argued that military might can be used to enforce economic arrangements in US interests. Empires prosper to the extent that the peace and good order they impose facilitate high economic output. Some of the additional income may be remitted to the imperial power and used by its military to maintain the peace. But as Britain found when nationalism broke out in its colonies, the military burden of maintaining a rebellious empire exceeds the remittances from it. In any case, such adventurism would be negated within a decade or two by the actions of the remaining economic powers (whose combined GDPs are already about double that of the US).

It seems likely that the US dollar will lose its dominance as the international medium of exchange, coming to share this role with the euro. There will be some loss of seigniorage, the advantage a currency issuer gets from others using its currency, but it will also become harder for the US to fund its budget deficit (or to maintain a huge US public debt at little cost). The economic strength of the US has allowed it to get away with inefficient fiscal management (and an inefficient health service and major military spending). It is not obvious that this can continue without the US losing sufficient economic power to undermine its hegemonic status even sooner.

The US will not lose its relative economic dominance suddenly. Rather, it will slide away. Most Americans will not even recognise the transition until long after the rest of the world has done so.

Britain faced similar difficulties in the twentieth century. Even in the 1960s, when its economy was one-fifth the size of the US economy, and it had suffered the debacle of the 1956 Suez invasion (when Britain ignominiously retreated at US insistence), there was still a popular sentiment among the British that their country remained a world power. (Its 'empire' was treated as meaningful long after it had fallen apart: the 'empire' appellation was not dropped from the Commonwealth Games until 1970.)

While empires have been common in world history, the hegemon is a peculiarity of a globalised world with costs of distance high enough for it to be bifurcated into a Rich and a Poor Club. In global terms there have been only two hegemons – other candidates, such as the Roman Empire, controlled very small parts of the world (and that control was moderated by the difficulties of the centre exercising authority at a distance). The adjustment will be even more difficult for Americans, for there will be no replacement hegemonic power. Britons were able to acknowledge their more restricted role when they could see that the US was dominant.

Thus the issue is not who will replace the current hegemon. US airport bookstalls are brimming with such anxieties. But hegemony is not moving to Europe or Japan or China or whomever. The US's dominance will slowly give way to a multipolar world of great powers, each of which can make a major – but not unilateral – difference. Those who see the last two centuries of a globalised world as 'normal' will find it hard to understand what will replace it.

It will be hard enough for those who have grasped that there will be no hegemon to understand this new world order. Economics has good explanations of how markets work when there is a dominant monopoly (a hegemonic actor), and of pure competition (when no individual agent has power). It has some understanding of markets where there is a duopoly (such as the bipolar political world of the American and Soviet nuclear powers). However, economists have found oligopoly – where a number of large firms compete in a market – far more difficult to analyse.

A multipolar world is similarly difficult to come to terms with, because the possibilities for alliance between powers are so numerous. Yet in such a world, indeterminancy is the reality. Much of the world's future is not inevitable, and it can be influenced if we go about it the right way. To do so requires systematic thinking, including understanding the processes which shape the global economy and contribute to the politics of the new world order.

Epilogue • Democracy in a Globalised World

As an economics student I was struck by Paul Samuelson's notion that the marketplace was a 'democracy' in which consumers expressed their preferences by their purchases.[1] But it is a democracy in which votes are allocated on the basis of how much each has to spend – a democracy of dollars, not of people.

In an ideal world, the market 'democracy' and the political democracy would be independent of one another. In the real world, they are not. Instead, there is considerable tension between them: dollar-votes are used to influence person-votes, and person-votes are collectively used to override dollar-votes. Much of the nineteenth and twentieth centuries involved a struggle in liberal democracies to find the right balance.

That (complicated) story belongs to another venue. Here we observe that just when many rich countries seemed to have found a domestic balance, globalisation exacerbated the tension. As an economy increasingly engages in international intercourse, international actors get involved in the domestic economy, increasing the number of dollar-votes and reducing the power of person-votes.

This is not an unmitigated disaster. Globalisation increases the usefulness of the dollar-vote, giving consumers more bang for their buck. However, it reduces the total dollar-votes of some. Others – as we saw in relation to the hollowing out of the middle class – gain little; still others benefit from globalisation. The paradox is captured by steelworkers who bemoan the loss of jobs to China, while wearing Chinese-made clothes they have bought in preference to more expensive local products. Recently they have been joined by ICT workers, who were largely indifferent to the pressures on blue-collar workers – and indeed were pleased to pay less for cars made from lower-priced steel – but who have become outraged now that their jobs too are being offshored.

Public understanding is not helped by the more uncritical 'free-market' advocates of globalisation, who emphasise its success and rarely mention that almost inevitably someone will be worse off. While we may ponder whether we live in the best of all possible worlds, change does not mean everyone will be better off (Rabin rules, OK?).

The reality is more subtle. The dollar-vote method for resolving the economic questions of what should be produced, and how, for whom, where and when, results in much higher material output than the non-market alternatives – especially as products become more complex and varied. An individual who is worse off as a result of a particular economic change is nevertheless likely to be considerably better off than had there been no market supply at all.

The uncritical anti-globalisers who mention only the downsides of globalisation are equally unhelpful. Perhaps they judge that to acknowledge any positives would strengthen the pro-globalisers (who might well make a similar argument with respect to the limitations of anti-globalisation arguments). But how is anyone to make sense of a debate dominated by such extremism? It is harder to make, and to understand, a balanced perspective, one which takes account of both the good and the bad, the winners and the losers.

This framework seeks a rebalancing of dollar-votes and person-votes in a globalised world. It is not a matter of rejecting globalisation, and like Cnut commanding the tide to turn. (In fact the king was demonstrating to fawning courtiers that he was *not* omnipotent.) There is a need to think about the degree to which dollar-votes should influence that which the market delivers badly, and the degree to which person-votes should influence that which the market does well. As Jesus said, 'Render unto Caesar the things which are Caesar's, and unto God the things that are God's'.

The nation-state may have increasingly less unilateral control over commercial transactions across its borders, but international commerce should not try to control non-commercial activities inside domestic borders, even where these involve the use of resources. The outcome may be that we end up with less political democracy than we once thought we had, but more market democracy.

I was struck by how distorted the public debate has become when I told people I was studying globalisation. The almost invariable reply was, 'Are you for it or against it?' My response is summarised at the end of the prologue, which is also a good way to end the book.

Marx's last thesis on Feuerbach states that 'philosophers have only interpreted the world in various ways; the point is, to change it.' But effective change depends on good interpretation. That has been my goal in writing this book.

Notes

Preface
1. MIT Press, Cambridge MA, 1999.

1. Globalisation: An Introduction
1. J. Anderson and E. van Wincoop, 'Trade Costs', *Journal of Economic Literature*, vol. 42, 2004, pp. 691–751.
2. A complicating factor is that while a reduction in general distance costs may release resources which can be redeployed for other productive purposes, a cut in tariffs has no such effect.
3. 7th edition published by Addison-Wesley, Boston MA, 2006.
4. N. Crafts and A. J. Venables, 'Globalization in History: A Geographic Perspective', in M. D. Bordo, A. M. Taylor and J. G. Williams (eds), *Globalization in Historical Perspective*, University of Chicago Press, Chicago, 2003, pp. 323–69.
5. A reduction of the tariff on an input may result in the expansion of an industry using the input, even though the activity is inefficient. This situation is common in developing countries (and, historically, in developed countries), where priority industries are characteristically favoured by high tariffs on their outputs and low tariffs on their inputs.

2. The Significance of Location: Samoa and Hawaii
1. Tikopia in the Solomon Islands, first studied by the New Zealand anthropologist Raymond Firth, is the most famous of these outliers.
2. Named after a contemporary Lord of the Admiralty, the eponymous inventor of the sandwich.
3. G. Daws, *Shoal of Time: A History of the Hawaiian Islands*, University Press of Hawaii, Honolulu, 1968, p. 428.
4. D. Oliver, *The Pacific Islands*, University Press of Hawaii, Honolulu, 1989, p. 152.

3. When Distance Changes: New Zealand
1. R. W. Fogel, *The Escape from Hunger and Premature Death, 1700–2100: Europe, America, and the Third World*, Cambridge University Press, Cambridge, 2004.

4. Regions and Economies of Scale: The United States
1. G. R. Taylor, *The Transportation Revolution, 1815–1860*, Rinehart, New York, 1951.
2. The exposition assumes firms sell at cost, and do not take advantage of any monopoly power to raise their prices.
3. It would be anachronistic to condemn Fogel for this omission, since the relevant theory about economies of scale was not well understood until after his pioneering research.

5. The Forces of Agglomeration: New York
1. An adjustment has been made for boundary changes.
2. M. Fujita and J.-F. Thisse, *Economics of Agglomeration: Cities, Industrial Location, and Regional Growth*, Cambridge University Press, Cambridge, 2002, p. 8.

7. Offshoring: India
1. The outside supplier may be wholly or partly owned by the outsourcing business.
2. Some experts use the term only when there is a formal ongoing contract between supplier and purchaser.
3. R. Coase, 'The Nature of the Firm', *Economica*, vol. 4, no. 16, Nov. 1937, pp. 386–405.
4. Despite the label, the source of the service may be on the same land mass.
5. The factory management may comprise a handful of skilled expatriates who are collectively paid more than the far more numerous process workers.
6. An exception arises if the consumer is willing to accept advice by telephone, as occurs with computer help desks and even in medicine.

8. Intra-Industry Trade: Motor Vehicles
1. Intra-industry trade data varies according to how fine or coarse the definition of industry or product is.
2. Executive Office of the President, *Economic Report of the President*, Government Printing Office, Washington DC, 1998.
3. Other definitions of monopolistic competition envisage quite different market structures. This follows E. H. Chamberlain's seminal contribution.
4. A New Zealand car assembler tells of importing CKD (completely knocked down) packs of 2½ cubic metres at a cost of about $140 a cubic metre for a car retailing for about $5000. In order to get their costs down, component manufacturers began to make larger 'bits' which could not be nested and took up more space. The last car he assembled came in an 18.7-cubic-metre pack at an additional cost of $2268. This is a nice illustration of how the costs of distance can be more important than a tariff. M. Webster, *Assembly: New Zealand Car Production 1921–98*, Reed, Auckland, 2002, p. 164.
5. By setting up in North America without having to carry various costs of the established motor industry sites, with their labour unions and retirees, the new producers were able to undercut the established firms.
6. R. B. Reich, *The Work of Nations: Preparing Ourselves for 21st-Century Capitalism*, Knopf, New York, 1991, p. 128.
7. T. L. Friedman, *The World is Flat: A Brief History of the Twenty-first Century*, Farrar, Straus & Giroux, New York, 2005, pp. 515–23.

9. Migration: Mexico

1 The ratio was 4.1 in 1998 – $27,300 vs $6655, measured in international dollars. The largest relative differential I have been able to find is across the Greek–Albanian border, where it is close to 4.5. Ratios in excess of 3.0 are common between rich European countries and their poorer eastern neighbours. In 1990, at the time of reunification, the ratio between West Germany and East Germany was 3.6 (Maddison Data Base).
2 Ignoring the effect of gains from economies of scale.
3 On rare occasions migrants have been more skilled than the population among whom they arrived. This was true of the Jews who fled Europe in the 1930s and 1940s.

10. Locating the World's Population: Aging

1 The statistical basis for this chapter is a series of publications by the Population Division of the United Nations' Department of Economic and Social Affairs, in particular *World Population Prospects: The 2004 Revision*, New York, 2005; and *World Population Ageing, 1950–2050*, New York, 2002. These forecasts are unlikely to be revised so dramatically as to alter this chapter's thesis markedly.
2 Other important factors are family policy and the social and cultural environment.
3 The UN defines the 'more developed world' as Australasia, Europe, Japan and North America, roughly corresponding to the membership of the Rich Club in 2000.
4 Since 50/70 = 71%. Various assumptions are made here, including that the average real return on investment equals the average growth of productivity – which seems to be roughly true.
5 Extrapolated from *World Population Prospects*, 2002, which gives scenarios based on two assumptions about migration.
6 New immigrants from poorer countries may go through the fertility transition more quickly than those they leave behind. (Samoan women in Samoa average about 2.0 daughters each; when they come to New Zealand they have 1.5.) And their children may seek more skilled jobs, leading to a future deficit of unskilled workers.
7 This section makes extensive use of B. R. Chiswick and T. J. Hatton, 'International Migration and the Integration of Labour Markets', in M. D. Bordo, A. M. Taylor and J. G. Williamson (eds), *Globalization in Historical Perspective*, University of Chicago Press, Chicago, 2003.
8 Within continents, the largest movements were eastward in the Russian Empire.
9 While the early twentieth-century figure covers only intercontinental migrants from Europe, that for the late twentieth century includes both non-Europeans and migration within continents. The ratio would probably exceed three if comparable definitions were used.
10 Figures from *World Population Prospects*, 2004. This includes relatively short-distance migration, such as cross-border movements from China to Hong Kong and from Kazakhstan to Russia.
11 It is assumed here that the relative incomes of the elderly will not fall, because they will become politically more influential as they make up a growing proportion of the population.

11. Sovereignty: Time

1 The draft Multilateral Agreement on Investment is available at http://www1.oecd.org/daf/mai/pdf/ng/ng987r1e.pdf.

12. The Nation-State: Germany

1 This summary of Aristotle's *Politics*, iii, 9, 1280a, 26-40 & 1280b, 1-40, was provided by Jim Flynn, Emeritus Professor of Political Studies, University of Otago.
2 P. Munz, *Beyond Wittgenstein's Poker: New Light on Popper and Wittgenstein*, Ashgate, Aldershot, 2004. Munz's argument is specifically about language, but is readily generalisable (if there can be culture without language).

13. Cultural Convergence: Canada

1 This section is informed by J. R. Saul, *Reflections of a Siamese Twin: Canada at the End of the Twentieth Century*, Viking, Toronto, 1997.
2 *OECD Fact Book*, 2005. The Canadian proportion is exceeded among rich countries by only Australia (23.1%) and New Zealand (19.5%), and probably Luxembourg and Switzerland, for which there is no data – they report 37.5% and 19.7%, respectively, of their population as foreign nationals. The US proportion is also exceeded by Sweden (11.4%).
3 http://www.dooneyscafe.com/print.php?sid=369.

14. The Diaspora: Australia

1 OECD, *Fact Book* 2005.
2 Southern Cross, *Estimates of Australian Citizens Living Overseas as at 31 December 2001*, http://www.southern-cross-group.org/archives/Statistics/Numbers_of_Australians_Overseas_in_2001_by_Region_Feb_2002.pdf. An astonishing 330,000 Australians – 1.7% of the resident population – were reported to have been overseas on census night 2001. Some of these may be included in the diaspora statistics.
3 These 2001 figures are based on consular records of the Australian Department of Foreign Affairs and Trade. No doubt other Australians were below their radar.
4 The figures are reported in G. Hugo, D. Rudd and K. Harris, *Australia's Diaspora: Its Size, Nature and Policy Implications*, Committee for Economic Development of Australia,

Information Paper No. 80, Melbourne, 2003.
5 D. S. Raj, *Where Are You From? Middle-class Migrants in the Modern World*, University of California Press, Berkeley, 2003, p. 4.

15. The Social Market Economy: The European Union

1 The EU already had an informal constitution of treaties, regulations and practices, rather like the British constitution. The referendum was about whether this would be replaced by a 'basic law', an arrangement more familiar to most Europeans.
2 US constitutional arrangements make far greater use of common law, a heritage from Britain, than is the practice in most European countries.
3 B. Jesson, *Fragments of Labour: The Story Behind the Labour Government*, Penguin, Auckland, 1989.
4 The exceptions were the United Kingdom, the Netherlands and Ireland.
5 For the source and destination countries combined, there is likely to be a reduction in income inequality.
6 This strictly applies only where the offshoring involves 'unskilled' workers. Where there are skilled (high-paid) workers it is conceivable that income inequality will narrow.
7 For instance, all the other Australian states and New Zealand followed Queensland's elimination of death duties, to remove that reason for retiring in Queensland.

16. Policy Convergence: Health Care

1 In the two most authoritative studies, the economic impact of alcohol abuse is calculated to lower effective GDP by around 1%. See B. Easton, 'Alcohol Consumption: The Social and Economic Impacts', in *The Encyclopaedia of Public Health* (forthcoming from Elsevier).
2 Luxembourg is not discussed in the text. Its data tends to be distorted by the number of workers who live outside its borders.
3 See http://www.who.int/tobacco/framework/download/en/index.html.

17. The International Trading System: The World Trade Organization

1 For instance, the deal involved New Zealand eliminating import licences by creating special ones for Australian imports, the value of which steadily increased until they became irrelevant. The new licences were often given to the manufacturers who had been protected by them.
2 TRIPs deals with copyright and related rights, such as rights of performers, producers of sound recordings and broadcasting organisations; geographical indications, including appellations of origin; industrial designs; integrated circuit layout designs; patents, including the protection of new varieties of plants; trademarks; trade dress; and undisclosed or confidential information, including trade secrets and test data. Among the multitude of other agreements which the WTO supervises are Agreements on Agriculture (AOA), Textiles and Clothing (ATC), Trade-Related Investment Measures (TRIMs), Technical Barriers to Trade (TBT), Sanitary and Phyto-Sanitary Measures (SPS), Subsidies and Countervailing Measures (SCM).
3 See http://www.wto.org/english/thewto_e/whatis_e/10ben_e/10b00_e.htm.
4 Friends of the Earth International, *The World Trading System: How It Works and What's Wrong With It*, 2003, available at http://www.foei.org/publications/pdfs/worldtradesystem.pdf. For another list, see http://www.globalexchange.org/campaigns/wto/OpposeWTO.html.

18. The International Financial System: The IMF

1 Sometimes this role as a standard of deferred payment (e.g., to pay debts) is separated out.
2 Almost. The coiner usually kept a little gold to cover the costs of production – the 'seigniorage'.
3 The next few pages have benefited from P. Blustein, *The Chastening: Inside the Crisis That Rocked the Global Financial System and Humbled the IMF*, Public Affairs, Oxford, 2001.
4 Critics often add the 'World Bank' to the pantheon of wickedness. Yet nowadays the International Bank for Reconstruction and Development (to give it its correct title) is a minor player in the provision of long-term capital to developing countries, compared to private capital sources.
5 This account is based on past failures, almost all of which involved fixed exchange rates. The next round of failures may be rather different if they occur in countries with floating exchange rates.
6 The other economies which experienced financial crises in this period were, in chronological order, Mexico (8th treating the EU as a unity), Thailand (13th), Indonesia (11th), Russia (7th), Brazil (6th), Turkey (14th) and Argentina (17th). The share of world GDP of the largest, Brazil, was 2.7%.
7 All banks make some loans which become bad debts. This is allowed for in their balance sheets. But sometimes the bad debts far exceed expectations.
8 Blustein, *The Chastening*, p. 212.
9 There has been debate about the extent to which the cuts should contract the economy. There is a strong – and in my view plausible – view that in the 1990s the IMF measures often reinforced the economic contraction which was already occurring as a result of the run on the bank. The IMF now appears to acknowledge that it would act less harshly were there to be a repetition of these crises.
10 For a discussion of the practicalities of the belling process, see M. Ul Haq, I. Kaul and I. Grunberg (eds), *The Tobin Tax: Coping with Financial Volatility*, Oxford University Press, New York, c. 1996.

19. Foreign Direct Investment: McDonald's

1 That the outlets are franchised adds another indigenous dimension, for locals take some of the profits – and much of the risk.
2 Eventually, as at first some may be retained and reinvested.
3 A legitimate grumble is voiced when political or corporate kleptocrats raise the loan on behalf of the country or company, loot the proceeds, and leave others to bear the debt servicing or losses.
4 For a summary of the evidence, see J. Bhagwati, *In Defense of Globalization*, Oxford University Press, New York, 2004, pp. 170–8.
5 P. De Grauwe and F. Camerman, 'Are Multinationals Really Bigger than Nations?', *World Economics*, vol. 4, no. 2, 2003, pp. 23–37. The individual members of the EU are treated separately.

20. How Economies Develop: Smith to Solow and Beyond

1 A. Smith, *An Inquiry into the Nature and Causes of the Wealth of Nations*, first published 1776, Book I, Chapter 1, 'Of the Division of Labour'.
2 R. Solow, 'Technical Change and the Aggregate Production Function', *Review of Economic Statistics*, vol. 39, no. 3, Aug. 1957, pp. 312–20.
3 T. Balogh and P. P. Streeten, 'The Coefficient of Ignorance', *Bulletin of the Oxford University Institute of Economic and Statistics*, vol. 25, no 2, May 1963, pp. 97–107.

21. Resources: Oil

1 These are primary fuels. Some may be used to generate hydrogen, which may be used for transport.
2 Part of the pressure in 2005 was a shortage of oil refinery capacity, rather than of oil production capacity.
3 The calculations may implicitly assume that the energy cost of inputs is about US$35 a barrel, ignoring the circularity of the production process. If this is allowed for, the long-run price will be higher.
4 Global warming melting the Arctic ice may enable the use in summer months of the Northwest Passage between the Atlantic and the Pacific Oceans to the north of Canada.
5 This early nineteenth-century notion was revived by Garrett Hardin in 'The Tragedy of the Commons', *Science*, vol. 162, 1968, pp. 1243–8.
6 Readers trained in economics a couple of decades ago may be surprised that the term 'externality' is not used in the chapter. An externality occurs when decision-makers do not take into account all the consequences of their decisions. The industrialist who is not charged for the firm's emissions into the air and water and so ignores their polluting impact on the ecosystem is a good example of externality. The fisher who ignores the impact of fishing on the stock of fish and the ecosystem is another. In recent decades economists have realised that in many cases externalities reflect a lack of proper ownership of the resource being desecrated – the river used for sewerage, the fish over-exploited. The two approaches give similar conclusions; this chapter has used the more recent one.
7 Where the oil reservoir lies under jurisdictional boundaries – as between Iraq and Kuwait, and some undersea reservoirs below EEZ boundaries – the determination of ownership can be more difficult.
8 The theory is due to Ronald Coase, who was awarded an Economics Prize in honour of Alfred Nobel in 1991.
9 Shell is also based at The Hague in the Netherlands.

22. Information: The World Wide Web

1 A. Hourani, *A History of the Arab Peoples*, Faber, London, 2002, p. 303.
2 http://en.wikipedia.org/wiki/Main_Page.
3 Seeking the exact quote, I ended up finding it in Wikipedia.
4 Wikipedia's discussion of its recipe (currently) provides three different reverse-engineered formulations.

23. Technology Transfer: Japan

1 While the term 'meta-technology' is not widely used, it encapsulates a set of standard economic ideas that have become more prominent in recent years.
2 D. C. North, *Institutions, Institutional Change, and Economic Performance*, Cambridge University Press, Cambridge/New York, 1990, p. 15. See also W. J. Baumol, *The Free-market Innovation Machine: Analyzing the Growth Miracle of Capitalism*, Princeton University Press, Princeton, 2002. The literature on 'innovation systems' does not really engage with North's approach, and pays less attention to international technology transfer than would seem warranted.
3 The Maddison Data Base groups Austria, Belgium, Denmark, Finland, France, Germany, Italy, The Netherlands, Norway, Sweden, Switzerland and the United Kingdom as the West European 12. The six Asian Tigers – discussed later in the chapter – are Hong Kong, Malaysia, Singapore, South Korea, Taiwan and Thailand.
4 The annual figures suggest that the secular trends changed abruptly in about 1970 (the postwar catch-up was over) and 1990 (when Japan reached the level of those at the top of the OECD).
5 West Europe also suffered from wartime devastation. Some heuristic estimates suggest that its 'latent' production capacity in 1950 was about 50% higher than actual GDP per capita.

Japan's latent capacity immediately after the war was about double its actual capacity.

6 A good source of Deming's ideas is his *Out of the Crisis*, Massachusetts Institute of Technology, Cambridge MA, 1986.

7 M. Olson, *The Rise and Decline of Nations: Economic Growth, Stagflation, and Social Rigidities*, Yale University Press, New Haven, 1982.

8 Japan and some of the other East Asian Tiger economies did protect their domestic markets, building a strong domestic base from which to export. This strategy is becoming increasingly less possible, because the world trading regime is unwilling to give easy access to exporters with protected domestic markets.

9 The belief that the Japanese were not particularly (technologically) creative was a canard based on the view that all they could do is copy (which we have seen is not true for meta-technologies). Japan has recently been very innovative in some areas, including robotics and computer games.

10 Perhaps entrepôt ports such as Hong Kong and Singapore servicing large, lower-productivity regions should be treated as a part of a larger economy. The city of New York is another such example, but because the statistics are collected across a larger region, we do not always see the parallel. Statistical (and jurisdictional) boundaries may not correspond to economic boundaries.

24. The Rich Club: Argentina

1 Measured by GDP per capita (using the Maddison Data Base). Here Western Europe comprises the twelve countries used in the previous chapter, although Finland should probably be omitted until around 1950 (and Luxembourg added).

2 The term was coined in 1988 by W. J. Baumol and E. N. Wolf in 'Productivity Growth Convergence and Welfare', *American Economic Review*, vol. 78, no. 5, pp. 1155–9. For a rich recent review, see S. Dowrick and J. B. DeLong, 'Globalisation and Convergence', in M. D. Bordo, A. M. Taylor and J. G. Williamson (eds), *Globalisation in Historical Perspective*, University of Chicago Press, Chicago, 2003, pp. 191–226.

3 The oil-based rich countries are omitted from the club because they have such a different economic structure. I am also not sure that we should treat small entrepôt economies such as Hong Kong and Singapore as having the same economic structure as the other members of the Rich Club. They are more like New York.

4 'Whatungarongaro te tangata, toitū te whenua: People come and go but the land endures.' I am grateful to Richard Benton for the precise saying.

5 Comprehensiveness requires mention that very often calls for 'reform' in Rich Club countries involve different notions of the common good, or even amount to little more than proposals to shift the income distribution in favour of the proposers of the reform, or their clients.

6 Dowrick and DeLong, 'Globalisation and Convergence', use a broader definition for their 'Convergence Club', arguing that at various times other economies have been about to join but did not succeed. One might think of them as reaching take-off mode but not getting airborne.

7 Argentina's per capita income as a percentage of the West European 12 was 103 in 1913, 73 in 1960 and 49 in 1998. (Uruguay's was 90, 65 and 44 respectively.)

8 Argentina's religion – Roman Catholicism – has been blamed, but this does not explain the fact that Ireland, Italy, (South) Germany and Spain are club members.

9 During the twentieth century, Argentina, Uruguay, New Zealand and Australia grew at 0.9, 0.8, 0.7 and 0.4% per annum respectively below the Rich Club average. Next on the list is the United Kingdom (0.3% per annum slower). Its poorer relative growth was due to it being the first to industrialise. The others have caught up. (In the last third of the century, Australia became a substantial exporter of minerals, and began growing faster than the Rich Club average.)

10 See D. Sheinin, 'Defying Infection: Argentine Foot-and-Mouth Disease Policy, 1900–1930', *Canadian Journal of History*, vol. 29, Dec. 1994, pp. 501–24.

11 The data source used here is the Oxford Latin American Economic History Database, http://oxlad.qeh.ox.ac.uk/.

12 It was the same for New Zealand. See B. H. Easton, *In Stormy Seas: The Post-war New Zealand Economy*, University of Otago Press, Dunedin, 1997.

13 Asian service industries not subject to such external pressures have performed less impressively. Exporters to Japan find that its inefficient wholesale and retail trade sectors add unusually high margins to the landed export price. This is an example of an informal protection which discourages importing.

25. Poor Countries: Africa

1 Unless otherwise specified, the data in this chapter comes from the Maddison Data Base.

2 More than 50 sovereign states have populations of less than a million. Not all these micro-states belong to international institutions such as the UN.

3 The choice of $3500 per annum is explained in the next chapter.

4 Libya is not included in the Maddison Data Base, but may be above the poor country threshold because of its oil exports.

5 The per capita incomes of a number of poor countries, including China and India, appear to have fallen in the first half of the twentieth

century.
6. Spain is an exception. It might be argued it was a member of the Rich Club in the eighteenth century, lost this status for the next 150 years, and has recently regained it.
7. The United Nations *World Population Prospects*, 2004, expects the HIV-AIDS epidemic to reduce the world's population by about 10 million a year.
8. Definitive conclusions are dependent on the reliability of the Chinese statistics.
9. P. Lindert and J. G. Williamson, 'Does Globalization Make the World More Unequal?', in M. D. Bordo, A. M. Taylor and J. G. Williamson (eds), *Globalisation in Historical Perspective*, University of Chicago Press, Chicago, 2003, pp. 227–76.

26. The Insignificant Middle Club: The Bifurcation Model

1. The geometrical choice of thresholds – each being double or half the adjacent one – is because commonly income distributions arranged this way appear normally distributed – as in the conventional 'bell curve'. (They are 'log-normally' distributed.)
2. A Very Poor Club, with average GDP below $1750 per annum, would have 44 members, 13.6% of the world's population, producing 2.5% of its GDP. Its average income would be 18% of the world's. Over half would be African states. A Very Very Poor Club with average GDP below $875 per annum would have about 17 members (all but 4 of them African) with 4.9% of the world's population and 0.6% of its GDP. Its average income would be 12.5% of the world's.
3. Kuwait, Oman, Qatar, Saudi Arabia, Trinidad and Tobago, United Arab Emirates, Venezuela.
4. Czech Republic, Estonia, Greece, Portugal, Slovakia, Slovenia.
5. Above the $14,000 per annum dividing line, Hong Kong, Singapore and Taiwan were already members of the Rich Club in 1998.
6. Further examples are Ireland and Spain, and the Asian Tigers.
7. The two biggest European manufacturers in 1750 were Russia and France. Germany, Austria-Hungary, and Italy also led Britain, which did not become Europe's (and the world's) largest manufacturer until about 1810. The US became the world's largest manufacturer in about 1890.
8. 1750–1913: P. Bairoch, 'International Industrialization Levels from 1750 to 1980', *Journal of European Economic History*, vol. 11, Fall 1982, pp. 269–333. 1938: C. Simmons, 'De-Industrialization, Industrialization, and the Indian Economy, c. 1850–1947', *Modern Asian Studies*, vol. 19, no. 3, 1985, pp. 593–622.
9. Population share interpolated from Maddison Data Base. Manufacturing share from P. Bairoch, *Economics and World History: Myths and Paradoxes*, Harvester Wheatsheaf, New York, Table 8.1.
10. M. Fujita, P. Krugman and A. Venables *The Spatial Economy: Cities, Regions, and International Trade*, Cambridge, 1999, Part IV, especially around section 16.5.
11. Landowners may be worse off because there are fewer workers on the land.

27. The Pattern of World Development: China

1. Insofar as the model has changing costs of distance this is also technological change; and when these fall there is also a boost to consumption.
2. P. A. Samuelson, 'Why Ricardo and Mill Rebut and Confirm Arguments of Mainstream Economists Supporting Globalization', *Journal of Economic Perspectives*, vol. 18, no. 3, Summer 2004, pp. 135–46.

28. Options for Nations

1. Maddison data for 2002. The next largest economies are Brazil (2.7%), Russia (2.1%), and Mexico, Canada, South Korea and Indonesia (all 1.9%). Note that Germany, France, Britain, and Italy, all larger, are subsumed in the EU.
2. Maddison data for 2002. Indonesia (3.5%), Brazil (2.9%), Pakistan (2.4%), Russia (2.3%), Bangladesh (2.2%), and Nigeria (2.1%) all have larger populations than Japan.
3. Austria, Finland and Sweden ceased to be EFTA members when they joined the EU in 1995.
4. A. Alesina and E. Spolaore, *The Size of Nations*, MIT Press, Cambridge, 2005.

29. A Confederation of Nations?

1. Subtitled *War, Peace, and the Course of History*, Knopf, New York, 2002.
2. Failure to meet Kyoto targets is meant to lead to more stringent targets in the next period. But sanctions had little effect on the big economies of the European Monetary Union which failed to keep within the agreed limits for government deficits. Unenforceable penalties are almost irrelevant to big nations.

30. A Multipolar World

1. In the last 50 years, US GDP has fallen from about 27% of the world total to 21%. In the last fifteen years, Japan's proportion has fallen from about 8½% to near 7%.

Epilogue: Democracy in a Globalised World

1. P. A. Samuelson, *Economics: An Introductory Analysis*, 4th edn, McGraw-Hill, New York, 1958, p. 39.

Bibliography

Books

Adams, D., *Hitchhiker's Guide to the Galaxy*, Pan, London, 1979.
Aghion, P., and J. G. Williamson, *Growth, Inequality and Globalization: Theory, History and Policy*, Cambridge University Press, Cambridge, 1998.
Alesina, A., and E. Spolaore, *The Size of Nations*, MIT Press, Cambridge, 2005.
Aveni, A., *Empires of Time: Calendars, Clocks and Cultures*, Tauris, London, 1990.
Bairoch, P., *Economics and World History: Myths and Paradoxes*, Harvester Wheatsheaf, New York, 1993.
Baumol, W. J., *The Free-market Innovation Machine: Analyzing the Growth Miracle of Capitalism*, Princeton University Press, Princeton, 2002.
Baylis, J., and S. Smith (eds), *The Globalization of World Politics: An Introduction to International Relations*, 2nd edn, Oxford University Press, Oxford, 2001.
Beck, U. (translated by Patrick Camiller), *What is Globalisation?*, Polity, Cambridge, 2000.
Bhagwati, J., *In Defense of Globalization*, Oxford University Press, New York, 2004.
Blainey, G., *The Tyranny of Distance: How Distance Shaped Australia's History*, 3rd edn, Sun Books, Sydney, 2001.
Blustein, P., *The Chastening: Inside the Crisis That Rocked the Global Financial System and Humbled the IMF*, Public Affairs, Oxford, 2001.
Bobbit, P., *The Shield of Achilles: War, Peace, and the Course of History*, Anchor Books, New York, 2003.
Bordo, M. D., A. M. Taylor and J. Williamson (eds), *Globalisation in Historical Perspective*, University of Chicago Press, Chicago, 2003.
Cairncross, F., *The Death of Distance*, Harvard Business School Press, Cambridge, 1997.
Chamberlin, E. H., *Theory of Monopolistic Competition*, Harvard University Press, Cambridge, 1933.
Chernow, R., *Adam Hamilton*, Penguin Press, New York, 2004.
Cohen, D., *Globalisation and Its Enemies*, MIT Press, Cambridge, 2006.
Daws, G., *Shoal of Time: A History of the Hawaiian Islands*, University Press of Hawaii, Honolulu, 1968.
Deming, W. E., *Out of the Crisis*, MIT Press, Cambridge, 1986.
Denmark, Government of, *Progress, Innovation and Cohesion: Strategy for Denmark in a Global Economy*, Copenhagen, 2006.
Easton, B. H., *In Stormy Seas: The Post-war New Zealand Economy*, University of Otago Press, Dunedin, 1997.
Eichengreen, B., *Globalizing Capital: A History of the International Monetary System*, Princeton University Press, Princeton, 1996.
Elkan, P.G., *The New Model Economy : Economic Inventions for the Rest of the Century*, Pergamon Press, New York, 1982.
Executive Office of the President, *Economic Report of the President*, Government Printing Office, Washington DC, 1998.
Fogel, R. W., *The Escape from Hunger and Premature Death, 1700–2100: Europe, America, and the Third World*, Cambridge University Press, Cambridge, 2004.
Fogel, R.W., *Railroads and American Economic Growth: Essays in Econometric History*. Johns Hopkins Press, Baltimore:, 1964.
Frank, T., *One Market Under God*, Doubleday, New York, 2000.
Frank, T., *What's the Matter with Kansas? How Conservatives Won the Heart of America*, Henry Holt, New York, 2005.
Friedman, T. L., *The Lexus and the Olive Tree*, 2nd edn, Anchor Books, New York, 2000.
Friedman, T. L., *The World is Flat: A Brief History of the Twenty-first Century*, Farrar, Strauss and Giroux, New York, 2005.
Fujita, M., P. R. Krugman and A. J. Venables, *The Spatial Economy: Cities, Regions and International Trade*, MIT Press, Cambridge, 1999.
Fujita, M., and J.-F. Thisse, *Economics of Agglomeration: Cities, Industrial Location and Regional Growth*, Cambridge University Press, Cambridge, 2002.
Galison, P., *Einstein's Clocks, Poincaré's Maps: Empires of Time*, Sceptre, London, 2003.
Giddens, A. (ed.), *The Global Third Way Debate*, Polity, Cambridge, 2001.
Gomoroy, R. E., and W. J. Baumol, *Global Trade and Conflicting National Interests*, MIT Press, Cambridge, 2000.
Gould, B., *The Democracy Sham: How Globalisation Devalues Your Vote*, Craig Potton, Nelson, 2006.
Helpman, E., and P. R. Krugman, *Market Structure and Foreign Trade: Increasing Returns, Imperfect Competition, and the International Economy*, MIT Press, Cambridge, 1985.
Hoekman, B. M. and M. M., *The Political Economy of the World Trading System*, 2nd edn, Oxford University

Press, Oxford, 2001.
Holland, S., *The Global Economy: From Meso to Macroeconomics*, Weidenfeld and Nicolson, London, 1987.
Hourani, A., *A History of the Arab Peoples*, Faber, London, 2002.
Hugo, G., D. Rudd and K. Harris, *Australia's Diaspora: Its Size, Nature and Policy Implications*, Committee for Economic Development of Australia, Information Paper No. 80, Melbourne, 2003.
Hutton, W., *The State We're In*, Jonathan Cape, London, 1995.
Hutton, W., *The World We're In*, Little Brown, London, 2002.
Hutton, W., and A. Giddens (eds), *Global Capitalism*, New Press, New York, 2000.
Jesson, B., *Fragments of Labour: The Story Behind the Labour Government*, Penguin, Auckland, 1989.
Kelsey, J., *At The Crossroads*, Bridget Williams Books, Wellington, 2002.
Keynes, J. M., *The Economic Consequences of the Peace*, Macmillan, London, 1919.
Klein, N., *No Logo: No Space, No Choice, No Jobs: Taking Aim at the Brand Bullies*, Flamingo, London, 2000.
Krugman, P. R., *Currencies and Crises*, MIT Press, Cambridge, 1992.
Krugman, P. R., *Development, Geography and Economic Theory*, MIT Press, Cambridge, 1997.
Krugman, P. R., *Geography and Trade*, MIT Press, Cambridge, 1993.
Krugman, P. R., *Pop Internationalism*, MIT Press, Cambridge, 1996.
Krugman, P. R. (ed.), *Strategic Trade Policy and the New International Economics*, MIT Press, Cambridge, 1986.
Krugman, P. R., and M. Obstfeld, *International Economics: Theory and Policy*, 7th edn, Addison-Wesley, Boston, 2006.
Lamberton, D. (ed.), *Managing the Global: Globalization, Employment and the Quality of Life*, Tauris in association with the Toda Institute for Global Peace and Policy Research, London, 2002.
Landes, D., *Revolution in Time: Clocks and the Making of the Modern World*, Viking, London, 2000.
Landes, D., *The Wealth and Poverty of Nations*, Little Brown, London, 1998.
Lipsey, R. G., K. I. Carlaw and C. T. Bekar, *Economic Transformations, General Purpose Technologies and Long-Term Economic Growth*, Oxford University Press, Oxford, 2005.
Maddison, A., *Growth and Interaction in the World Economy: The Roots of Modernity*, AEI Press, Washington DC, 2004.
Maddison, A., *The World Economy: A Millennial Perspective*, Development Studies Centre of the OECD, Paris, 2001.
Munz, P., *Beyond Wittgenstein's Poker: New Light on Popper and Wittgenstein*, Ashgate, Aldershot, 2004
North, D. C., *Institutions, Institutional Change, and Economic Performance*, Cambridge University Press, Cambridge, 1990.
OECD Fact Book, OECD, Paris, 2005.
Oliver, D., *The Pacific Islands*, University Press of Hawaii, Honolulu, 1989.
Olson, M., *The Rise and Decline of Nations: Economic Growth, Stagflation and Social Rigidities*, Yale University Press, New Haven, 1982.
O'Rourke, K. H., and J. G. Williamson, *Globalisation and History: The Evolution of a Nineteenth-Century Atlantic Economy*, MIT Press, Cambridge, 1999.
Polyanyi, K., *The Great Transformation: The Political and Economic Origins of Our Time*, Farrar and Rinehart, New York, 1944.
Porter, M. E., *The Competitive Advantage of Nations*, Free Press, New York, 1990.
Raj, D. S., *Where Are You From? Middle-class Migrants in the Modern World*, University of California Press, Berkeley, 2003.
Ravenhill, J. (ed.), *Global Political Economy*, Oxford University Press, Oxford, c. 2005.
Rawls, J., *A Theory of Justice*, Harvard University Press, Cambridge, 1971.
Reich, R. B., *The Work of Nations: Preparing Ourselves for 21st-Century Capitalism*, Knopf, New York, 1991.
Rostow, W. W., *The Stages of Economic Growth; A Non-Communist Manifesto*, Cambridge University Press, Cambridge, 1960.
Samuelson, P. A., *Economics: An Introductory Analysis*, McGraw-Hill, New York, 1958.
Saul, J. R., *Reflections of a Siamese Twin: Canada at the End of the Twentieth Century*, Viking, Toronto, 1997.
Schumacher, E. F., *Small is Beautiful*, Blond and Briggs, London, 1973.
Schwartz, H. M., *In the Dominions of Debt : Historical Perspectives on Dependent Development*, Cornell University Press, Ithaca, 1989.
Schwartz, H. M., *States Versus Markets: History, Geography, and the Development of the International Political Economy*, St Martin's Press, New York, 1994.
Slaughter, A., *A New World Order*, Princeton University Press, Princeton, 2004.
Smith, A. (ed. E. Cannan), *An Inquiry Into the Nature and Causes of the Wealth of Nations*, Random House, New York, 1937.
Sobel, D., *Longitude: The True Story of a Lone Genius who Solved the Greatest Scientific Problem of His Time*, Walker, New York, 1995.
Soros, G., *The Crisis of Global Capitalism: Open Society Endangered*, Public Affairs, New York, 1998.

Strange, S., *The Retreat of the State: The Diffusion of Power in the World Economy*, Cambridge University Press, Cambridge, 1996.
Stiglitz, J. E., *Globalization and Its Discontents*, Norton, New York, 2002.
Stiglitz, J. E., *The Roaring Nineties*, Norton, New York, 2003.
Stiglitz, J. E., and A. Charlton, *Fair Trade for All: How Trade Can Promote Development*, Oxford University Press, Oxford, 2005.
Taylor, G. R., *The Transportation Revolution, 1815–1860*, Rinehart, New York, 1951.
Tomasi di Lampedusa, G. (translated by Archibald Colquhoun), *The Leopard*, Collins and Harvill Press, London, 1961.
Ul Haq, M., I. Kaul and I. Grunberg (eds), *The Tobin Tax: Coping with Financial Volatility*, Oxford University Press, New York, 1996.
United Nations Department of Economic and Social Affairs, Population Division, *World Population Ageing, 1950–2050*, United Nations, New York, 2002.
United Nations Department of Economic and Social Affairs, Population Division, *World Population Prospects: The 2004 Revision*, United Nations, New York, 2005.
Von Thünen, J. H. (translated by C. M. Wartenberg), *Isolated State*, Pergamon Press, Oxford, 1966.
Wade, R. H., *Governing the Market*, 2nd edn, Princeton University Press, Princeton, 2004.
Webster, M., *Assembly: New Zealand Car Production 1921–98*, Reed, Auckland, 2002.
Whitrow, G., *Time in History: The Evolution of Our General Awareness of Time and Temporal Perspective*, Oxford University Press, Oxford, 1998.

Articles

Anderson, J., and Eric van Wincoop, 'Trade Costs', *Journal of Economic Literature*, vol. 42, no. 3, 2004, pp. 691–751.
Bairoch, P., 'International Industrialization Levels from 1750 to 1980', *Journal of European Economic History*, vol. 11, Fall 1982, pp. 269–333.
Balogh, T., and P. P. Streeten, 'The Coefficient of Ignorance', *Bulletin of the Oxford University Institute of Economic and Statistics*, vol. 25, no. 2, May 1963, pp. 97–107.
Baumol, W. J., and E. N. Wolf, 'Productivity Growth Convergence and Welfare', *American Economic Review*, vol. 78, no. 5, 1988, pp. 1155–9.
Coase, R., 'The Nature of the Firm', *Economica*, vol. 4, no. 16, Nov. 1937, pp. 386–405.
Coase, R., 'The Problem of Social Cost', *Journal of Law and Economics*, vol 3, no 1 1960, pp. 1–44.
De Grauwe, P., and F. Camerman, 'Are Multinationals Really Bigger than Nations?', *World Economics*, vol. 4, no. 2, 2003, pp. 23–37.
Easton, B. H., 'Towards an Analytic Framework for Globalisation: The Political Economy of the Diminishing Tyranny of Distance', *Journal of Economic and Social Policy*, vol. 8, no. 1, Summer 2003, pp. 72–86.
Elkan, P.G., 'A Model of Industrialization and Trade with Internal and External Scale Effects', *Oxford Economic Papers*, vol 22, no 2, July 1970, pp.194-219.
Hardin, G., 'The Tragedy of the Commons', *Science*, vol. 162, 1968, pp. 1243–8.
Samuelson, P. A., 'Where Ricardo and Mill Rebut and Confirm Arguments of Mainstream Economists Supporting Globalization', *Journal of Economic Perspectives*, vol. 18, no. 3, Summer 2004, pp. 135–146.
Sheinin, D., 'Defying Infection: Argentine Foot-and-Mouth Disease Policy, 1900-1930', *Canadian Journal of History*, vol. 29, Dec. 1994, pp. 501–24.
Simmons, C., 'De-Industrialization, Industrialization, and the Indian Economy, c. 1850–1947', *Modern Asian Studies*, vol. 19, no. 3, 1985, pp. 593–622.
Solow, R., 'Technical Change and the Aggregate Production Function', *Review of Economic Statistics*, vol. 39, no. 3, Aug. 1957, pp. 312–20.

Index

abacus, 170
absolute advantage, 40, 41, 203
Adams, Douglas, 152
advertising, 51, 108, 109, 152
Afghanistan, 78, 215
Africa, 78, 85, 132, 153, 211, 213–14; economy of, 174, 175; migrants from, 58, 66; population of, 62, 63; standard of living in, ix, 118, 169–76
African-Americans, 59
aging population, 61, 62–64, 66–67, 101, 103, 211; *see also* China
Agreement on Trade-Related Aspects of Intellectual Property Rights (TRIPs), 115
agriculture, 13, 31, 32, 47, 60, 181, 182; *see also* farming
aid, 95, 128, 173, 175
Al Qaeda, 33
Albania, 171
alcohol, control of, 105–8, 109
Allende, Salvador, 133
Alsace-Lorraine, 81
Amazon rainforest, 129
American Federal Reserve Bank, 125
Anderson, James, 3
Argentina, 51, 78, 121, 163–8, 170, 178, 179, 189, 212; currency of, 194–5; economy of, 165–8; migration to and from, 165, 195; terms of trade of, 167
Aristotle, 83, 205
Asia, viii, 78, 197, 198, 201, 211, 212, 213, 214; and banking system, 122, 124; and trade, 194; and transport, 7, 11, 13, 34, 93, 145; economy of, 60, 103, 162, 189, 190, 195; free trade area, 118; manufacturing in, 3, 46, 54, 168; migration to and from, 58, 59, 66, 94; standard of living in, 169, 171, 172
Asian Development Bank, 123
Asian financial crisis, 128, 162
Asian Tiger economies, 157, 159, 161–2, 163, 168, 174, 188
Atatürk, Mustafa Kemal, 197
Auckland, 19, 194
Auckland Islands, 70
Austen, Jane, 170–1
Australasia, 4, 22, 27, 47, 57, 61, 65, 93, 97, 98, 99, 100, 112, 143, 146–7, 163, 210
Australia, 4, 18, 71, 78, 206; and CER, 112–14; and farming, 166–7, 168; and Kyoto Protocol, 206; and New Zealand, 19, 92–93, 112–14, 193–4, 195, 198; and transport in, 93, 137; and US, 133; economy of, 51, 165, 193, 199, 214; identity as Australians, 88, 93–94; migration to and from, 92–94, 95, 96; population of, 92, 165, 193, 199; standard of living in, 172
Australia and New Zealand Closer Economic Relations and Trade Agreement (ANZCERTA) *see* Closer Economic Relations
Australian Football League, 93
Austria, 78, 105, 106, 165

Baldwin, Robert, 86
Balogh, Tommy, 139
Bangladesh, standard of living in, 172
banking, 116, 122–5, 126–7; *see also*, American Federal Reserve Bank, Asian Development Bank, European Central Bank, World Bank
barriers, 3, 28, 31, 60, 111; protective, 53, 113, 213; tariff and non-tariff, 3; to trade, 116, 117; *see also* protection, tariffs
barter, 120
Basques, 89, 193, 202, 204; *see also* Spain
Baumol, William, 158–9
Belgium, 55, 78, 82, 105
Bering Strait, 34, 72
Berlin, viii, 71, 79
Berlin Wall, xiii
bilateralism, 116, 117, 118, 196, 198, 205, 214
Blainey, Geoffrey, 4
Blustein, Paul, 125
Bobbitt, Philip, 205, 206
books, x, 45, 151–2, 188, 210, 216
borders, 3, 28, 53, 54, 56, 60, 77, 87, 96, 105, 109–10, 127, 173, 199, 203, 218
Bordo, Michael, 9
Bosnia, 204
Boston, vii, 33, 37
Brazil, 22, 72, 129, 145, 188, 194, 214; economy of, 190, 214; manufacturing in, 189
British East India Company, 186
British, identity as, 95
British North America Act, 1867, 86
British Petroleum, 144, 148
British Standard Time, 69, 73; *see also* Greenwich Mean Time
Buenos Aires, 170
Burger King, 131

Calderón, Sila, 195–6
Cambodia, 189
Canada, 35, 66, 71, 84, 85–91, 95, 96, 144, 145, 166, 180; and farming, 166; and US, 75, 85, 88–89, 91, 104–5, 153; economy of, 163, 165, 172, 180, 214; health care system of, 104–5; identity as Canadians, 87–88, 95, 102; incomes in, 163; manufacturing in, 32, 180; migration to and from, 57, 89, 92; population of, 85–87, 92; separatism in, 193, 202; standard of living in, 172
Cape Horn, 34
Cape of Good Hope, 7
capitalism, 87, 101, 138–9, 141–2, 160
Caribbean, 33, 34, 78, 132, 195
Catalonia, 89, 193, 202, 204, 206; *see also* Spain
Catherine the Great, 26, 27
Closer Economic Relations (CER) Agreement, 198, 214; between Australia and New Zealand, 112–14, 193, 194, 198
chaebol, 122
Charlemagne, 78, 80

Chile, 127–8, 133, 178; economy of, 190
China, 7–8, 10, 12, 38, 39, 73, 92, 114, 147, 160, 162, 186, 215, 216; aging population of, 211; and environmental problems, 190, 211; and trade, 114, 186; and US, 215; as super-economy, 213; economy of, 162, 183, 184–90, 192, 211, 213, 214; incomes in, 172, 173; labourers from, 12, 14, 48, 217; manufacturing in, 34, 47, 145, 180, 181, 189–90, 217; migration to and from, 58, 65, 66, 86, 92–93; population of, 47, 48, 62, 162, 172, 192; standard of living in, 172, 173
Chinese: calendar, 72–73; language, 91
Chirac, Jacques, 97
Christchurch, vii
cities, importance and role of, 2, 7, 29, 30–31, 33, 34, 36, 37, 83, 144; *see also* Auckland, Berlin, Boston, Buenos Aires, Christchurch, Constantinople, Doha, Istanbul, Johannesburg, New York, Paris, Sydney, Tokyo, Washington
Civil War (US), 82
coal, 55, 82, 144, 149
Coase, Ronald, 45, 46
Coca-Cola, 153
Colbert, Jean-Baptiste, 101
colonialism, 15, 89; *see also* Great Britain
Columbus, Christopher, 7
communism, ix, 26
comparative advantage, 20, 21, 24, 38, 40–41, 42, 47, 50, 55, 168, 194, 198
competition, 8, 24, 39, 42, 129, 166, 216; direct, 59; foreign, 98, 99, 117; monopolistic, 50, 51
competitive advantage, 24, 38, 40, 41, 42, 50, 54, 55, 57, 156, 161, 168, 194, 213
computers, 39, 45, 48, 55, 70, 75, 153, 170, 188, 189, 211; *see also* Dell, software
Congress of Vienna, 80
Constantinople, 7
Convention for the Metre, 1875, 71, 73
Convention on Cultural Diversity (UN), 90, 91, 204
Cook Islands, 15, 16
Cook, James, 10–11, 12, 14, 18, 27, 71
copyright, 42, 153, 154
Corn Laws, 20, 21
Costa Rica, 78
country-of-origin rule, 118
coups, 7, 12, 167, 179; role of multinationals in, 132–3
cultural convergence, 9, 62, 67, 75, 77, 84, 85–91
cultural diversity, 2, 9, 62, 86, 87, 90, 91, 116, 193, 196, 204
cultural independence, 90, 195, 202–3
cultural pluralism, 81, 90
culture, xi, 10, 16, 37, 56, 64, 65, 66, 74, 80–81, 102, 104, 105, 134, 200–1, 202, 215; change, 67, 91, 134; effects of migration on, 64; *see also* symbols and myths
Cyprus, 197
Czech Republic, 78, 193, 202
Czechoslovakia, 89, 193, 202

Darfur, 204
debt redemption, 173
Dell, 54, 55
Deming, W. Edwards, 160

democracy, 83, 158, 196, 217, 218
Denmark, 78, 105, 106, 189, 199
Depression, 97
developing countries, 93, 153, 179
di Lampedusa, Guiseppe Tomasi, 91
Dias, Bartolomeu, 7
digital information, 39, 210
distance: costs of, ix, xi, 2, 3, 4–5, 6–7, 8, 9, 10, 17, 21, 22, 23, 25, 29, 30, 31, 32, 33, 37, 43, 47, 50, 51, 57, 58, 60, 65, 71, 81, 92, 93, 96, 98, 99, 117, 129, 137, 145, 152, 154, 175, 177, 181, 182, 184, 185, 188, 209, 210–11, 213, 215; effects on trade and investment, 18, 28, 40, 46, 48, 52–53, 54, 55, 129, 137, 153; tyranny of, vii, viii, xii, 20, 29, 165; *see also* transport, travel
Doha, 117
Doha (Development) Round, 117–18, 119
dollar (US), 120, 122–3, 124, 126, 194–5, 215
Dominican Republic, 72, 73
Donne, John, 110
drugs, illegal/illicit, 109
DuBois, William E. B., viii
dumping, 117, 167, 168, 174
Durham, Lord, 86

Easter Island, 10, 11, 16
economic development, x–xi, 10, 36, 44, 95, 131, 146, 155, 157, 163, 170, 174, 177, 180, 181–3, 185, 187, 189, 194
economic merging, 79, 192–9
economic theory, x–xi, 147, 148; and formal model of economic trade, 20–23; on convergence process, 163–4; on economies of scale, 30–32, 33, 35–36, 47, 51, 52, 55, 89, 135, 168, 175, 177, 182–3, 184–5; on growth, 2, 137, 138–9, 142, 159, 186; on tariffs, 3–4, 5
economies: export-oriented, 161; import-oriented, 161; integration of, 81; large, 75, 117, 119, 180, 198, 213–14; of scale, xi, 2, 6–7, 17, 21, 26–32, 33, 35, 38, 41, 46–47, 50–51, 52, 53, 55, 58, 81, 89, 135, 141, 181–3, 184, 185, 198, 199, 210, 211; small, 75, 118, 199, 211, 214; *see also* individual countries
Economist, 127–8
Einstein, Albert, 70
El Salvador, 78
'electronic herd', 127
employment, 62, 87, 93, 98, 100, 101, 115, 123, 147
English language, 47, 48, 86, 87, 91, 141, 188, 211
environmental factors, 11, 17, 18–19, 108, 115, 116, 119, 129, 130, 147, 158, 190, 196, 199, 206–8, 211; *see also* China, Kyoto Protocol
equality, 48, 97, 100–1, 103, 115, 117, 119, 175–6, 183, 211
Erasmus, 8
Erie Canal, 29, 34, 35
Estonia, 107
ethnic cleansing, 81–82
ethnic composition, 66, 67, 211
ethnic diversity, 34, 81, 95
ethnic nationalism, 59, 81, 82, 83, 84, 87, 88, 90
ethnic problems, 66, 87
euro, 120, 123–4, 196, 215
Europe, viii, 7, 8, 18, 19, 26, 28, 47, 78, 81, 82, 84, 87, 97, 101, 165, 171, 172, 192, 200, 201, 202, 203,

213, 215, 216; and trade, 40, 51; and transport, 33–34, 81, 145; economy of, 2–3, 159, 160, 161, 162, 163, 165, 187, 192; effects of plague in, 174; in history, 8, 79, 151, 174; incomes in, 169, 171–2, 178; manufacturing in, 180, 185, 187; migration to and from, 57–58, 59, 61, 65, 66, 92, 94, 197, 198; perspective of, x; population of, 57, 62, 117; standard of living in, 169, 172, 178; wage rates in, 48; workers in, 46
European Central Bank, 123
European Coal and Steel Community, 55, 82
European Economic Association (EEA), 196, 214
European Economic Community (EEC), 82, 197
European Free Trade Association (EFTA), 196
European Monetary Union, 124, 194, 196
European Single Market, 196
European Union (EU), 28, 54, 79, 82–83, 97–98, 99, 100, 101, 102, 105–8, 109, 114, 117, 122, 149, 163, 168, 193, 204, 207, 214; as super-economy, 213; confederation of, 2–3, 39, 55, 97, 200–3; growth of, 196–8; population of, 192
Exclusive Economic Zone (EEZ), 146–7, 207
exploration, 7–8, 10–12, 13–15, 18–19, 20, 185–6; *see also* Columbus, Cook, Dias, Magellan
Export Oriented Industrialisation (EOI) *see* industrialisation
exports, 5, 8, 12, 19, 24, 50, 95, 99, 167, 175, 189, 190, 194–5, 199; of farm produce, 165, 167; of manufacturing, 3, 182, 212

farm products, 20, 23, 24, 163, 165, 168, 182, 183, 185, 204, 212
farming, 12, 18, 20–22, 23–24, 26–27, 34, 44, 45, 60, 117, 146, 166–7, 184, 185; *see also* agriculture
Fawcett, Brian, 88
Feuerbach thesis, ix, 218
Fiji, 10, 15
Finland, 38–40, 42, 105, 106, 107, 165
First Peoples, 16, 65, 66; of Australia, 18, 94; of Canada, 86; of Hawaii, 13, 16; of New Zealand, 13, 16; of Samoa, 16
First World War, 36, 58, 65, 79, 81, 148, 165, 209
fishing, 143, 146–7, 149, 150, 166, 167, 204, 209
flying, vii, 145
Fogel, Robert, 20, 29–30, 31
food, 20, 48, 57, 120, 134, 143, 146, 168, 187, 189; fast-, 44, 129, 130, 131, 134; GE-modified, 109; insecurity of 48, 116, 150
Ford, Henry, 52
Ford Motors, 50, 52, 54
Foreign Direct Investment (FDI), 130–1, 132, 135
forestry, 11, 19, 38, 39, 44, 166
France, 54, 55, 70, 71–72, 73, 74, 78, 79, 80, 81, 83, 88, 89, 105, 134, 165, 186, 201; and European Union, 97, 117
free trade agreement (FTA), 114, 133, 193; *see also* trade
free trade area, 55, 118
Friedman, Thomas, 54
Friends of the Earth, 115
fuel: alternative, 144–5, 149, 209; prices, 145, 210
Fujita, Masahisa, xi, 7, 36, 181

Gabon, 172
General Agreement on Tariffs and Trade (GATT), 115, 116, 117, 166
General Agreement on Trade in Services, 115
General Motors, 27, 53
German Democratic Republic (East Germany), xiii, 199; economy of, xiii, 193; economy and EU, 197, 198
Germany, Federal Republic of, xiii, 14, 54, 65, 71–72, 76, 88, 97, 105, 107, 148, 165, 193; and transport, 81; as nation-state, 77–84; economy and EU, 55, 197; ethnic minorities in, 81; manufacturing in, 189
global warming, 34, 128, 143, 149, 206–8, 209
globalisation, x–xii, 32, 55, 64, 77, 85, 89, 96, 97, 98, 103, 119, 135, 145, 174, 183, 192, 199, 200, 209, 210, 216, 217–18; and culture change, 90–91; and health care, 104–5, 108–9; and inequality, 172–3, 175–6; and nation-state, 77; and nationalism, 77; and notion of sovereignty, 69, 72, 75–76, 128, 203–4; and outsourcing, 46; and standards of living, 172–3; and WTO, 117; definitions of, 2–9, 138; early stages of, ix, 7–9, 10, 16, 143, 169; effects of, 33–36, 37, 101–2, 104, 106, 108, 154, 169, 172, 188; harnessing of, xi–xii; of information, 152, 156; of time, 69–76; pressures of, 88; regional, 31–32; *see also* cultural convergence, nation-state, policy convergence
gold, 19, 121, 144
Great Britain, 14, 20–21, 22, 24, 33, 69, 70, 71, 78, 82, 83, 89, 92, 105, 114, 148, 167; and colonialism, 26, 47, 86, 186, 215; and Irish, 193; and manufacturing, 186; and Scotland, 193, 202; and separatism, 193, 202; and US, 216; and Wales, 193, 202; economy of, 21, 22, 50, 180; health care in, 110; migration to and from, 65, 89; trade with China, 186; *see also* British
Greece, 92, 105, 106; economy and EU, 197
Greenwich Mean Time, 69, 71, 72, 73
Gregorian calendar, 69, 70, 72, 73, 74
Guadeloupe, 89
Guatemala, 78
Gutenberg, Johannes, 8, 45, 151

Hamilton, Alexander, 27–28, 82
happiness and income, correlation between, 170–1, 174
Harrison, John, 71
Hawaii, 6, 15, 16; and US, 12–13, 16; first contact with Europeans, 10–13, 14, 15; settlement of, 10; standard of living in, 13
health care, 44, 56, 63, 64, 66, 76, 87, 88–89, 93, 98, 101, 102, 103, 104–10, 115, 116, 171, 188, 198, 202, 205, 215; *see also* individual countries
Hegel, Georg, 210
Herder, Johann, 80–81, 84
Hitler, Adolf, 79
HIV-AIDs, 153, 174, 175
Holy Roman Empire, 78–79, 80, 84
homosexuality, 82, 89
Honduras, 78
Hong Kong, 111, 158, 161, 162, 163, 189
Hungary, 78

INDEX

Iceland, 196
imperialism, Western, 186–7
import controls, 99, 168
Import Substituting Industrialisation (ISI) *see* industrialisation
income, 16, 22, 56, 58–59, 63, 66, 75, 93, 100–3, 115, 139, 161, 163, 169–76, 182–3, 186–7, 189, 205, 211, 212–16; distribution of, 95, 99, 131, 160, 177–8; levels of, 213; of poor, 48, 169, 171–2, 175–6; per capita, 165, 169–71, 173–4, 190, 212; variation in, 162, 171; *see also* individual countries
India, 7, 44, 47–48, 117, 134, 145, 171, 186, 188, 211; and Great Britain, 186–7; as super-economy, 213; economy of, 162, 188, 190, 214; manufacturing in, 180, 181; migration to and from, 58, 65; population of, 62, 162, 172, 181, 192; standard of living in, 172
Individual Transferable Quotas (ITQs), 146–7
Indonesia, 65, 121, 122, 125–6, 162; standard of living in, 172
industrialisation, ix, 63, 163; benefits of, 175; export-oriented, 8, 112, 167–8, 176; human costs of, ix; import-substituting, 8, 112, 167–8
inequality, 48, 100, 101, 103, 115, 116, 175–6, 183, 211
information technology, 5, 8, 9, 46, 145, 217; *see also* computers, internet, software, telecommunications, World Wide Web
intellectual property rights, 116, 133, 153, 154; *see also* Agreement on Trade-Related Aspects of Intellectual Property Rights
International Energy Association, 148
International Monetary Fund (IMF), 114, 122–8, 200, 204
international rule of law, 111, 118–19, 199
International System of Units, 73
internet, vii, x, 31, 152, 155; *see also* World Wide Web
investment, 101, 102, 135, 140, 153, 158, 167; definition of, 130; foreign, 74–75, 130, 205; international, 102, 117, 122; overseas, 130–1; *see also* Foreign Direct Investment, Multilateral Agreement on Investment
Iran, 65, 78, 147
Iraq, xii, 65, 83, 147, 201, 214, 215
Iraq–Kuwait war, 149
Ireland, 54, 65, 78, 105, 106, 161, 163, 164; economy and EU, 197
Irish famine, 57, 65
Islam, 72, 134, 197
Israel, 118, 132, 147
Istanbul, 197
Italy, 55, 78, 82, 105, 107, 165
ITT, 133

Japan, 12, 51, 53, 62, 66, 78, 123, 148, 158, 164, 170, 172, 173, 213, 216; and manufacturing, 180; and US, 215; as super-economy, 213; economy of, 54, 157, 159–61, 162, 163, 165, 168, 180, 184, 187, 188, 189, 190, 192, 213; labourers from, 12; population of, 62, 192; standard of living in, 172, 173, 178, 179
Jefferson, Thomas, 29
Jews: diaspora of, 92, 94, 95–96; persecution of, 57, 82, 96

Johannesburg, 170
Jordan, 147

Kamehameha, 12
Karlsson, Thomas, 106
kauri gum, 19
Kazakhstan, 65
Keynes, John Maynard, viii, 143
Khrushchev, Nikita, 187
Kipling, Rudyard, 18
Kiribati, 72, 73
'knowledge' economy, 140–1, 154–5
Kroc, Ray, 129
Krugman, Paul, xi, 3–4, 7, 181
Kurds, 197
Kuwait, 149
Kyoto Protocol, 1997, 206–8; and Australia, 206; and US, 206, 207

labour, ix, 14, 21, 27, 28, 31, 32, 48, 53, 141, 160–1, 166, 174, 188; division of, 6, 137; mobility, 41, 56–61, 65, 97, 101, 103, 112, 156, 157, 198, 201; productivity of, 182; shortage, 48, 64, 66; size of labour pool, 66–67, 140; skilled and unskilled, 48, 98–101, 139, 158, 161; specialisation of, 95, 137
labour force, 37, 48, 65, 180; age of, 62–63; nationalities of, 12, 14; payment of, 132, 183; significance of, 10–17, 33, 34, 38, 49, 56, 70–71, 96, 98, 99–101, 145, 175, 197
labour market, 93, 195, 212, 214
Lafontaine, Louis-Hippolyte, 86
Lange, David, 127
Latin America, 58, 59, 158, 165, 171, 172; economy of, 211; income in, 190; standard of living in, 171, 172
Laurier, Wilfrid, 86
Lebanon, 132, 147
Liechtenstein, 196
Lindert, Peter, 175
location, 33, 34, 49, 70–71, 145; significance of, 10–17, 33, 34, 38, 96
London, viii, 4, 19, 33, 69, 71, 72, 95, 148, 152
Louis XIV, 101
Luther, Martin, 8, 80, 151
Luxembourg, 55, 78, 82, 105

Madagascar, 7
Maddison, Angus, xiii
Maddison Data Base, 159, 170, 172, 178
Madison, James, 27, 29
magazines, 90, 152, 210
Magellan, Ferdinand, 11
Magna Carta, 119
Malaysia, 128, 161, 162, 178, 179, 187
Malthus, Thomas Robert, 143, 146, 149, 150
Manhattan, 33, 89
manufacturing, 21, 44–45, 46, 47, 49, 50, 53–54, 98, 112, 145, 163, 166–7, 168, 177, 181, 182, 183, 184, 185, 186–7, 188–9, 190, 199, 212–13; costs of, 199; development of, 181, 182; offshore, 98; output in world, 180; *see also* individual countries
Mao Zedong, 160
Māori, 10–11, 13, 15, 16, 18, 163; impact on land, 19;

wars, 19; *see also* New Zealand
Marquesas, 10, 16
Mars Climate Orbiter spacecraft, 74
Marshall, Alfred, 35–36
Marshall Plan, 215
Marx, Karl, ix, 120–1, 138–9, 141, 142, 218
Maslow, Abraham, 80
Mauritius, 172, 178, 179
Mazda, 53
McDonald, Dick and Mac, 129, 131
McDonald's, 129–35
McLamore, James, 131
Melanesia, 10, 14
Mexico, 56–57, 58, 59–61, 65, 78, 121
Microsoft, 27
Middle East, 132, 147, 188, 197, 214
Middle Income Club, 177–9
migration, 7, 14, 21, 29, 32, 34, 57–61, 64, 86–87, 100, 175, 192, 211; effects of, 58–59; illegal, 56–61; restrictions on, 21; twenty-first century, 62, 66–67; *see also* individual countries
military, 13, 28, 53, 83, 197, 198, 200, 201, 205, 215; force used for economic ends, xii, 148–9; service, 95
Mill, John Stuart, 171
minerals, 19, 190, 194
mining, 44, 133
missionaries: in New Zealand, 19, 20; in Pacific, 12, 14
Moldova, 171
monetary system, global, 76, 128, 144; *see also* dollar, euro, sterling
monetary union, 114, 124, 194–5, 196, 214
monopolies, 35, 43, 50, 51, 84, 108, 125, 126, 216
Monroe, James, 29
most favoured nations (MFN), 114, 116
motor vehicles, 50–55, 217; *see also* Ford, General Motors, Toyota, Trabant
Motorola, 39, 43
Multilateral Agreement on Investment, 74, 90, 133
multilateralism, 111, 118, 205
multinational firms, 76, 119, 129–35, 148
multipolar world, 209, 216
Munz, Peter, 84
music, downloaded, 153, 210

Namibia, 172
Napoleon, 70, 79, 80
nation-state, x, xi, 2, 9, 14, 28, 65, 66, 78, 82–83, 90–91, 92, 94, 95, 96, 104, 118, 200–3, 205, 206, 208, 213, 214, 218; and globalisation, 76, 77, 104; and multinationals, 132–3, 135; and nationalism, 79–83; autonomy of, 90; future of, 190, 192–9; sovereignty of, 72, 75, 120, 126–7, 128, 202–4
nationalism, 77–79, 80–81, 82, 122, 215; civic, 83–84, 87, 88, 89, 90, 205; myths related to, 83–84; *see also* ethnic nationalism, globalisation
NATO, 132, 198
Nauru, 16
Netherlands, 33, 55, 78, 80, 82, 83, 105, 106; and European Union, 97
New York, vii, viii, 27, 28, 29, 33–37

New Zealand, 4, 10, 13, 18–19, 70–73, 198; agriculture in, 19–21, 23, 166, 167, 168; and adoption of International System of Units, 73; and Australia, 92, 193–4, 195; and CER with Australia, 112–14, 198; and health care, 110; and impact of European settlers, 19; and Samoa, 14, 15–16, 94, 96, 192–3; and trade, 19–25, 51; as nation-state, 77–78; economy of, 51, 165, 168, 172; in globalising world, xi; in multipolar world, 209–18; land acquisition in, 19; refrigeration in, 6, 18, 20, 22, 24, 30; settlement of, 10; standard of living in, 172; travel from, 5; women in, 24–25; *see also* Māori
New Zealand Australia Free Trade Agreement (NAFTA) 112, 113
newspapers, 127, 152, 210
Nicaragua, 78
Nigeria, standard of living in, 172
Niue, 16
Nobel, Alfred, 157
Nokia, 39–43
North America Free Trade Agreement (NAFTA), 56, 59–60
North Korea, 122
Norway, 78, 105, 148, 165, 196, 198
Novo Nordisk, 189
nuclear powers, US and Soviet, 216

Obstfeld, Maurice, 3
Organization for Economic Cooperation and Development (OECD), xiii, 74
offshoring, 44–49, 100, 101, 162, 168, 181, 188–9, 213
oil, 50, 52, 116, 129, 143–5, 146, 147–8, 149, 150, 167, 178, 215; countries, 51, 133, 142, 143–4, 148–9
Oliver, Douglas, 15
Olson, Mancur, 160
Opium Wars, 114, 186, 203
Österberg, Esa, 105
outsourcing, 45–46, 49, 50, 55, 142, 160
Oxford English Dictionary, 152

Pacific, European exploration of, 11–13, 15, 19; *see also* exploration
Pakistan, 65; standard of living in, 172
Panama, 132
Panama Canal, 5, 20, 34, 145
Paris, 55, 71, 72, 73
patents, 42, 141, 153, 205
Pepsi, 133
periodicals, 152
Peron, Juan, 179
Persky, Stan, 87–88
pharmaceuticals, 24, 109, 133, 141, 153, 174
Philippines, 12, 13, 65
Pinochet, Augusto, 133
Poland, 78
policy convergence, 75–76, 77, 88, 103, 104–10
Polynesia, 10–11, 12–13, 15, 16, 18, 65, 70, 94
Poor Club, 7, 165, 171, 173, 177, 178, 179, 181, 182–3, 184, 185, 187, 189, 215
Pope Gregory, 69
Popper, Karl, 84, 138

population, world, 62; *see also* individual countries
Porter, Michael E., 54
Portugal, 50, 78, 105
postal systems, 152
prices, 52, 144–5, 167
printed word, 8, 151; *see also* Gutenberg, women
production, primary, 50, 51, 163, 165
productivity, 23, 24, 29, 30, 31, 32, 48, 63, 99, 137, 139, 143, 145, 155, 166, 167, 174, 182, 183, 187, 212, 214
products, differentiation of, 38, 42, 50, 51, 53, 55
protection, 74, 90, 99, 100, 108, 111, 112, 113, 114, 116, 117, 123, 126, 153, 163, 166–8, 186, 196
Proudhon, Pierre-Joseph, ix
Prussia, 79, 81
Puerto Rico, 178, 195–6
Pufendorf, Samuel, 79

Rabin, Matthew, 111–12
Rabin's Law, 22, 112, 113, 116, 198, 217
radio, 39, 71, 108
Raj, Dhooleka, 95
Rawls, John, 175
Reformation, 151
refrigeration revolution, 165; *see also* New Zealand
refugees, 87, 94
Reich, Robert, 53
remittances, 16, 66, 95, 197, 198, 215
research and development, 102, 140–1
resource depletion, 142, 143–7, 149, 204, 209, 212
Ricardo, David, 21, 40, 50
Rich Club, xiii, 7, 65, 66, 67, 102, 103, 117, 162, 163–8, 169, 170, 171, 172, 173, 174, 175, 177, 178, 179, 181, 182–3, 184, 185, 187, 188–9, 190, 193, 198–9, 210, 211–13, 215
Roggeveen, Jacob, 14
Roman Catholic Church, 69
Roman Empire, 80, 169, 216
Romania, 171
Romer, Paul, 140
Rostow, Walt, 52
rule of law, 111, 118–19, 199
rural life, ix, 58, 85
Russia, 26, 57, 69, 71, 116–17, 121, 147, 158, 198, 214; income in, 190; trade with China, 186

Samoa, 6, 95–96; and aid, 95; and New Zealand, 96, 192–3; first contact with Europeans, 13–14, 15; migration to and from, 15–16, 94–95, 96; settlement of, 10–11; standard of living in, 193
Samoan identity, 94
Samuelson, Paul, 189, 217
San Domingo *see* Dominican Republic
sandalwood, 11, 12
satellites, 71
Saudi Arabia, 116, 118, 119, 134, 142
Saul, John Ralston, 84, 88
Scandinavia, 39, 65, 102
Schumacher, E. F., 138
Schumpeter, Joseph, 143
sealing, 11, 18, 19
Second World War, xii, 65, 79, 81, 82, 97, 148, 159–60, 167, 209, 215

Serbia, 132
Shakespeare, William, 69, 133
shipping, 3, 4, 5, 19–20, 33–35, 70–71, 72, 145, 215
Singapore, 158, 161, 162, 163
slavery, 27, 32, 33, 57, 65
Slavic peoples, 82
Slovakia, 193, 202
Smith, Adam, x, 28, 29, 137–8
Smithsonian Agreement, 144
smuggling, 109
social market economy, 75, 87, 97–98, 99, 100, 101, 102–3, 173, 198
Society Islands, 10, 15
software, 25, 45, 47, 48, 133, 154
Solow, Robert, 137, 139, 140
South Africa, 57, 65, 172, 174, 214; economy of, 175, 190
South America, 57, 65, 78; manufacturing in, 46
South Korea, 12, 109, 111, 121, 122–3, 126, 127, 162, 163, 178, 214; labourers from, 12
Soviet Union, 39, 48, 70, 158, 161, 187, 216
Spain, 13, 78, 89, 105, 107, 161, 163, 164, 165, 195; and separatism, 193, 202; economy and EU, 197, 202; *see also* Basques, Catalonia
standard of living *see* individual countries
steel, 7, 55, 82, 217
sterling, 120, 124
Streeten, Paul, 139
Suez Crisis, 215
Suharto, President, 125–6
Sweden, 105, 106, 107, 165
Swift, Jonathan, 23
Switzerland, 78, 196, 198
Sydney, 194
symbols and myths, 80, 83, 84, 86; *see also* nationalism
Syria, 147

Tahiti, 10, 16
Taiwan, 162, 163
tariffs, 3, 5, 21, 23, 44, 99, 112, 114, 115, 116, 168, 186, 203; protection of, 46–47
Tasman, Abel, 18
taxation, 66, 93, 100–3, 106–7, 108, 109, 114, 126, 128, 131, 194, 195, 202
Taylor, Alan, 9
technology, 11, 18, 30, 31, 40, 41, 85, 95, 131, 137, 142, 152, 155, 186–7, 210; and knowledge, 140–1, 151, 154–5; change, 42, 101, 184, 212, 213; definition of, 138–9, 155; for agriculture, 23–24, 31, 143; 'frontier', 155–6; importance of, ix, 23, 143; innovation, 42, 43, 142, 149, 155–6, 158, 164, 212, 213; of exploration, 11; new, 6, 24, 131, 138–41, 144, 149, 155–6, 157, 164; transfer, 157–62, 164, 165, 167–8, 186; *see also* research and development
telecommunications, 44–45, 46, 49, 92; *see also* information technology, radio, satellites, telegraph, telephones, television
telegraph, 20, 31, 39, 71
telephones, vii, 30, 39, 43; mobile, 38–43; *see also* Motorola, Nokia
television, 39, 80, 90, 108, 152

Terra Australis, 11, 18
terrorism, 33, 56, 91, 209; see also Al Qaeda
Thailand, 121, 122, 162, 187
Thisse, Jacques-François, 36
tobacco, control of, 105, 108–9
Tobin, James, 128
Tokelau, 16
Tokyo, 170
tolerance, 201; of diversity, 83, 89
Tonga, 10, 15, 16
Toyota, 50, 53, 54
Trabant, xiii
trade, 8, 40–41, 81, 90, 109, 182; free, 20, 22, 41, 47, 109, 111–12, 187, 198; increases in, 182–3; inter-industry, 50, 51; international, 7, 20, 56, 59, 85, 89, 104, 109, 117, 118–19, 120–1, 122, 126–7, 177; intra-industry, 7, 42, 50–55; liberalisation of, 22–23, 59; multilateral negotiations, 75; role of money in, 120–1; see also barter, free trade area, individual countries
translation services, 47
transport, 20, 26, 29–32, 36, 46, 97, 143, 144, 145; cost of, vii, ix, xi–xii, 3, 4–5, 21, 23, 30–31, 44, 46, 48, 53, 57, 92, 147, 210; effects of, 81, 93, 137; see also distance, individual countries
travel, overseas, 5, 10, 11, 16, 29, 34, 72, 92, 93, 103, 107–8
treaties, 90, 118–19, 186, 203, 204, 206; see also names of individual treaties
Treaty of Nanjing, 186
Treaty of Paris, 1763, 89
Treaty of Paris, 1951, 55
Treaty of Rome, 1957, 55, 82
Treaty of Westphalia, 1648, 72, 118, 203
Tunisia, 172
Tupaia, 10, 14
Turkey, 121, 147; and EU, 197–8
Tuvalu, 207

Ukraine, 117
unemployment, 21, 100, 123, 188, 194
UNESCO, 90, 204
United Nations (UN), 33, 34, 62, 64, 66, 114, 171, 192, 204; Development Program, 171; see also Convention on Cultural Diversity, UNESCO
United States Department of Agriculture, 166
United States of America, x, xii, 12–13, 14, 27, 33, 36, 39, 71, 78, 92, 101, 134, 143, 145, 148, 204, 205–6, 209; and Canada, 85, 104–5; and cultural convergence, 85, 91; and energy, 149; and Hawaii, 12–13, 16; and health care, 66, 104–5, 109, 205–6, 215; and IMF, 123–4, 126; and income, 56, 60, 172; and invasion of Iraq, 201, 214; and Kyoto Protocol, 206, 207; and Mexico, 56, 65; and migration to and from, 34, 56–61, 65, 86–87, 100, 206; and military, 12, 132, 133, 148, 201, 215; and motor vehicle industry, 52–53, 54, 188; and Puerto Rico, 178, 195–6; and Samoa, 15–16; and taxation, 102; and trade, 51, 113–14, 132, 133; and transport in, 29–31, 33–35, 36–37, 71, 81, 145; and war, xii, 28, 132; and WTO, 116, 117–18; as nation-state, 78, 82, 192, 205–6; as super-economy, 213; Congress, 59, 60, 114, 195, 196, 206; constitution of, 27, 32, 97, 158, 202, 204, 206; economy of, 2, 3, 26–30, 73, 81–82, 132, 159, 160, 161, 162, 163, 165, 168, 180, 182, 185, 192, 199, 201, 209, 214–15; federal arrangement in, 27–28, 31, 82–83, 200, 204; industrialisation of, 57; political hegemony of, 214–16; population of, 32, 57, 92, 117, 192; standard of living in, 172, 177; trade with China, 186, 188; wage rates in, 48, 163; workers in, 46, 111, 217; see also Canada
Uruguay, 78, 163, 164–5, 167, 168, 178, 189, 212
US Steel, 27
USSR, standard of living in, 172

van Wincoop, Eric, 3
Vatican City, 207
Venables, Anthony J., xi, 7, 181
videos, 133, 210
Vietnam, 189
Vogel, Julius, 20
Volker, Paul, 125
Volkswagen, xiii, 189
Voltaire, 79
von Moltke, Helmuth, 81
von Thunen, J. H., xi

wage: differentials, 56, 58, 59–60; rates, 99, 101, 131–2, 188–9
war, xii, 55, 57, 82–83, 119, 132, 146, 148–9, 159; see also Civil War, First World War, Franco-Prussian war, Iraq–Kuwait war, Māori wars, military, Opium Wars, Second World War, War of Independence
War of Independence, 28
Washington, 29, 37, 71, 72, 125
Washington, George, 27, 28
water (as resource), 12, 14, 34, 37, 40, 57, 143, 146, 147–9, 150, 155–6, 175, 190, 209
welfare state see social market economy
West Indies, 33
Western European Twelve, 159, 165
whaling, 11, 18, 19, 144, 146
Wikipedia, 152
Williamson, Jeffrey, 9, 175
wine, 24, 50, 51, 105, 106–7
women: and vote, 24; as commodities, 12; in workforce, 62, 101, 134; labour of, 155; literacy of, 151
wool, 19, 20
Wordsworth, William, 33
World Bank, 123
World Health Organization (WHO), 108–9
World Time Conference, 1871, 71, 75
World Trade Organization (WTO), 90, 108, 111–19, 154, 200, 203, 204, 207
World Wide Web, 91, 151–6, 207

Yugoslavia, 89, 193, 202

Zheng He, 7–8